MANAGING YOUR VENDORS

THE BUSINESS OF BUYING TECHNOLOGY

**A Complete Management Handbook for the
Procurement of Technology from Vendors:
Principles, Processes and Procedures,
with a Case Study.**

Florian A. Mikulski

PTR Prentice Hall
Englewood Cliffs, N.J. 07632

Library of Congress Cataloging-in-Publishing Data

Mikulski, Florian A., 1936
   Managing your vendors: the business of buying technology:
a complete management handbook for the procurement of technology
from vendors: principles, processes and procedures, with a case study/
 by Florian A. Mikulski.
        p. cm.
  Includes index.
  ISBN 0-13-221060-6: $26.25
   1. Industrial procurement--Management. 2. High technology--Purchasing.
3. Computer contracts--Case studies. I. Title.
HD39.5.M553 1993
658.7'2--dc20   93-4395
                                                  CIP

Editorial/production supervision: **Benjamin D. Smith**
Manufacturing buyer: **Mary Elizabeth McCartney**
Acquisitions editor: **Paul Becker**
Cover design: **Bruce Kenselaar**
Cover Photo: **Comstock**

 © 1993 by P T R Prentice-Hall, Inc.
A Simon & Schuster Company
Englewood Cliffs, New Jersey 07632

Printed in the United States of America

10 9 8 7 6 5 4 3 2 1

ISBN   0-13-221060-6

Prentice-Hall International (UK) Limited, *London*
Prentice-Hall of Australia Pty. Limited, *Sydney*
Prentice-Hall Canada Inc., *Toronto*
Prentice-Hall Hispanoamericana, S.A., *Mexico*
Prentice-Hall of India Private Limited, *New Delhi*
Prentice-Hall of Japan, Inc., *Tokyo*
Simon & Schuster Asia Pte. Ltd., *Singapore*
Editora Prentice-Hall do Brasil, Ltda., *Rio de Janeiro*

TABLE OF CONTENTS

PART 2: ESTABLISH THE INTERNAL RULES OF PURCHASING TECHNOLOGY

PART 3: HAVE A STANDARD APPROACH TO FIND THE BEST VENDOR

LIST OF EXHIBITS

PREFACE

Have you considered that one of the biggest risks you take in business is when you hire a vendor? It doesn't matter whether it's for facilities construction, computer systems, telecommunications networks or outsourcing.

How many failures to deliver technology using vendors has your organization had? How many lawsuits have you noticed? How often have losing vendors in competitive evaluations escalated or sued because of unfair or illegal practices? The major business dailies carry stories like this every day.

Oh sure, your personnel will tell you that they have a process for evaluating and selecting vendors. When you examine it, you will not find a process. You'll find multiple discrete activities, which when considered as a whole, are incapable of guaranteeing successful project or service completion.

Wouldn't you want a fail-safe way to find, evaluate and manage your vendors? Shouldn't your business **objective** be to buy from the best vendor, with the highest probability of successful on-schedule completion at the lowest cost without fear of litigation?

Managing Your Vendors is a complete unified philosophy, policy and practice of management fine-tuned over twenty years, and successfully used in procurements from under $50 thousand to $1 billion. It is applicable to large, medium and small companies, local, state and federal governments, institutions and nonprofit entities. Within these organizations, the audience for *Managing Your Vendors* are the CEO, COO, CFO, CIO, CAO, Contracts, Purchasing, Auditing, and technical managers and implementers. It certainly is applicable to vendors as well.

When you implement *Managing Your Vendors* within your organization, you will find it is a major cost avoidance tool, saves time, avoids project risk and large business and expense losses from unsuccessful projects. It is purposefully structured to avoid losses or delays from litigation, or opportunity costs associated with challenged vendor selections. *Managing Your Vendors* provides complete vendor management and control throughout the vendor relationship. At the same time, it assures a non-adversarial relationship with vendors.

Although the masculine singular has sometimes been used of necessity in this manual, nothing contained herein, including the use of the masculine singular, should imply that the feminine or neuter cannot be equivalently substituted for the masculine in the same context, unless the text clearly and unambiguously requires that the gender be masculine or feminine, as for example in the case study.

The case study originated as a tool to lighten and humanize the process described in the manual. Every name of a person or business used in the case study is totally a figment of my imagination, and any reference to anyone or anything that may actually possess such a name, living or dead is totally accidental and unintended. Furthermore, there is nothing in the case study that reflects any actual experience that I may have had in my career or those with whom I have been associated.

Editorial comments that I have made with respect to the performance of organizations and businesses are the direct result of my personal experience, or have been obtained from well publicized multiple reports in the media. These comments reflect my professional judgment, opinions and personal biases.

This manual is dedicated to my wife Ann, whose love, support and tolerance for her spouse over all these years has been magnificent. Special thanks to Rex S. Wolf whose keen mind, fast wit and incisive comments in reviewing the draft have helped made this manual immeasurably better.

Florian A. Mikulski

INTRODUCTION

WHAT IS THIS MANUAL ABOUT?

A business doesn't always buy from catalogs describing features, options, specifications and price. Even small companies have situations in which only customized products can provide a solution. This manual is about how to purchase customized or complex technology, and how to manage your vendor, so that you have a high degree of confidence in the project's success.

If you order a Chrysler with all the options, you select them from a limited set of possibilities. You know that it would be nearly impossible to alter any of those options once the order arrived at the factory. If you change your mind on your order for a Rolls-Royce, almost any option can be accommodated.

But in a business situation like the purchase of a computer application, the number of changes that can be implemented is virtually infinite.

Customized technology is equipment, services or software, that either does not exist in a form to meet the buyer's needs, or must have major modifications to meet that need. Customized technology can also include procurement of off-the-shelf technology on such a scale, that the size of the purchase and its deployment is immense, and therefore, contains a high degree of planning, schedule, and delivery risk. Customized technology also has the characteristic that the cost of customization is a large percentage of the total purchase price. Another characteristic is that it is usually purchased through a competitive bid and proposal process.

A custom designed software package to manage the operation of a refinery is customized technology. Installing a local area network on one floor, for a ten person work group, would not be customized technology, even if some modifications were made to the system, because it does not have adequate scope and risk. Purchase of packet network equipment to be deployed in fifteen countries meets the definition by virtue of the project size and distribution, even though the technology itself is off-the-shelf. Buying ten personal computers is not customized technology because there is little or no customization, and price is more important than minor differences in functionality.

The principles defined in this manual apply to any technology. The procurement of computer systems software is our example for presenting the thesis. Computer systems projects have a high degree of innovation, are complex and frequently fail, so they provide a good example of a more difficult and risky procurement.

The time frame over which the procurement takes place has a definite beginning and an end, and hence is a *Project*. The major events that occur between the beginning and end of the project are called *Milestones*. The whole process is called a *Project Life Cycle*. The management process to deliver the project is called *Project Management*. When a vendor is involved, it's called *Vendor Management*.

The *Vendor* or supplier is the source from whom you will buy the technology. In most cases your firm doesn't have the expertise to design or implement the technology, or you have other priorities that conflict with doing it yourself. Therefore, selection and management of the vendor with the best product is essential to success.

This manual presents its message in two ways. The first is the development of a set of reasoned rules, philosophies and concepts that are grouped under the term: "Principles." It's critically important to understand and adhere to the Principles. The second approach is to provide you with a set of checklists and procedures that will help you in improving your vendor selection and management process.

However, cookbook solutions aren't useful if they ignore your firm's specific circumstances. It is more useful to think clearly guided by fundamental principles than to be confused by a lot of process.

But there is a need for a standardized way of selecting and managing a vendor. A standardized methodology can be measured, and is easier to communicate and teach than ad hoc approaches. Standardized methodology, once embedded within a firm's culture, allows people to concentrate on the content of the project, and not on whether the process is reasonable and understandable. This manual provides a standardized approach that has successfully stood the test of time in selecting quality vendors and managing them to deliver satisfactory solutions.

WHY IS THIS MANUAL NECESSARY?

You might recognize one of the following situations. You bought a new car but because you didn't test drive it in your own neighborhood, you now find that it's underpowered for the hill you live on. You got a good deal on a new stereo system, but the speakers don't match the room acoustics because you weren't willing to have the store demonstrate the system in your home. You bought an off-brand washing machine, and now that you've moved, you can't get it serviced.

These annoying examples of simple mistakes, even in the selection of items that we think we understand, happen all too frequently. One would think we would learn by our mistakes. Yet, these mistakes are trivial in comparison with the mistakes businesses make when it comes to choosing customized technical products and services.

Even low-level technical procurements get screwed up. Remember the football stadium that was constructed some years ago without toilets?

The size of business that is impacted doesn't seem to matter much. The complexity of the technology and the dollar value may be different for a large firm than for a small one, but the relative impact of mistakes in procurement are invariably the same. Large companies can frequently overcome mistakes. A small company may not recover, with bankruptcy the result.

Mistakes are viewed by senior management as a disaster. Mistakes cost money and time. Mistakes cost loss in project time and management time. Time lost equates to opportunities lost because of the unavailability of the product or service. Careers are destroyed when procurement mistakes are made. So, it is essential to a business, and to its employees, that the risks inherent in buying customized technology are minimal, and recognized to be minimal. If you have the right tools to buy customized technology, then you will minimize the risks.

Since most businesses do not have research and development as their main line of business, they need to purchase technology from vendors. If the buyer and vendor operate by a reasonable set of procedures, they can reduce risk and avoid unpleasant situations. After all, an internal project can sometimes be covered up. It's the projects that involve outsiders that get the bad publicity, the acrimony and the lawsuits. Establishing a professional management process for delivering customized technology creates ownership and commitment by customer and vendor. That is risk avoidance at its best.

Although we use the commercial business world as the example, government and institutions are not exempt from the need to have successful technology implementations. Perhaps you remember the new computer system which the New Jersey Department of Motor Vehicles purchased from a vendor, and years later, it was still not functioning properly.

In government (municipal, state or federal, civilian or military) the restrictions on employee conduct in procurements are strict. Yet, there are frequent examples of fraud, conflicts of interest and contested awards.

If you adopt the methods in this manual, you will have high probability that:

- You have bought the best system at the best price.

- You will not be second-guessed by management about that procurement.

- You will not have contested awards, because the process is fair and the vendors will know it is fair.

The degree to which these methods are adopted will vary with company size, the degree of bureaucracy, the capabilities of the technical personnel, and how much the firm was burned by the last procurement disaster. We present a formal process because it is important to cover many of the possible types of problem situations. You should adopt what will work in your company.

However, there is a real difference between methods and principles. If you fail to adopt the principles upon which the methods are based, you will increase your risk and the probability of an unsuccessful procurement.

WHAT SIZE OF COMPANY CAN USE THIS MANUAL?

Let's examine two kinds of companies. If a company has at least $5 million annual sales, it's reasonable to expect that at some time it will need to buy some special technology costing as much as $1 million.

For example, a specialty garment manufacturer may need a modified computer controlled laser fabric cutter to improve quality and productivity. An expenditure of $1 million may not be unreasonable for that equipment. But a less expensive purchase could get the firm in trouble. A software program costing only a few thousand dollars, required for a special production run, could have enormous impact if its malfunctioning hampered the firm's ability to accurately cut its fabrics. Exhibit 1 has a graphic representation of a 150 person company with three levels of management. The discussion that follows analyzes this exhibit.

A company that has $5 million in annual revenue will likely have from $1 to $3 million in payroll costs, depending upon the industry and product. If we assume an average salary of $25 thousand per person, the total staffing level might be between 50 to 180. If you agree that a reasonable span of management control is 5-6 direct reports, then a 150 person company will have three levels of management: the boss, managers, and supervisors, plus the doers.

In this small firm it is probable that all three levels of management will be involved in any purchase of customized technology. The line manager (e.g. manufacturing) may not only be required to install the technology, but will likely be the principal user of it. Certainly the line manager will have "ownership" of the result. The functional manager (Information Systems) has to recommend the technology to the boss, and may have to do much of the technical analysis himself. As a member of the management team, he has a vital interest in the project's impact on his career. Top management is concerned about the expenditure, the risk, and the impact upon profitability and operations.

These individuals actually "wear several hats." The boss is a decision maker and a buyer; the functional manager is a recommender, a reviewer, and a project controller; and the line manager is an acceptor and a user. Meanwhile, the supervisor or project manager working for the functional manager will have to probably manage the day-to-day tasks of the project.

The concepts just introduced (e.g., decision maker, reviewer, buyer) will be more fully developed below for a larger company.

EXHIBIT INT-1

ORGANIZATIONAL STRUCTURE FOR A SMALL BUSINESS

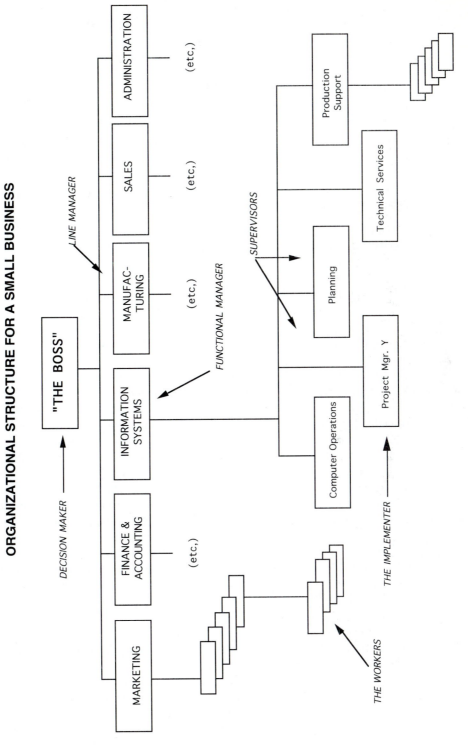

These managers must understand their role in the process of purchasing technology, and therefore, should be familiar with the principles of this manual to varying degrees. The two lower levels must be knowledgeable enough to know how to adopt the procedures to their scale. Thus, even if your company has only 150 employees and you are a supervisor or manager, you should be familiar with this manual because sooner or later you will be involved in a large project procurement.

A similar case can be made for a larger firm. In a larger firm the "hats" are worn by more bodies. It's not unusual for four or more levels of management to be involved in the process of selecting and implementing customized technology. A larger company also has more specialization in its organization. Thus the hierarchy involved with the purchasing decision and its implementation may also be specialized.

Exhibit 2 provides an organizational view of participants in a procurement in a larger firm. Use the Exhibit in the following presentation.

The following discrete functions or persons are likely participants in the selection and implementation of customized technology.

The *Decision Authority* is the person who can approve the spending of the money involved. This may be the CEO, a division general manager, a line of business manager, or even a special review committee to whom such authority has been granted. The bottom line is that this authority controls the expenditure of the dollars.

A *Recommender* is the person who has responsibility to ensure that the technical solution supports the business requirements. This individual is accountable to certify the qualifications of the vendor and the product and the propriety of the method of selection. He or she usually is also accountable to deliver the working result satisfactorily to the internal *Buyer* or *User* if there is one. The recommendee or a direct report, is the *Accountable Executive*.

In large companies, the *User* may very well be an operations component. Functional segmentation of back office operations from marketing, for example, may mean that customized technology will operate in the back office under the direction of a User.

The *Buyer* may be the executive of a line of business (e.g. marketing), whose profitability will benefit from the technology, but who will neither use it nor implement it. By definition, the *Buyer* pays for the project out of his budget. The User, the Recommender and the Implementer are effectively subcontractors who deliver the technology to the *Buyer*.

The *Implementer* is the person accountable for the actual planning and implementation of the project. These are usually high level technical managers who manage others who do the work.

A *Project Manager* is usually assigned to hold primary responsibility for the vendor management. The *Project Manager* has a dedicated or seconded team of technicians assigned to assist in implementation of the project.

HOW MUCH OF THIS MANUAL SHOULD YOU KNOW?

The *Decision Authority* should know the principles well enough to understand that they are essential, and that they are followed when a vendor is recommended for his approval.

The *Buyer* and *User* should know the principles of sound vendor management. They should have confidence that the process will provide high probability that a solution meet-

EXHIBIT INT-2

PROCUREMENT PARTICIPANTS IN A LARGE FIRM

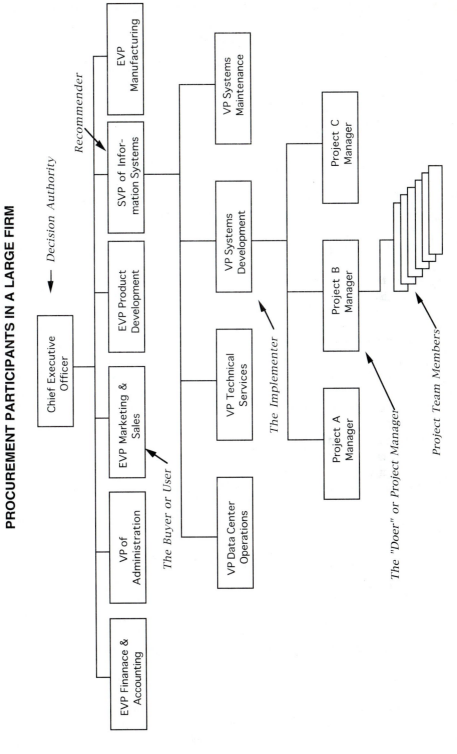

ing the business needs will be delivered in a timely and cost effective manner. Each has a vested interest in the total project (not just the vendor approval) because each is affected by the project's results.

The *Recommender* may be the Director of Research and Development, the Chief Information Systems Officer, Director of MIS, or any other person whose principal responsibility includes satisfactory implementation of the technology. The recommender is also the *Accountable Executive*. This individual is responsible for the creation of the policies and procedures that must be followed by the implementers. He or she is also responsible to ensure that the policies are actually followed, and that projects are successfully delivered. The *Recommender* is the person who is responsible for the final results of the project. Therefore, the *Recommender* is the "owner" of this manual or its equivalent within the company.

Implementers include people from a variety of technical organizations and disciplines. They are active participants in the planning for the technology, the selection of vendors, and implementation or operation of the technology. Implementers must be familiar with the procedures enacted within their firm. They are then responsible to ensure that their projects are actually implemented in accordance with the procedures.

The *Project Manager* must know every element of this manual and should want to use this manual as a day to day guide throughout the project life cycle. The *Project Life Cycle* is the total activity in a project, from specification generation through approval, implementation, test, and operations. This manual ties project life cycle activities into a unified methodology.

You buy customized technology because a *Vendor* has a capability which you can't duplicate. The vendor should know, understand and abide by the set of rules which your company is following. The vendor is in partnership with you for the period of the project. The higher the probability of success and the lower the risk, the more likely the vendor will be that the vendor will be profitable and receive follow on sales. Therefore, this manual is also required reading for any vendor.

HOW IS THIS MANUAL ORGANIZED?

The contents of this manual are logically divided into five parts with twelve chapters and two appendices:

Part 1. Know What You Want To Accomplish

This part is internally focused. It provides insight and procedures on how to plan within your company so that you can be successful in buying technology. It illustrates pitfalls in planning for technology projects when the culture or timing are inappropriate. Then we analyze how and why the preparation of requirements are so important, and various ways of specifying requirements to improve the probability of success while reducing risk and costs. Chapters 1 and 2 comprise Part 1.

Part 2. Establish the Internal Rules of Purchasing Technology

This part establishes the methods, procedures and rules about who within the company deals with vendors and how the company approves the choice of the vendor. It develops the need for a Systems Contract Administrator, the advantages of a Preferred Vendor Policy and the need for a Vendor Evaluation Policy. Special emphasis is devoted to examining why you should require separate technical, management and cost proposals from vendors. Part 2 includes Chapters 3 and 4.

Part 3. Have a Standard Approach to Find the Best Vendor

This part discusses how to collect information about vendors in order to create a vendor inventory and a qualified vendor list. It examines ways in which to exercise leverage over various types of vendor cultures. It examines activities you might conduct to assist in the procurement process, including Requests for Information (RFIs), Requests for Quotation (RFQs) and site visits. Then a structured and unified way of preparing the Request for Proposal (RFP) is presented in depth. The presentation emphasizes the need for uniform formats, especially the importance of Work Packages in controlling vendor responses. An actual script of a Request for Proposal is included. Chapters 5 through 9 and Appendix B comprise Part 3.

Part 4. Select the Best Vendor and Negotiate the Best Deal

This part provides a detailed walk-through of how to evaluate vendor proposals and shows how to negotiate the best contract once you know that you've selected the best vendor. The need for evaluator's worksheets, tool kits and questionnaires is developed. A detailed way to quantify the scoring of proposals is developed, and the case study examines scoring and evaluation processes and meetings. The requirement for sensitivity analyses, risk analyses and real costs review is demonstrated. The chapter on negotiation provides examples of actual negotiating tactics and the need for a negotiation worksheet with several negotiating positions. Part 4 includes Chapters 10 and 11 and Appendix A.

Part 5. Manage the Vendor You've Selected

This part discusses how to manage the vendor so that what you've bought works successfully. Emphasis is placed on those areas where the highest risk is present. Part 5 includes Chapter 12.

Format

Four styles have been used to distinguish differences in the text. Most of the presentation matter is in a type style such as this sentence.

> An inner paragraph like this will call attention to additional information, alternative approaches, examples which are not in the direct flow of the current topic, or, will point to exhibits that follow.

> When a fundamental principle needs to be emphasized, or attention directed to a highly important point, the point will be made in this style.

To add additional relevance to the presentation material, a case study approach will be used. When discussion reverts to use of the case study, the presentation format will be changed to this style.

## Chapter One

UNDERSTANDING MY COMPANY

Implementing a customized system is difficult enough without burdening yourself with internal enemies, misguided projects or questionable priorities. When you participate in the mainstream of your company's planning and can ally yourself with the line of business managers, you won't have to fight internal battles while you are trying to manage a vendor. Knowing how your company works, and how it can work for you, will help your chances of success in any project.

NO ONE LIVES IN A VACUUM

A stock market crash or a major recession makes us aware that circumstances can affect us all. Companies don't need crashes to change plans and behavior dramatically. Market forces and competitive pressure, as well as mismanagement or poor timing can influence decisions. These decisions in turn impact the technical support staff.

> Assume that you were a telecommunications manager for the Allegis Corporation, the holding company of United Airlines back in 1987. You have a charter to integrate the various networks of its subsidiaries. In January, you might have been trying to convince the general managers of Hertz and the Westin Hotel chain to sign up for your common corporate network. By October (if you hadn't followed your company's painful reorganization in the press) you might be taking down the network that was no longer relevant to the new United Airlines.

> You must be aware of current corporate business issues. Otherwise, what you technically propose may be irrelevant to the firm's future.

At top levels in a company, executives participate in strategic business planning. Because strategy can involve sales of nonperforming divisions, layoffs of personnel in troubled times, or acquisition of another business, these sensitive activities are usually confidential. Some of these activities also fall into disclosure constraints of *Insider* knowledge, as defined under the Securities and Exchange Commission Regulations. Therefore, much planning and analysis goes on that is not commonly known to employees. Yet, when corporate decisions are made, the fallout on current plans can be enormous.

Strategic planning in a small firm may be equivalent to a long daydream by the founder. Or there may be an annual off-site planning session to review where the firm should be in the next few years. The degree of precision and formality of the plan will likely differ greatly from a large firm. Sophisticated or not, at some point the plan must be given to others for execution.

THE CASE STUDY

John Sparks is Senior Vice President for Systems Development at Baccarat Bank and Trust Co. (BB&T). Baccarat came into existence in the last century, with its assets presumably being created at the card table. Despite its questionable beginning, BB&T is a well managed institution with over $1,500 million in assets and a return on assets of 1%. It has a well regarded, if stodgy reputation. The primary growth of the bank has been in commercial and real estate loans and management of pension trusts. John reports to the Executive Vice President for Operations and Systems, Lisa Moore, and is responsible for the planning and implementation of systems applications within the bank. John and his peers manage their areas of responsibility with a high degree of autonomy, tempered by some shared management objectives.

Some months ago in October, Lisa had asked John to make an assessment of commercially available software packages, including systems that integrated wholesale and retail processing. John considered that packages were a waste of time. BB&T had always developed its applications in the past. John felt that he had an excellent systems staff and could develop anything the bank required. He knew of only one major current systems problem. Around the time of Lisa's request, John concluded that the existing commercial loan system needed to be rewritten. Seven years of modifications and improvements to the system has led to operational inefficiencies and difficulty in implementing new modifications. Although considered obsolete by today's standards of efficient code, the system did the functions it needed to. However, John was from the school of "only the best technology for us."

John subdivided the research team investigating integrated systems, and initiated a project to begin a new commercial loan system using fourth generation techniques. After four months of effort the team itemized existing system problems and documented the new system requirements.

On Wednesday, February 7, John triumphantly provided Lisa with a presentation on the new system requirements. He also requested approval for a half-million dollars in additional funds to implement the system. Lisa responded extremely coolly to the presentation. She also asked John for the status of the integrated system pack-

age analysis. John protested about the study, and reaffirmed his certitude that the only system BB&T should be doing is a new loan system. No useful resolution came out of the meeting, and they agreed to meet again Friday.

At a major press conference on Thursday, BB&T announced the acquisition of the Mimosa Street Bank, an $800 million bank with a retail branch network, on-line tellers and Automated Teller Machines. Most of the customers of Mimosa Street Bank are individuals and small businesses. Mimosa Street Bank uses a service bureau for its data processing.

On Monday, Fred Everet set about picking up the pieces in John's organization as his replacement.

John's fate is not uncommon in the careers of highly concentrated persons. They get so focused on their relationship to technology that they ignore the signals around them. John didn't believe the last annual report or the strategic plan outlining an aggressive diversification and growth strategy for BB&T. If he had, he might have anticipated that the bank was no longer complacent to keep its current niche, and that change was in the wind. If diversification were likely, especially into retail banking, an integrated bank computer system would be needed. Therefore, the request from Lisa was more than curiosity. Based on her knowledge of confidential corporate plans, she had been trying to anticipate a business need for a new system without disclosing her inside knowledge.

An organization chart of the senior management of the Bank is in Exhibit 1-1.

Baccarat Bank and Trust (BB&T) is fictitious, as are all the characters and other entities in this case study. We chose a medium-size bank because it has multiple lines of business: personal, small-business retail, large commercial business, real estate, trust, credit card and perhaps a leasing subsidiary. The mission of banking is to provide financial services to customers. The interaction of many products within multiple lines of business, regulatory restrictions, and a diversified customer base makes banking a difficult business to plan, manage and control. Technology supports that mission. Since the banking business is complex, so too are the systems supporting the business. A complex example will enable the reader to better understand more of the issues of vendor management than a simpler case study.

The case study example is the procurement of a "Branch Integrated Transaction System" or BITS, as the staff of BB&T will call it. BITS will be a total retail bank processing system designed to integrate the operations of the acquired bank with the existing wholesale systems of BB&T. Purchased computer systems software seldom fit perfectly and usually need significant revision. The case study will follow how BB&T manages the procurement of a customized system for BITS from a vendor.

EXHIBIT 1-1

SENIOR MANAGEMENT OF BACCARAT BANK & TRUST

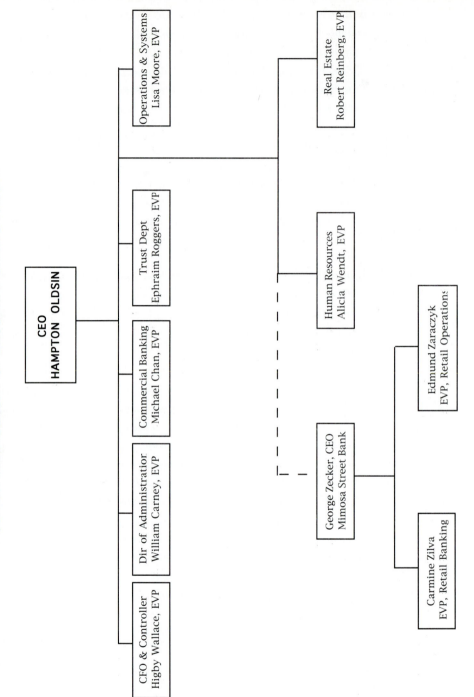

A corporation with many lines of business increases the difficulty of planning for the allocation of resources. It has a concurrent demand for resources from the technology support staff. Some requirements transcend one line of business and incorporate multiple user needs, and sometimes, the entire corporation. Reconciling multi-client or multi-user requirements are among the most difficult issues faced by technical management.

A small company can be a single-product firm or have a limited set of products. A multi-product company is concerned with allocation planning among its products. A multi-division company with independent product lines may treat each division as autonomous. Integration only happens at the corporate consolidation level in that case. The planning process is simpler, and the systems implications are easier to manage in each example above. But, there is always more demand than funds available. Decisions on resource allocation are made through the budgeting process.

CORPORATE CULTURE

What a business can do in technology is dependent upon what the business is willing to attempt. What is ventured will depend upon how decisions are made, and what the firm's previous experience has been in implementing technology. In a highly centralized company, strategic decisions are usually made at the top. Supporting the CEO as decision maker may be staff or review committees who pass judgment on proposals. These committees are invariably viewed by the systems staff as bottlenecks to getting the systems job done. Yet, they need not be.

Staff review groups often do what the proposal author should do in the first place: assess risk; determine economic benefits; estimate costs accurately; and ensure that all affected parties have an opportunity to concur. The only way to pass through the filter of these staff groups is to establish a shared professional concern for corporate values, not just technical. If you enlist their counsel the very first time you have a proposal, and accept their input, you will usually find that subsequent proposals get a more favorable review. You've made their job easier by paying attention to the values they are entrusted to protect.

In many firms, staff groups support senior level management committees entrusted by top management to act as a business and technical review committee. As more persons become involved in review, audit, concurrence and the like, the more important it is to have standard ways of communicating information.

Exhibit 1-2 provides an illustration of how a formal project approval mechanism might involve many key corporate participants.

Top down organizations have the benefit that everyone knows what to expect and how to react to what the boss wants. That may mean conformity and a lack of innovation and risk taking. Or, a top down focus may reflect a well considered view of major issues, with decisive decisions quickly made. The way a company considers risk may dictate the degree to which your proposal must conform to the culture.

A decentralized company with delegation may allow proposals to be approved by the decentralized components. Often, decisions happen faster without staff groups, and propos-

EXHIBIT 1-2

EXAMPLE: CORPORATE PROJECT APPROVAL HIERARCHY

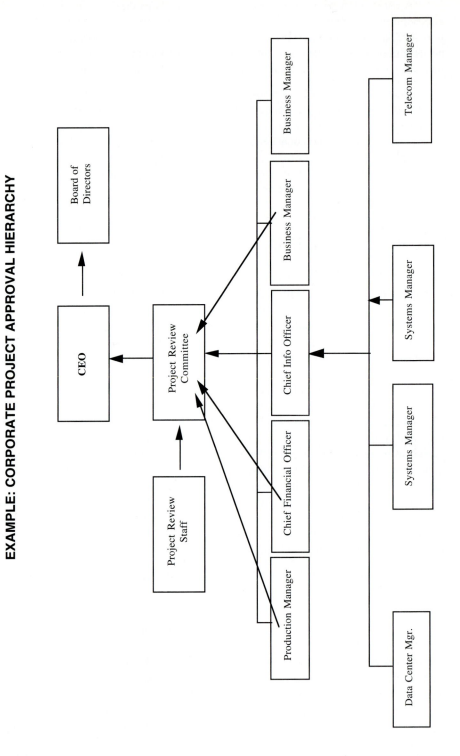

als may require less supporting information. The increased risk in not having peer review may be offset by a much closer working relationship between the technical personnel and the business unit. Signing up clients to support a multi-user project may be much more difficult in a decentralized culture, since there are more people with an "I'll do it for myself" mentality. A conglomerate culture is frequently a funeral pyre for multi-user projects.

Whether the culture is centralized or decentralized, the technical manager must know how to negotiate for his proposal. It helps if the climate is one in which the technicians are viewed as partners with the business managers, and not as necessary evils.

If the culture is complex, any proposal for innovation will take longer. You must allow for increased coordination and review time. If not, your credibility is damaged when the project is delayed. It won't matter that the internal bureaucracy contributed to the delay. After all, it's "your" project, not theirs. Therefore, the bottom line for any manager is to find a way in which the project will fit in with the corporate culture.

> Trying to change (or violate) corporate culture is best left to CEOs, and not to the technology components.

THE BUSINESS PLAN

Technology assessment begins with the Strategic Business Plan. Almost every business of any size has a business plan. A venture capitalist wouldn't even consider an investment in a start-up without a business plan. Why should an on-going business have any different need to document its plans than a start-up?

The *Business Plan* provides the goals, objectives, strategies and sometimes tactics that management needs to communicate to its constituencies. These are the shareholders, customers, suppliers and employees. The business plan specifies what, and how, top management expects its constituents to assess its performance. Therefore, the business plan is not just a piece of paper. It represents management's sense of priority and commitment, and its vision of the future. Presumably, management's bonuses depend on how well that plan is completed. We include decisions to do business reengineering within the context of a business plan.

The case can be made that the business plan is an ideal, and does not conform to the corporate reality. That may be partially true. However, the business plan represents a valid point of departure for discussion about options, contingent strategies, and the impact of unforeseen economic or competitive situations. As a technology member of the company, you are obliged to have conversations with your business counterparts about technology implications of the plan. No technical manager can ignore the need to take this initiative.

> **The Business Plan is the starting point for the collection of requirements needing technology support.**

Corporate management of BB&T had communicated their intentions to diversify in their previous annual report, and in a formal business plan that was circulated to all senior level officers, including John.

BB&T Management had defined the acquisition strategy in consumer banking to diversify its portfolio, find a lower cost source of funds and expand geographically. The business plan and the current year's budget allocated funds for further studies. The balance sheet was strong, and the price to earnings ratio high because of the good return on assets. In a climate of banking failures, it was clear that BB&T would be an acquiring bank.

Lisa tried to anticipate the retail bank acquisition by tasking John to investigate integrated banking systems. John Sparks ignored all the signals. He kept on doing his thing, without working with his internal business clients to see how the change in corporate strategy might affect them and him.

The first clue to anticipating the need for new technology is to know as much as possible about how your company communicates its intentions. Reading of annual reports, 10Ks and business plans are just the beginning. Aggressive line of business managers are also eager to take advantage of new opportunities. They need to understand the technical and operational implications of any opportunity.

In any company where technology is a service function, the technical staff must learn the income producer's business to be a productive part of the team. This also means trying to communicate with the client in the client's language, not the technologist's. The businessman certainly won't make the effort to learn the technology.

The technical manager should hold frequent talks with internal clients to figure out if what he is developing for them is still relevant. Feedback has to be a constant process. Monthly, if not biweekly, meetings between the technical manager and his line of business counterpart will do much to ensure that when the time comes to operate the new system no "we vs. they" situation arises.

Corporate plans are made under a set of assumptions about the economy and about the industry. In a capital intensive business (e.g., manufacturing), if interest rates climb severely in the coming months, and the assumption has been that they would be flat, an astute technical manager will anticipate that funding for all but extremely high priority projects will not be available. The cost of money will rise, increasing the firm's liabilities and reducing its cash flow. The technical manager should be much less assertive about promoting expensive new solutions under such circumstances.

> **Technology implementation is a partnership activity with the business unit requiring the product or service.**

Consider the smaller business. The business plan for a small business may be as informative for what it doesn't say, than for what it does. Since the small business can be somewhat simple, the business plan might be very simple as well. It may assume that growth and profitability will continue along current rates. We would interpret that to mean that the business will be in a "business as usual" mode for the foreseeable future. The present course is the future plan as well! Keep doing what you are doing. The plan or set assumptions may be correct or not. However, if the plan must be changed, everyone will be aware of the change because the culture has already communicated the baseline plan.

Management may be oblivious for the need to have a documented vision of the future and the approach to get there. Without written guidance, managers lower down in the organization may have difficulty making decisions in harmony with the future direction. A poor plan can be corrected. To have no plan is to invite chaos.

THE TECHNOLOGY PLAN

John Spark's career at BB&T might have been longer if Lisa also had had a formal program of technology planning in response to the strategic business plan.

Known as "*Business Systems Plans, Systems Plans, Information Systems Plans, Technology Annexes*" or by similar names, the Technology Plan is a formal interpretation by the technology component about the technical implications of the business plan execution, the projects anticipated, and an estimate of the funding required. In other words, the technology plan is the technologist's interpretation of what would need to be done technically to support the business plan. These could be programs to lower costs, increase capacity, reengineer operations, improve accuracy, or provide a new system for transaction processing.

The business plan has appendices that contain preliminary capital, project and operating budgetary estimates for the plan period. These should include a technology component. By reviewing the technology budget estimates to their plan, business managers can anticipate the development and operating costs that their plans may incur. After review, business plans may be altered, or technology responses scaled back. In this way, the corporation obtains a responsible and responsive feedback from its technology component.

As a corollary to constructive conversations between technologists and business units, when spending proposals for technology are presented during a budgetary planning cycle, they are easier to approve. The preliminary estimates will have been incorporated into the business unit's budget, or in the technical unit's budget. In any event, the business component will have concurred in the technical plan. The periodic dialogue between the business manager and the technology unit will also ensure that these estimates are refined as business situations change.

Technology management is a business in itself. The technology plan also includes components of planning and budgeting unique to the technology organization alone. For example, new disk drives, additional memory, or diagnostic systems are self contained expenditure elements that get reviewed and approved as part of technological support to the whole corporation.

A more difficult situation arises when a business plan has a corporate-wide impact, affecting multiple lines of business. The technical response to a corporate wide plan may be a large system. Many components may be affected. Reconciling the technical plan becomes a two-fold task. One must negotiate the corporate response with the component designated to represent the corporation, and simultaneously negotiate with all impacted parties to find what they gain or lose with the new technology. This process is difficult, but is useful for large and small firms alike, since internal needs are clarified and priorities reconciled.

A valid reason for the widespread move away from centralized management of a business is the incredibly difficult job of building systems that satisfy multiple users. The compromises necessary in a multi-user system to make enough components happy all too often lead to the building of a camel when one needs a horse.

In the case study example, the Branch Integrated Transaction System (BITS) is a multi-user system. Hence, it has high risk. Remember that the multi-million dollar write-off some years ago for a failed Trust System at Bank of America was a multi-user, multi-state and multi-bank system! CONFIRM, the hotel and car rental reservation system, was another multi-user, multi-business system that failed dramatically.

THE BUDGET PROCESS

When you can anticipate the future, you can plan for it. Since implementing technology is dependent upon when the business unit decides to move ahead with its plans, anticipating when to budget for project capital and expense funding is another challenge facing technical management.

Technology development has a long lead time. Technical managers, therefore, need to plan for multi-year programs. In many companies, the budgeting process for next year doesn't have such a look-ahead provision. If that's the case, technical management will need to work with the budget planning staff to get such a provision incorporated. Then management won't get surprised by multiple-year project expenditures.

Assuming a calendar year fiscal cycle, many companies begin a preliminary round of budget submissions in May or June. Formal reviews start at the executive level in September. Revisions are then made to reflect current year earnings through three quarters. The final budget is approved by the Board of Directors in December for the coming year.

A May submission is much too late to present the technology part of the budget. If a line of business is paying for the project, they won't have a chance to agree with you on the appropriate level of expense before the schedule of budget submissions gets beyond their ability to control. If your submissions are integrated by the corporate staff, and you wait until May to coordinate with the business unit, they will be miffed because they didn't get the first review. Your proposed budget effects their profitability. As a consequence, the technical unit often gets only part of what they request, since budget estimates may not have been changed to reflect their contribution (or cost).

We've found the following useful. In January of the year before the budget will take effect, submit a preliminary one-page estimated budget to each line of business you support. List by category, the line item to be funded, and its connection to the business plan. Then discuss the estimated budget that you expect to submit in May with the line of business manager.

Exhibit 1-3 contains an example of how such a one-page preliminary budget proposal to a line of business might look.

If the funds are in the business' budget, you have sufficient time to get your budgetary requirements included. If they are in your budget, you have time to get the concurrence you need. In either case, you have good communications with your line of business partner, and you won't get hammered by their lack of agreement during the formal budget review cycle in September.

You can imagine how difficult it is to anticipate budgetary expenses for projects between 11 and 23 months before they begin. It is better to submit what you will require in January, and change it as the process moves, than to be under-funded and embarrassed by a lack of planning and teamwork. It goes almost without saying that if you propose a budget and don't reduce it when better estimates are available, you will lose every bit of credibility you established by getting your contribution in early.

> **When it comes to budget planning, the technical manager must be early, anticipatory, and the first to reduce the budget when the funds aren't needed.**

So far we found that none of the above has occurred at BB&T. The strategic business plan was not backed up by a technology plan. The technical staff did not have a dialogue with the business components. A budget for new projects was not proposed.

Presumably because BB&T has not had dramatic change over many years, institutionalization of business-technology coordination was done informally rather than formally. The net result was that even senior technology managers had few guidelines to follow, and few relationships developed with business counterparts. Furthermore, technology efforts emphasized internal systems development that no one requested. We think John Sparks replacement, Fred Everet, has a real problem.

EXHIBIT 1-3

BUDGET PLANNING PROPOSAL

Baccarat Bank & Trust

Preliminary Systems Support Budget

Business Component:

Commercial Loan
Department

Business Executive:

Michael Chan,
EVP

Business Requirement:

> Increasing commercial loan volume, and an increase in the variety and features available in loan proposals has created a situation in which current automated systems cannot cope with the unique repayment scenarios. The bank is at risk of not being able to adequately determine its exposure under these new options.

Project Description &
Systems Requirement: **Priority:**   Moderately High

> Initiate the first stage of a systems requirements analysis to determine the scope of changes required to implement either new accrual calculations and an increased database, or, conversely, determine the scope of a new system to replace the existing Commercial Loan System.

Financial Proposal: $(000)

Proposed Capital:	$250.0	**Current Year Capital:**	$0.0
Proposed Budget:	$200.0	**Current Year Budget:**	$50.0
Total Expenditure:	$450.0	**Total Expenditure:**	$50.0

Benefits:

> Accurate loan accounting information. With a loan portfolio of $400 million, a 1% level of inaccuracy could expose the bank to fraud or collection problems of $4 million in additional risk.

Requesting Officer: John Sparks,
SVP

## Chapter Two

PROJECT REQUIREMENTS

WHAT ARE REQUIREMENTS?

A *Requirement* is a statement of need. Requirements are the conceptual blueprints from which the vendor develops the software. A requirement can be originated by a business component, an operations unit, or the technical unit. When applied to a systems procurement, a requirement is translated into specifications that dictate the performance characteristics of the system to be procured.

Systems *Analysis* is the process of translating non-technical business needs into quantified, technical specifications. A *Systems Analyst* is a person who understands the business person's language and the technical language of the resultant specification. After the systems analyst translates the business need into technical information, he must review what he has created with the business person to confirm that his interpretation is correct. If the requirement is not fed back and approved, there is little likelihood that the business person will really understand the technical performance specifications which result. It is up to the analyst to provide the necessary interpretation between the language of business and the language of technology.

Exhibit 2-1 Requirements Validation Process shows a flowchart of the process by which the original expression of need gets translated into detailed performance specifications. This Exhibit will be useful in the discussion that follows.

Monday afternoon, the Chief Executive Officer of Baccarat Bank and Trust (BB&T), Mr. Hampton Oldsin, gave a briefing about the acquisition of the Mimosa Street Bank (MSB), to the Officers of the Baccarat Bank and Trust. Mr. Oldsin pointed out the marketing synergism of the acquisition, the broadened base of deposits that would provide a lower cost of money to BB&T for loans, and the lowered risk to earnings that a diversified portfolio and client base would provide. He expected that regulatory approval for the merger would be obtained late in the year. He named seven

EXHIBIT 2-1

REQUIREMENTS VALIDATION PROCESS

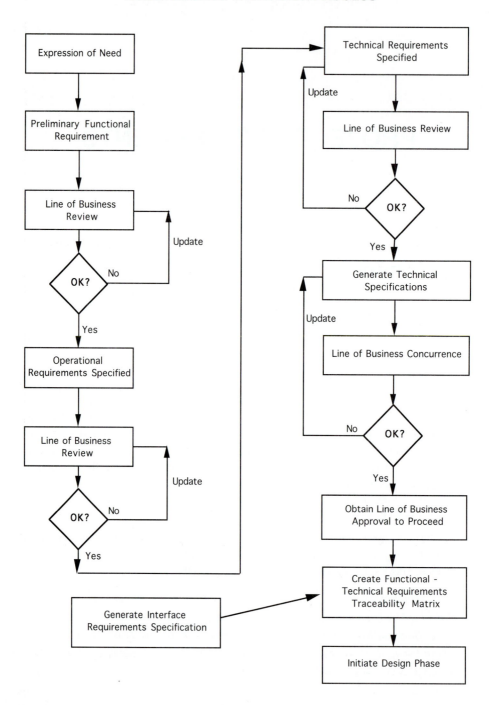

task forces, staffed by members of both banks, who would immediately work on planning for the management of the combined bank. Since combined operations could not begin before regulatory approval, and since end-of-year peak business must not be hampered by organizational dislocations, the actual start date of a fully integrated bank would begin after the end of the following year's first quarter, or on April 1.

As Fred and Lisa walked out of the auditorium, Fred tried to remove the glaze from his eyes caused by the shock of knowing that a corporate decision had been made and he had a nearly impossible task to do. He asked Lisa: "Didn't you tell him integrating operations and systems is impossible in this time frame?" Lisa said: "I was so persistent that I'm lucky to be still employed. The Board of Directors and Oldsin would not hear of it. We must get the two banks together. There are other activities planned that make the date unalterable. I can't discuss them."

"Fred, I'm leading the integration task force on operations. You will have to lead the way in doing the systems integration and development. By the way, since the Mimosa Street Bank uses a service bureau, they essentially have no systems staff either. You'll need to get requirements directly from the marketing and branch operations functions of the MSB. We cannot continue to use the service bureau. That's a mandate. The MSB has too many audit exceptions for that processing. It's also one of the reasons why they were a low-cost investment."

As Fred sat in his office, he cursed at the mindlessness of management in dictating inviolate target dates without their understanding the difficulty in achieving the results they wanted. They probably didn't care at all about his difficulty!

After a bit, Fred calmed down and began to take stock of the situation. Since there was no long range plan or budget, and this was a corporate directive, obtaining funding approval to spend what he needed would not be a problem. BB&T has a good data center with extra capacity on the mainframe, so hardware acquisition won't be necessary. It's unlikely that we have the knowledge to develop the retail system in-house, so a vendor solution is probable. But that can wait. First, we have to find out what is required to create an integrated bank.

How often have you been faced with a similar situation? Unreasonable schedules, unknown requirements and unknown risks, with top management looking sternly over your shoulder?

In some industries like Wall Street, impossible systems requirements are the norm. When a new financial product is created, millions of dollars are at stake. It's critical to be the first to offer the product. The back office must be capable of processing the new type of transaction in order for the product to be sold. Systems implementation becomes the critical path item pacing successful entry of the new product. Somehow, these "impossible" systems do get completed, but the stress level is very high.

The case study is an example of a top down requirement. The origin of requirements can take a number of forms.

BUSINESS DRIVEN REQUIREMENTS

Requirements which originate from top management or the marketing or sales units of the organization are *Business Driven Requirements* because these units are the revenue generators of the company. They are the primary and most influential sources for defining systems needs.

> For a rug manufacturer, an order-entry system may be the most important system for the business. A distributor's order is entered, and production, shipping and installation activities all follow.

> An oil exploration company may find that the computer system that does seismic analysis is its most important system. Without accurate modeling and analysis capability, the company may be unable to identify likely oil fields. Its dry holes will increase and drilling costs will be too high. A quality seismic model will be the differentiating factor in its competitive position and profitability.

A bank may have several business driven requirements: calculation of loan accruals; balancing cost of funds versus pricing of loans (if the difference or "spread" is too narrow, the bank is unprofitable); consolidating customer relationship exposure to meet legal lending limits; or, monthly statements consolidating all customer accounts—checking, savings, certificates of deposit, credit card and home mortgage. These requirements stem from the need to manage money prudently and lend prudently, or to provide a product (consolidated statement) that may differentiate the bank from its competitors and attract new customers.

If the requirement is for a new product (e.g., a consolidated monthly statement) a systems analyst will meet with the business manager and discuss the ideas for inclusion in the new statement. Let's assume that the manager suggests the following: "I believe the statement should show end-of-month balances and each transaction for the customer's checking account, savings accounts, money market, certificates of deposits, consumer loans and real estate loans."

This list includes a lot of informational products and it is likely that each will have its own transaction processing system, accounting system and output processing. In his statement of business need, the marketing person is oblivious to the infrastructure surrounding these products. Only a broad description of what should be aggregated has been offered as the requirement. These broad statements of requirements are called *Functional Requirements*. "Group the products into one report" is a functional requirement because it specifies what, not how, nor to what degree of accuracy, nor to what format. Exhibit 2-1 tracks the scenario of requirements development that follows. The period in which this process occurs is called the *Functional* or *Definition Phase* of a project.

> The following example may help your understanding. If I say I want a two door automobile that has good acceleration, braking and handling, I've defined a few functions: a functional requirement. If I specify that my automobile must go from 0 to 60 in less than 5.9 seconds; brake from 60 mph to full stop in less than 250 feet; pass NASCAR's slalom testing standards for maneuverability; have a top speed of not less

> # A broad, nontechnical statement of a need
> # is called a Functional Requirement.

than 128 mph; and have a six speaker 100 watts rms per channel sound system, etc., etc. I am very specific about what I want. These are more than needs, these are specifications.

Because this second set of automobile requirements can be supplied by Porsche, Corvette, BMW, Ferrari and several other cars, does not alter the fact that I have eliminated more cars than I have included. The detailed performance requirements are called Requirements Specifications. These are discussed later.

The analyst will collect the requirements, do some research, and come up with a few ideas on what can or cannot be done. One response to the business counterpart might be the following: "All the systems you want consolidated can be consolidated into one statement except the real estate and loan systems. Each has specialized accounting and a rigid processing schedule. Because we must process customers' statements on a cyclical basis, we can't match these systems with the statement. Including the real estate and loan information would only be useful to 5% of our customers whose statement days match the loan and mortgage days. Everyone else would be very confused. We can consolidate the other systems, and they would be issued on statement date, not at month end."

Cyclical statements are mailed by businesses that have a huge number of customers. It is impossible to process all customers' statements on one day at month end. Therefore, companies use a rotating schedule for this process, called the cycle date. Banks do the same, only they call it statement date.

The manager agrees to the new proposal. The exceptions were OK because the analyst took the time to explain why the number of systems had to be limited. The business requirement was fed-back to the originator and the recommended changes were accepted.

OPERATIONAL REQUIREMENTS

After completing the sessions with the business manager, the systems analyst visits the production managers for each product. They discuss the changes that would be required of their operations to produce a consolidated statement. It might be necessary to move the start of processing credit card accounts up by two hours, in order for the statement consolidating software to have access to all the completed product files in time to do its own processing. That might have an operational consequence of requiring some employees to start work two hours earlier. Two hours may be an estimate, to be refined when the system is closer to operating. However, the need for an operational change is noted, and included in the aggregation of the requirements for the consolidated statement. It is possible that human resources and the legal department (for labor issues) may have to approve a change in operating schedules.

Even personnel a bit removed from the direct production process may need to be consulted. The mailroom supervisor might need to know the increased size or increased weight of envelopes that will be handled. The mailroom supervisor might even suggest that the increased weight of the combined statement pages may increase postage by an ounce an item.

TABLE 2-1
CONSOLIDATED STATEMENT IMPACT ON POSTAGE COSTS

YEAR	NUMBER OF MONTHLY ENVELOPES	COST PER ENVELOPE, $	TOTAL NET COST, $	SAVINGS, $
MULTIPLE STATEMENTS, *One ounce each*				
Year 1	1,600,000	0.22	352,000	
Year 2	1,600,000	0.25	400,000	
Year 3	1,600,000	0.30	480,000	
CONSOLIDATED STATEMENT, *One Ounce*				
Year 1	1,000,000	0.22	220,000	132,000
Year 2	1,000,000	0.25	250,000	150,000
Year 3	1,000,000	0.30	300,000	180,000
CONSOLIDATED STATEMENT, *Two Ounces*				
Year 1	1,000,000	0.39	390,000	-38,000
Year 2	1,000,000	0.45	450,000	-50,000
Year 3	1,000,000	0.55	550,000	-70,000

As shown in Table 2-1, the bank has 400,000 customers using each of the four products. Then the current monthly mailing is 4 times 400,000 or 1,600,000 envelopes. At postage rates prevailing in Year 1, the monthly postage cost was $352,000. When postal rates went up in Year 2, the cost rose to $400,000 and to $480,000 when each ounce increased to $.30 in Year 3.

Assume that by consolidating several products into one statement, the total number of statements that would be mailed would drop to 1 million. As you can see from the table, if the mailing could be done at a cost of one ounce per envelope, the consolidated statement would save $132,000 per month in Year 1, $150,000 in Year 2 and further savings as postal rates increase in Year 3. If the consolidated statement included more pages containing enhanced detail or promotional literature, so that the weight per envelope increased to two ounces, then the consolidated statement would be more expensive than current costs. The impact is indicated in the last three rows in Table 2-1.

Has the business manager's profit analysis included a scenario that anticipates this possible expense contribution? We don't know. Once the systems analyst presents this data to the manager, there will be a greater awareness of operational consequences of marketing initiatives. The analyst's feedback in this example might be the key factor in the success or failure of the project.

TECHNICAL REQUIREMENTS

Technical requirements include two classifications. The first stems from the analysis of a business requirement. The example we have been using can be extended to cover technical requirements.

To complete the preliminary analysis of requirements, the systems analyst visits the data center manager. They discuss what the business manager needs, and the technical impacts. They then estimate the computer resources necessary to do the consolidation. Let's assume that the computer has enough capacity to meet the requirement. But, when they investigate the volume of paper (including promotional materials) that would be created per day by the new consolidated statement, they estimate that a new laser printer would be required at a cost of $300 thousand. The technology currently available cannot do the job without a major investment. After investigating options, the data center manager suggests that if the statements leave out the lines of promotional material and truncate the descriptions of the transactions to forty characters, the existing equipment will be sufficient.

The analyst returns to the business manager and presents the option: find $300 thousand to pay for your new requirement, or modify the requirement so we can meet it with existing equipment. The business manager would revise the business plan financial forecast to include the laser printer expense, choose the limited text option, or withdraw the requirement entirely because the resulting statement will not be of sufficient quality to generate new business to merit the investment.

This process of iterative communication is the proper way in which requirements should be identified, modified and validated. Blind acceptance of the business need by operations or systems might have caused excessive cost or operational problems. Getting all who are affected involved in the process avoids problems. This is why requirements collection and systems analysis is frequently the longest part of the development cycle.

> Requirements collection and validation must be iterative. Compromise is essential if reasonable solutions are to be found.

The systems analyst completes documenting the business, operational and technical requirements. Many details are still left out of the requirements in this preliminary stage. Performance criteria are absent. But the information collected thus far can serve as the starting point for further refinement.

A second type of technical requirement is the need to change technology within the technology component itself. When a mainframe computer begins to deliver slower response to terminal users, the technology unit must define its own requirements to upgrade computer capacity to meet its standards of performance. These are internally generated technical requirements. Most firms today have standard procedures for management review and approval of these technology infrastructure enhancements.

INTERFACE REQUIREMENTS

So far we've considered the requirements process as though it was occurring in a vacuum, free from external or internal influences. The personal computer is the only stand-alone system, and even these are networked to an ever increasing degree. Almost every new system will have an interface with other systems.

Systems that either feed or receive data from the system being developed must define the rules by which that linkage is to be made. Because the new system can cause processing problems to existing systems, the new system must conform to the existing standards if risk is to be minimized. The interface must be rigorously specified. A set of technical, electrical, physical, logical and timeliness requirements must be specified. The custodians of each of these interfacing systems (or manual activities) will guarantee their side of the interface by signing an *"Interface Agreement"* or *"Interface Specification."* This agreement includes assurances that their side of the interface will not be altered, thereby assuring compatibility when the new system is delivered.

An *Interface Requirements Specification* is a formal agreement between the owners/operators of two systems, documenting the specifications that govern the transfer of data between them. In a static operation, complying with interface requirements is usually not a problem. Only the system under development undergoes extensive change and must have its design conform to the other systems.

On the other hand, if there are multiple systems concurrently under development, special effort must be made to monitor the interfaces between these systems and the processing performed as a consequence of the interface. In parallel developments, new requirements and design changes inevitably occur, and must be tracked. Changes must be audited and tested. Risk is increased for each system because of the combined uncertainty of the compatibility of the simultaneously changing systems.

Special test cases must be developed to reduce the risk. It is prudent to allow extra time for testing of all interfaces. An additional degree of prudence would dictate freezing all system changes at a specified date before integrated testing begins, to be assured that the individual systems are stable.

If possible, avoid situations of parallel development of interfacing systems. The risk of one or both systems failing increases by much more than the sum of the individual risks.

> An Interface Requirements Specification must be created for every system or activity that feeds or receives data from the new system.

> An Interface Requirements Specification is as critical to project success as the System Requirements Specifications of the system being developed.

REQUIREMENTS SPECIFICATIONS

The period when detailed requirements are developed from functional requirements is called the *Requirements* or *Definition Phase* of a project. The documentation produced from this activity is a *Requirements Specification*. It's a specification because it lists detailed quantitative performance specifications that the completed system must meet. We retain the name requirements because the degree of detail is not so specific that it effectively dictates the actual design of a system. The ultimate implementation can still take many forms, as our automobile example above illustrates.

The process of creating definite project phases or cycles started in the late 1950's when the projects to build the earliest missiles, satellites and the Early Warning Radar Systems became incredibly complex. In order for anyone to understand the schedule and what was to be built, the project was divided into discrete phases. Each phase was further subdivided into smaller, understandable and measurable tasks.

Almost every major business has adopted some form of this process, usually called a "*Project Life Cycle* or *Systems Development Life Cycle*" for their systems development. We totally subscribe to this process.

Exhibit 2-2 provides an outline of the generally accepted phases of a systems development project. The completion of all phases completes the project life cycle. These phases will be discussed only in the context of the vendor relationship.

The preparation of the Requirements Specification is the first technical phase of the project. The systems analyst begins documenting requirements in a standard format, listing performance criteria as quantitatively as possible.

Exhibit 2-3 provides a simple example of the difference in quantitative and qualitative precision between a functional requirement and a requirements specification. The example illustrates the purchase of a Private Branch Exchange (PBX) telephone switch.

One approach frequently taken in the documentation of requirements for a specification is to categorize a requirement as either mandatory or optional. We prefer to add a third category of requirement that we call "valuable."

Mandatory requirements are those that cannot be omitted from the final system. If the iterative process of reconciling business, operational and technical requirements has been followed, then the mandatory requirements will reflect exactly what is necessary to be included in the system. By definition, mandatory requirements must be implemented as specified by their Requirements Specifications.

EXHIBIT 2-2

PROJECT LIFE CYCLE PHASES

This table contains descriptions of the typical phases
and sub-phases in a systems development chart.

Major Phases	Subphases (Synonyms)	Description	Deliverables
Requirements	Functional Requirements Requirements Specifications (Definition Phase)	Defines the reason for the system.	Budget Proposal Functional Requirements Requirements Specification
Analysis	(Planning)	Research conducted to validate performance requirements and find potential solutions.	Systems Analysis Report Interface Specifications Project Plan
Procurement	(Acquisition)	Process of finding, evaluating, choosing a Vendor and negotiating the contract.	Request for Proposal RFP Guidance Document Vendor Proposals Evaluation Package Vendor Selection Report
Design	Preliminary Design Final Design	Process of translating requirements into specific design elements which will be implemented.	Design Specifications Prototype
Development	Code, Debug, Document Subsystem Test (Implementation) (Code & Module Test)	Software coding and documentation and initial testing of machine readable instructions.	Source Code Object Code Program Documentation
Integration	(Installation) (System Test) (Test & Acceptance) Interface Testing Acceptance Testing Operations Training	Testing multiple assemblies of programs until the total operational system is tested.	Test Plans Test Scripts Integration Test Plans and Scripts Test Results Training Materials
Conversion & Parallel	Data Conversion Parallel Operations Cutover	Conversion of all data to new files and parallel operations to confirm the accuracy and precision of the new system compared with the old.	Data Files Comparative Results Tests Contingency Plan Cutover Schedule
Maintenance	(Operations) Post Completion Review	Day-to-day use of the accepted system. Verification of Benefits	Operations Manuals Run Books Final Documentation

EXHIBIT 2-3

COMPARISON OF FUNCTIONAL REQUIREMENTS VERSUS REQUIREMENTS SPECIFICATIONS

FUNCTIONAL REQUIREMENTS	REQUIREMENTS SPECIFICATIONS
1.0 STATIONS. The PBX will have the capability to support up to 100 stations.	1.0 STATIONS. The PBX shall have the capability to support up to 100 stations only by the addition of line cards into the same cabinet. The PBX will be wired in the backplane to meet the maximum capacity of the cabinet. The initial equipment configuration shall be for 50 stations or the nearest greater integer conforming to station card equipment.
2.0 LINES. The PBX will be equipped to handle the traffic requirements of 100 stations.	2.0 LINES. The PBX shall be capable of handling 100 station calls in which 60% at any one time shall be station calls and the remainder shall be tie line or trunk calls, either incoming or outgoing. The tie/trunk lines shall be of any mix without requirements for unique circuit card provisioning. The initial provisioning and the provisioning of central office lines shall be such that the probability of not achieving CO dial tone access shall be less than 0.01 during the busy hour.
3.0 FEATURES. The PBX will be equipped to provide standard advanced features including: call pick up, call waiting, abbreviated dialing, etc.	3.0 FEATURES. The vendor will indicate which of the following features are not supported, and if not, what is the alternative approach to be used to implement that capability: call forwarding, call forwarding-busy, call pick-up from groups, call hold, camp-on, call transfer, conference and add-on, data privacy, last number redial, differential ringings, call waiting, call restriction, class of service.

Not all requirements are as important as others. The most important are usually obvious. Those of slightly lesser criticality can still be very important, but not at all cost. Sometimes the person specifying the requirements doesn't know the cost to benefit balance between what he requested and what can be implemented.

A *Valuable Requirement* is one in which the case cannot be made for an absolute need at any cost. The term valuable comes from a concept of applying an analysis of worthiness or value to something. *Value Analysis* means quantifying as objectively as possible the benefit of the requirement, and matching the benefit against the projected cost to see if the price versus performance is acceptable.

One way of determining the value of a set of possible solutions to a requirement is to assign a numerical value (for example: plus or minus five, with zero being the value of the reference point) to each proposed solution according to its cost effectiveness. An intrinsic value for each alternative is established.

Suppose that a manager having a new telephone system (PBX) installed, insists each person also should have connection to a mainframe. A systems analyst might integrate the data requirement into the PBX specifications. A value analysis of the cost of the enhanced PBX capability might show that the cost of the PBX would increase by 100%. (See Table 2-2, row 2).

TABLE 2-2
PBX-Mainframe Data Connectivity Options

% Connectivity & Option		Relative Price	Value
0%	Basic PBX	100	0
100%	PBX + Data Connectivity	200	-5
100%	LAN Equipment & Cable	155	-1
15%	Limited LAN	135	+2
15%	PBX + Modem Pooling	110	+5

Further analysis shows that the same technical capability can be provided by local area network (LAN) equipment, independent of the PBX (row 3), for an incremental cost of 55%, since additional cabling has to be installed.

The analyst finds an external LAN equipment solution for a 15% population does not have the same economics because full cabling would still have to be done, even though some equipment would be saved. This external 15% LAN solution might cost an additional 35% of the cost of the PBX (row 4).

The analyst then learns that only 15% of the users require simultaneous connectivity. The PBX could provide that capability by a modem pooling approach for only 10% additional cost (row 5).

Taking these costs into consideration, the systems analyst then assigns a value of +5 to the 15% PBX connectivity solution, +2 to the limited LAN solution, -1 to the 100%

equipment solution for a LAN, and -5 to the 100% PBX data solution because this solution is too expensive.

A way to give the requirement a value was found. Data connectivity was a valuable feature, but not at the cost of doubling the telephone switch cost. A functionally equivalent and lower cost alternative was identified: PBX modem pooling. The business requirement was fulfilled at a reasonable cost.

In the above analysis on value, one should not overemphasize the numerical rating. Virtually any logical and consistent method of appraising value will suffice. The major benefit stems from a disinterested assessment of the options and their cost implications. This enables the analyst to avoid becoming enamored with the latest technical gadgetry. Identifying requirements as valuable will allow vendors to use ingenuity to solve the requirement, and provide a low-cost solution.

Another way of considering value analysis in determining whether requirements should be implemented, is to maintain the posture that everything is negotiable. In that way, "sacred cows" can be shown to be too expensive, and alternate, less expensive but adequate solutions can be found.

Still, in this imperfect world, the implementer must sometimes bow to the want of the business unit, even when the want might be a whim, or a gold plated feature. Many technologically unsophisticated business managers will readily identify enhanced status or prestige with a capability they want, even if they can't show a bottom-line benefit for it.

We call this the "*esteem value*"of the requirement. We shouldn't necessarily argue too strongly against these kind of requirements if they cost nothing. Esteem value or sex appeal requirements can have the benefit of establishing "ownership" of the system by the business entity. Sometimes, business managers are not even aware that these are not mandatory requirements.

One manifestation of an esteem value situation might be the continued rejection by the business unit of the analyst's interpretation of a requirement. This continued and unreasonable rejection might reflect that the "real" requirement is not being addressed. Analysts should be culturally sensitive to this occurrence of subjectivity.

Some financial officers kept rejecting a mock-up of the reports that they needed to monitor risky loan situations. Step-by-step review of each element included in the reports confirmed the requirement, but the reports were again rejected.

Finally the project manager had a small program written for a personal computer, with the identical data displayed in graphic format. The financial people, uncomfortable with the printed results, but unable to articulate why, accepted this format immediately. The graphics gave them the ability to visualize trends. One might say that the graphics were a frill to the basic requirement. Nevertheless, the "enhanced" requirement was the only acceptable solution.

> The sources of requirements do not always understand
> their real need, and it may be necessary to suggest
> a variety of alternatives to crystallize the requirement.

As the iterative dialogue occurs and the spirit of give-and-take between businessman and analyst improves, a better set of requirements results, and a good relationship is established.

Does this iteration process make systems more expensive? Probably not. Does it place greater onus on the technologist to work with the business or operations functions to solidify requirements? Yes it does. Does it take more time? Yes. However, it avoids the situation when on system delivery the business manager says: "This is not what I asked for."

The final category of requirements are *"Optional Requirements."* Optional Requirements have low or no value, or they are the residual requirements that are derivative of a mandatory requirement. If you are buying an existing software system, optional requirements could be part of the existing system that you don't particularly need, but also don't want removed by the vendor. However, you won't pay extra for it. (It would cost the vendor money to deliberately exclude it. If he has to exclude it, you will pay for it.) By specifying the components as optional, you preclude the vendor from trying to price the component as an unbundled feature.

Optional requirements are features that make the system easier to use, operate or maintain. There are a variety of equivalent optional requirements that can substitute for one another, and optional requirements have multiple ways of being implemented.

Optional requirements in the aggregate may not be optional because the system would not function if all optional requirements were omitted from it. They are optional on a case by case review of any single requirement.

Let's look at an example: Every report in a system that will be used only by the systems department must have the date and time included. That requirement is mandatory. You could generate an optional requirement that the date had to be the American standard: Month/day/year.

It's likely you wouldn't pay extra for modifications if the software package already displayed the date in European format as: Day/month/year. The difference in the requirement and the implementation is negligible. The solution is satisfactory. The requirement as specified could be waived, and should be optional. Fortunately this illustration was settled long ago by user selectable options. For example, Microsoft's Excel spreadsheet program permits five different ways of displaying the format for date or the time. It has macros in which you can invent your own format if you wish.

This trivial example of an optional requirement will have corresponding analogies in every requirements process.

You have to include optional requirements so the vendor can understand the full scope of the requirements to be delivered. In many situations, the vendor's creativity will be demonstrated by the elegance with which valuable and optional requirements are satisfied. Certainly the vast proliferation of word processing software packages available for personal computers is testimony to the need for optional features; the quality of which determines a best seller from a loser. One vendor might differentiate from others merely by the elegance of solutions offered for optional requirements.

Exhibit 2-4 provides an example of a method of specifying mandatory, valuable and optional requirements for the PBX requirements specification.

REQUIREMENTS SPECIFICATION PRECISION

Is it necessary to specify all the mandatory, valuable, and optional requirements for the procurement of customized technology? If you are knowledgeable about the business that the technology should support, you should specify requirements as rigorously as you can.

In a *Rigorous Requirements Specification* all input and output will be completely specified, including formats and forms or screen layouts. Processing functions will be specified, specific algorithms for calculations or logic flow will be mandated and degrees of precision stipulated. Audit, control and parameter requirements also will be specified. Data element descriptions will be known; field and record sizes specified. Processing times for transactions, and response time criteria for on-line interaction will be similarly specified. If the computer system hardware and operating system are mandated, then the requirements specification must include all the configuration elements of that environment.

The amount of effort required to specify rigorous requirements is significant. The time spent in requirements collection, analysis and specification can represent 50% of the total project schedule. Once a rigorous requirements specification is completed, the design and implementation tasks become much easier because ambiguity has been removed from the system. It is reassuring to a vendor to know that you know what you want.

When a rigorous requirements specification is included in the Request for Proposal, the vendor responses should be easily comparable. Technical differences in design should easily trace to your requirements and the prices should fall into a narrow band. It can be fairly said: "You know what you need."

If we pursue the analogy of the specification of an automobile a little further, we might get to the following details: valves: 12; compression ratio 9.5 to 1; EFI; computerized telemetry of 76 essential operating functions with visible and audible alarms; interior black leather with teak paneling; and so on.

We don't think of this process as a rigorous requirements specification, but it is. It is just that the manufacturer has taken most of the work from us by providing a large variety of options. In a systems procurement, there is no one to reduce the degree of diligence that you must expend to insure that you get what you need.

EXHIBIT 2-4

SPECIFYING MADATORY, OPTIONAL & VALUABLE REQUIREMENTS

(Excerpt from the Requirements Specification of an RFP for the purchase of a PBX.)

Rqmt #	Requirement Description	M,O,V[1]	Rationale for M,O,V Decision
6.0	**PBX Features**		
6.1	Stations. The PBX shall be designed to handle at least 600 stations, shall be wired for at least 400 stations, and shall be equipped for 300 stations.	M	A design which is capable of growth, with internal wiring in the cabinet for 400, so expensive rewiring is not required, and the minimum initial number of line cards must be 300 for day-one operations.
6.2	Analog/ Digital. The PBX shall be either analog or digital, conforming to all signaling requirements of central office configurations in 1992 without change except by software instruction.	V	This requirement gives the vendor the opportunity to offer either a digital PBX fully ready for ISDN compatibility, or, a lower price analog offering, but which he may be required to provide external hardware for ISDN connectivity at no cost when the timing requires it. The purchaser is looking for the best combination of price and future technological compatibility.
6.3	Automated Attendant. The PBX shall be capable of providing Automated Attendant Services in addition to standard operator features.	O	The purchaser can implement such a capability within the PBX, or, buy equipment from another vendor's equipment externally connected to the switch. Therefore, if the vendor has the capability, and the cost is comparable, the feature may be purchased. If the vendor lacks the feature there will be no evaluation penalty.
6.4	Station Message Detail Recording (SMDR) The PBX shall be equipped with equipment to measure, track and record all messages on magnetic medium for more than one million messages.	M	For charging calls internally, the purchaser must have all the call information that the switch handles.
6.4.1	SMDR. The PBX shall be capable of having its magnetic medium recording device interrogated and down line loaded by an external poll from a Brand x computer using X.25 protocol.	M	The data needs to be collected. Note that the type of magnetic media is not specified, so that is an optional design feature left to the vendor. The protocol for communication however, has been strictly specified (probably because the buyer already has a computer with that protocol). We would suggest that specifying the protocol to this level is extreme, since a simple ASCII bit stream can be accommodated by most computers. This could be a costly and restrictive requirement.
6.4.2	SMDR. The PBX shall be capable of having its message detail polled and downline loaded in real time by monitoring the SMDR data immediately prior to recording on the magnetic medium.	O	This is a nice requirement for flexibility and reliability purposes in case the magnetic recording device is malfunctioning. The requirement is optional because whether or not it is necessary will depend upon the type of recording device and its reliability. Thus the buyer will assess costs and reliability versus flexibility for items 6.4.1 and 6.4.2.

1. M, V, O: M = Mandatory; V = Valuable; O = Optional Requirement.

> A rigorous requirements specification is the best guarantee one can have in predicting successful implementation of a customized system.

The above is not the only way things are done, but it is the ideal. One or more constraints of time, staff resources, changing business climate or emergencies will frequently prevent a rigorous requirements specification process from occurring. Instead of total rigor, the systems analyst concentrates on the most critical mandatory requirements and the highest valuable requirements. Requirements which are less critical are not as well specified.

We might label this approach a *"Semi-rigorous"* requirements specification. Many of the technical performance characteristics will be omitted, but the business needs will be specified, even if the description may be uneven from one requirement to the next. Screen and report formats may be left for the vendor to create as part of the design. Project management may decide that some requirements can be specified more accurately as the project proceeds. If contracted to a vendor, there might be a staged process for design to conform to the staging of the requirements.

This use of semi-rigorous requirements specifications has utility under two sets of circumstances. In one, you may be purchasing an existing system that needs considerable rework in selected areas. You work rigorously on those areas of the greatest change, accepting the implied requirements of the existing system where little change is needed and allowing the vendor flexibility in altering the package to meet your needs without having to rewrite the entire system. You can save a considerable amount of money by ignoring the obviously satisfactory or immaterial solution. Semi-rigorous specifications also might be used in a circumstance of state-of-the-art development. State-of-the-art development is a sail into uncharted waters. One can only estimate what the performance will be.

The advanced technology aerospace programs are of this nature. It is impossible to specify all the weight, thrust, aerodynamics, payload and electronics systems, and know if they can be combined into a vehicle that performs ideally in all respects. This can be an iterative trial and error process of requirement-design-revision until the desired results are achieved.

Vendor responses to semi-rigorous requirements may be characterized by a higher degree of creativity, more variance among the technical performance proposals of the vendors, and a wider disparity in quality and price. It will be more difficult to choose the best vendor, and you have higher risk of making a wrong decision because you have greater ambiguity in both the specifications and the resultant design. The cost may also be higher, and there is a higher probability of schedule delays, because of the technical uncertainty. But, if you are making modifications to an existing system, you will save on schedule, cost and risk for those portions of the system that do not need modification. These savings usually exceed the negative elements stated.

In some situations the buyer wants the vendor to exercise his best ingenuity, irrespective of whether the requirement is mandatory, valuable or optional. One way to achieve that is to be much less precise in the degree of specificity of the requirement. We would describe this form of requirement as a "*loose*" requirements specification. Sometimes this may be not much more than adding a few performance criteria to a functional requirement. In other cases it may include listing some features and performance criteria, letting the vendor fill in the details based upon his design.

The problem with loose specifications is comparing one vendor's response with another to figure out which is better. Since you don't really know what you want, how can you judge which response is superior? If you really don't care about the manner in which the requirement is fulfilled, then all vendors are equal in their response and should be evaluated accordingly.

Loose specifications might be adopted in the first phase of a program in which prototypes will be built. Evaluation of the prototypes will then lead to rigorous specifications for the final product. This approach is much more likely for equipment than for systems projects.

There might be a situation where the requirements originator has only a vague idea of what should be implemented. A manual process is currently performing the functions, and the business unit wants to reduce costs, but has no idea what should be added, changed, or removed from the manual process.

Another example might occur when the business is so complex or arcane, that the systems analyst can't interpret the functional requirements.

> Computerized arbitrage program trading in the stock market may be an example of an arcane business. Even those who use the tools have been quoted as saying they didn't really understand what they were doing. The highly sophisticated mathematics required to implement this trading has led to the recruitment of mathematicians and scientists who previously would have joined the aerospace industry. This has resulted in Wall Street labeling these people as "Rocket Scientists."

In a situation of arcane requirements, it is conceivable to give the functional requirements to a vendor in the hope the vendor knows more about the subject and can satisfy the need. The vendor establishes a direct relationship with the business unit. The technical staff merely monitors the implementation. This can be dangerous for all concerned. Start with a communications gap between internal company components; add a difficult and not easily understood business; add one eager vendor who will by-pass the technical project team to communicate with the business manager; add no requirements that can be tested to determine if the vendor has truly delivered; and you have all the ingredients for disaster; and disaster frequently happens.

When a situation arises where the business unit cannot adequately specify what it needs, it is best to assign a number of systems analysts to join the business unit as clerks, production staff, or whatever is necessary to begin to understand the business. Unfortunately this is a strategic approach, and timely delivery of systems under competitive business duress does not often permit this luxury.

Another approach would be to schedule the requirements definition process and development in mini-phases so the business unit can make immediate response to the viability of a solution. It is also reasonable that the system itself be developed as a pilot project of very modest scope so the business unit can see results. This may cause better crystallization of the requirement specification. The goal is to be responsive, without jeopardizing the business or the technologists' careers.

In the securities business it is extremely difficult to tell a dealer making millions for the firm and for himself, that his weird request is unreasonable. Arcane projects have burned so many systems personnel, that they tell the dealer that they have other projects scheduled that they can't respond. This is the "ostrich" response to client needs. Systems personnel put their heads in the sand. The business unit then tries to do the project itself. Without systems discipline the results can be expected to be disastrous, with the added impact of bad feelings toward the uncooperative technologists.

We don't recommend loose specifications, but we do recognize that they can be forced on the technology component. When such a situation starts to develop, it is best to discuss the issue with top management for resolution.

This manual can't help you much about arcane or even stupid requirements when they come from the very top of the firm. However, we do know a printer who will print your resume at a reasonable price.

CASE STUDY

Now let's see how Fred handled his challenge.

Fred had previous experience with transaction based systems in the airline industry, but not sufficient to transfer that directly to banking. In any event as a senior manager, it was far more important for Fred to think about a strategy that might accomplish the corporate goal, but would avoid as much risk as possible. The extremely short time frame for integrated operations cutover represented more than enough organizational and coordination risk. Fred didn't want to compound that risk by taking an excessive systems development risk.

BB&T's systems architecture was a loosely coupled environment of production systems linked through a database architecture tied to the general ledger. Fred thought that if a retail banking system could be found to provide all the processing requirements in a self-contained mode, then it could be loosely interfaced with the BB&T systems in limited ways. An inelegant solution to be sure, but one that would allow safety. If the impact on existing BB&T processing and systems could be minimized, there might be a chance to meet the deadline.

If a self-contained retail system could not be found, then it would be necessary to take one of two other approaches. They could do parallel systems development, revising the existing BB&T systems, while developing a retail system within the current BB&T architecture. Conversely they could decide that all existing systems would be replaced by a total new banking system incorporating both the wholesale and retail functions.

The biggest risk in the former case, would be if every existing BB&T system had to be extensively modified to include the retail processing. In the second case, Fred's previous experience told him that an integrated de-novo system was marginally possible to do in fourteen months, but the supporting manual processes could not be revised in that time frame. The risk was too high.

Why not still treat the two banking requirements as independent, and interface and integrate them only where it made sense? A higher level of integration could be accomplished later, when all the staff of BB&T had some experience in operating a retail bank as well as the commercial bank.

Fred thus created BITS, a Branch Integrated Transaction System that would fulfill Mr. Oldsin's requirement at less risk than redesigning everything, or starting from scratch. Fred decided to act on his analysis, confident he could convince Lisa and her management team that this was the approach to take.

On reviewing his managers' experience, Fred found that Ulrich Schmidt had six years of experience with a Savings and Loan Association, and three years of systems development management experience with a large bank. Ulrich was currently managing the initial design of a trading system that would now be abandoned. He could be shifted to manage this BITS project. The manager responsible for the loan system design could be shifted to Ulrich. Ulrich had several limitations in relationship management with users. Therefore, this effort was going to require a lot more resource than Ulrich and his development team. It would require support from every member of Fred's staff.

An organization chart of Lisa Moore's direct reports can be found in Exhibit 2-5. Fred's organization is found in Exhibit 2-6. Note that Lisa's direct reports have surnames beginning in "E". Fred's direct reports have surnames beginning in "S".

Tuesday, at 2 p.m., Fred convened a staff meeting to announce the following assignments and actions:

1. *Ulrich Schmidt would immediately assume Project Manager responsibility for the BITS project.*
2. *The activity on a new commercial loan system initiated by John Sparks would be terminated. That manager would now report to Ulrich on BITS.*
3. *Rip Scali and three analysts would work full time in support of Ulrich in liaison with the designated representatives from MSB to define the retail system requirements for BITS.*
4. *Tony Scerbo and two of his staff would work with all internal components of BB&T to define a set of interface specifications. As the meeting continued, they identified that the following systems would have to be linked: the General Ledger, Income and Expense Accounting, Central Liability and Customer Profitability. Others were sure to be identified, but these would serve as a start for Tony's efforts.*

EXHIBIT 2-5

BACCARAT BANK & TRUST OPERATIONS & SYSTEMS ORGANIZATION

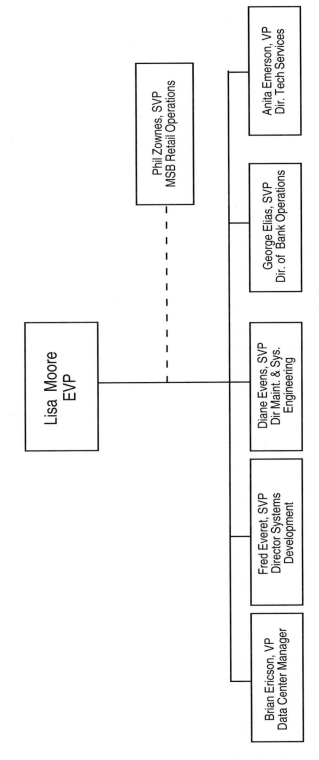

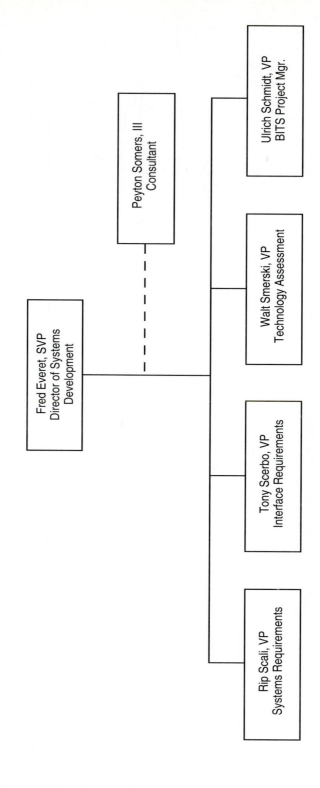

EXHIBIT 2-6

BB&T BITS SYSTEMS DEVELOPMENT ORGANIZATION

Fred Everet, SVP
Director of Systems
Development

Peyton Somers, III
Consultant

Rip Scali, VP
Systems Requirements

Tony Scerbo, VP
Interface Requirements

Walt Smerski, VP
Technology Assessment

Ulrich Schmidt, VP
BITS Project Mgr.

5. *Walter Smerski and two analysts would immediately begin a literature search of available retail systems. Walt would also contact his associates in other banks to get their recommendations on systems that might be candidates for BITS, and in the extreme, totally integrated retail and wholesale banking solutions.*

6. *Assuming Lisa approved, Fred would hire Peyton Somers, III, a renowned consultant on retail banking processing to help the effort.*

Fred assumed that he would have to modify some of these assignments after Lisa's staff meeting at 5 p.m. However, he felt it was good for his staff to have preliminary direction. This would avoid unnecessary anxiety.

Fred knew he was making a big assumption in believing there was a retail system available from a vendor that could be modified to fit BB&T's needs. But, what else was there? Other options are losers. Fred strode down the corridor to Lisa's conference room determined to have his way.

Fred's thought processes are pretty good. However, his assumption that a new total solution for the bank is inappropriate needs a little more examination. A totally new system would include all the requirements of the existing BB&T systems and the retail requirements as well. If it were obtainable from an outside vendor, multiple systems development would not be needed.

Although intellectually viable, few would pursue this approach unless they had much more time to carry it out. The effort in converting all data to reside in the new system, and the turmoil of parallel operations in two banks would be too great. Such a development would make the bank truly integrated, for everything in both banks would be brand new. But there would be little stability and no frame of reference to what worked before.

The situation might be different if BB&T's systems were already obsolete, and a strategic plan existed to replace them. If the timing was right, a totally integrated solution would be appropriate because it would position the bank for future requirements without a patched up systems environment. This was not the situation for BB&T.

One other obvious point about the integrated solution should be mentioned. If it were to be done, the requirements specification activity would double, since two banks would be changing, not one.

Technical personnel love the thought of building grand new edifices to current technology. The business minded technology manager knows that success comes from implementing the minimum needed solution, and going on to other victories.

> Successful systems projects strive for minimum change in manual operations when time is limited.

RELATIONSHIP OF VENDOR SYSTEMS TO REQUIREMENTS

As Fred plans his requirements collection and documentation, he needs to consider the rigor of those specifications. Where the practices of MSB and those of BB&T are unique, considerable detail will have to be given to the vendors. But the specification of requirements should not be done in a vacuum removed from the reality of the current situation. Fred has an intrinsic assumption that a system exists that will meet or nearly meet the BB&T requirements.

Theoretically, the requirements specifications should emphasize mandatory requirements and avoid restating needs that are already defined and implemented in the system to be bought.

There is a bit of chicken and egg aspect to this activity. If you don't have your requirements, you don't know which system conforms the best. If you evaluate many systems, you find many interpretations of how requirements are solved. Therefore, you don't have to define them. The easy solution is to generate semi-rigorous requirements and allow the vendor to perform. But what the vendor has solved does not conform to your needs. Without good requirements, you will not be able to design a test plan that proves that the vendor's modifications have met your requirements. A test plan based on the vendor's specifications tests what the vendor already has, not what you need. Therefore, there is no escape from a good requirements specification.

What can be done? Once selected, a review of conforming and non-conforming elements of the vendor's design can be conducted, and valuable and optional requirements can be compromised to meet the vendor's design. You can thus avoid spending funds on non-critical changes to the existing system that do not have an impact on mandatory requirements. Note that the emphasis made in the above statement is on reducing costs associated with changes, not in compromising your real needs or ability to test the system the vendor delivers.

There are two ways in which a purchased system might be implemented. The first way is to procure what is called the "plain vanilla copy." The vendor software requires little or no modification to meet your requirements. Title headings on reports are modified to conform to the buyer's company. Other non-critical features are altered slightly for cosmetic purposes. Tables may be modified to include a few new entries. But, record lengths, field sizes and algorithms remain unaltered. What you buy is what is already designed.

You can get this system for minimal increases over the vendor's published list price. Plain vanilla copy is obviously the least risky system to procure, install and operate. Once the system is operational, the business units, operations and technical staffs can determine if modifications are needed to meet some previously unrecognized deficiency. If you've bought source code, these can be done at your convenience in-house, or further changes can be contracted with the vendor for implementation at a non-critical time.

There is much merit in not pushing advanced technology. Simple functionality is obtained at lower cost and lower risk. The Soviet military approach to weapons procurement followed this method: create a fundamental design (e.g., AK-47 rifle or rocket boosters) and perpetuate it over long periods of serviceability.

Unfortunately, requirements for most large systems don't seem to have a good match with what the vendor has already developed. The larger the company the greater the disparity between perceived requirements and operational software. But that is natural. A larger firm has more components, more interfaces and more functions impacted by a new system. Thus a second type of systems procurement is the norm. Most systems will require significant modification. We define significant modification to mean that between 30-50% of the system must be customized to meet your requirements.

It's difficult to quantify the difference between 30% and 50% modification. You can be assured that when the vendor is marketing the system, a 15% modification will be described, and when the vendor is negotiating the price, a 75% modification will be quoted. You can expect that a 30% modification will impact virtually every module and major routine in the system.

Both parties, purchaser and vendor, have a strong desire to implement modified systems. The vendor (for a good fee) gets to improve his system at your expense, and then resell it later to others. The purchaser believes that time and money will be saved. For the most part both beliefs are warranted. The systems do get built faster and less expensively than new systems, but it is never easy.

Sometimes, retrofitting a system to meet new requirements may be technically unwarranted, and almost unfeasible. Design changes thought to be easy are discovered to be much more difficult to implement. One usually doesn't recognize the problem until well into the design phase. Sometimes the problem avalanches to impact other modules in the system. Then it's a serious emergency. A panic mode follows to fix the problem. Additional funds are spent, and the project overruns its budget. Finally some sort of adequate but non-optimum solution is found. The ultimate consequence is that the purchaser gets a system that doesn't meet performance specifications, and costs are more than originally planned. The vendor believes he is underpaid for the extra effort, and will have lost sales opportunities with other less demanding clients. No one is happy with the result.

An example of the above might be helpful. Suppose your requirements are semi-rigorously specified. Suppose that the vendor is able to demonstrate in the proposal that his system is in total conformity to your requirements. Because of a design idiosyncrasy never exercised before, it takes ten minutes for the system to process a single transaction. Although design conformity to a requirement may have been realized the practical value of that conformity is horrendous. You'll need to fund a change order to fix the problem. This can happen to anyone. Even rigorous requirements may not help you in determining the adequacy of the design to meet performance criteria.

> Do not assume because a vendor's system design meets requirements, that the performance processing of that requirement will be fully satisfactory.

Despite these obstacles, buying and customizing vendor systems are more the norm than the exception.

The requirements specification process shouldn't get silly. It doesn't make much sense to specify items if you are going to accept what the vendor has already designed. Years ago it was fashionable for the systems analysts to pride themselves in writing specifications that were totally neutral to the actual system's design. At current prices, installed mainframe equipment and software costs are enormous. The cost to develop from the ground up with new equipment is financially prohibitive. Thus, an implied hardware platform is almost inherent in every set of requirements specifications. One might as well limit the universe of possible solutions to the minimum set likely to give a pragmatic solution to the need.

An intrinsic assumption must be made that whatever system BB&T will purchase, it will operate on BB&T's existing mainframe computers.

At the 5 p.m. meeting with Lisa, Fred convinced all there to accept his recommendation to adopt a strategy of minimal changes to existing systems, and search for a vendor supplied system for BITS. Lisa instructed each manager to assign a full-time representative from their divisions to join the project team. She approved the need for the consultant. Ulrich Schmidt was approved as the project manager. Fred was instructed to adopt a project schedule and recommend a process by which success could be assured. A progress meeting was scheduled for Monday, the 19th.

Fred tasked his staff to begin the detailed planning for the project. The group concluded that the most immediate tasks were to establish the ground rules for the requirements that were to be specified, and to identify all personnel in the BB&T and the Mimosa Street Bank who would be needed to help in requirements identification, assessment and approval. Since the top executives in both institutions were enthusiastic about the merger, obtaining cooperation from MSB personnel should not be difficult.

A major problem was the lack of a data processing function in MSB that could add retail banking knowledge to the requirements definition activity. Since the bank examiners' audit had shown so many control problems in the service bureau system, it was of little use as a valid source of requirements.

After a bit of deliberation they agreed upon the following approach. The processing functionality of the service bureau would be totally ignored. All requirements for retail banking would be collected from the operations staff of MSB, and business requirements collected from product managers in MSB. Participants would be chosen from credit card operations, personal loans, student loans, term deposits, savings and checking accounts. The audit issues would form the basis of specifying a rigorous set of control requirements for the new system.

Peyton Somers, using his encyclopedic knowledge of retail banking, would construct a set of minimum processing requirements. The group assumed that the vendors would have solutions that would exceed these requirements. The solutions that would be most favored would be ones that: permit a high degree of flexibility for future change as BB&T learned more about retail; conformed to the existing database architecture of BB&T's systems; contain account numbering systems that would suit BB&T's checking account system so two different systems would not be required in the combined bank; and provide strong controls and audit traceability features.

On the other hand, if minimum change to existing BB&T systems were to be guaranteed, then rigorous interface specifications would have to be formulated. How well the vendor could satisfy these requirements would be a heavily weighted factor in the selection of the winning vendor. Systems, operations and business representatives were identified within BB&T to contribute to documenting that the interface requirements would be accurate and rigorous.

Exhibit 2-7 summarizes the conclusions reached by the staff on how the requirements would be specified.

With an understanding of the priorities completed, Fred's staff could now establish a schedule in time for Lisa's meeting. On his part, Fred began to schedule one-on-one meetings with every department head in both banks to brief them on the approach and solicit their support. The cultures of the two institutions could be meshed by the common goal of a successful systems development project.

At this point Fred has risen to the occasion. He clearly understands his role in working with the culture of his bank and bringing into that culture the members of the MSB. He has made some critical decisions: requirements, opting for controls, only one system to be modified (reducing risk), and not over specifying what he doesn't understand. Your project planning should have a similar vision: "I know what I want to accomplish."

EXHIBIT 2-7

BITS REQUIREMENTS RIGOR SPECIFIED BY BB&T

Requirement Adherence Category	Requirements Specification Precision		
	Rigorous Specification	Semi-Rigorous Specification	Loose Specification
Mandatory	Interface Specifications to: General Ledger, Commercial Loan, DDA, Leasing System, Certificates of Deposit. Data Base Specification. Audit, Controls, & Transaction Traceability.	Current retail banking operational procedures.	Baseline retail banking processing and performance requirements including: Credit card, personal loans, student loans, term deposits, savings accounts.
Valuable		Product improvement requirements from MSB line of business managers.	
Optional	Support requirements to national credit card entities: Visa, Mastercard.		Other retail banking products and features not currently part of MSB's product set, but which the Vendor's system supports.
Esteem	Not Allowable	Not Allowable	Not Allowable
Arcane	Not Allowable	Not Allowable	Not Allowable

## Chapter Three

PROCUREMENT ISSUES

BUILD OR BUY?

"*Build or Buy*" is the phrase used to suggest whether a technological development will be completed by internal resources, or whether it will be contracted to a vendor. In our context the term buy includes rental, leasing and all variations. The criteria for deciding to rent or lease versus buying are usually financial, not infrastructural. We want to examine the infrastructure issues related to a build or buy decision.

Fred has already decided that BB&T does not have the resources to develop the retail system internally. You shouldn't jump to that conclusion without understanding why you should, or should not seek vendor assistance.

In many companies the project manager responsible for delivery of the solution is delegated the option to develop a system internally or seek external support. Technical personnel with pride in their skills will prefer to develop systems themselves. This insures job preservation for the period of the development. They also maintain that no one can do it better than they can. This classic NIH (Not Invented Here) syndrome is much more prevalent than one would think. Such beliefs are a manifestation of intellectual arrogance and are unprofessional. No one has a monopoly on brains.

The problem with a corporate policy or philosophy that delegates build or buy decisions to an implementer is that finance, personnel, schedule and risk issues can extend far beyond the domain of the person making the decision, imperiling other activities. Priority projects might be affected as well. Those who will be directly involved in the project are not sufficiently disinterested to be able to judge the opportunity cost of doing it themselves. We believe that build or buy should be a senior level decision based upon a rational set of criteria and communicated as a corporate policy.

The criteria that senior management would have to consider in a build or buy decision include:

- The willingness of the firm to do the project internally. Willingness implies that internal development is consistent with corporate culture and that precedence exists for such development. If not, the proponent of the internal project will have more to explain to management than otherwise.

A mundane example of this philosophy would be a firm's preferences to do everything internally, while others contract externally for services exclusively. Security guards, cafeteria services, cleaning and maintenance, and fleet management all have their internal and external proponents.

As systems have evolved, nearly all firms do a little of each. However, like a pendulum, even some giant firms are moving to a total service bureau concept for systems and telecommunications operations.

Willingness also implies that the project is perceived to be desirable to do internally. The opposite of NIH, reluctance to do a project internally may indicate low level importance, or that the project is a "loser." If either is true, one should reconsider doing it at all.

- The capability to do the project internally. Capability includes the talent and experience to complete the project. Is there sufficient capacity? Can you really spare the quality and quantity of resources required? Do you have the specific application knowledge to implement the system? One possibly compelling reason to develop a system internally is to develop the knowledge about the application and maintain that knowledge for long term advantage.

Is this project necessary to do internally to retain essential staff? If so, you have a personnel problem, and justifying the system on such a rationale is wrong. You still may not have eliminated your personnel problem when the project is done. Find another way to retain staff.

- Do you have the financial resources to commit to either a build or buy decision? Internal costs are fixed whether you do the project or not. If you must increase staff, budget growth may be unacceptable. External projects can be capitalized while internal ones must be expensed. Which option is better suited to the current situation?

If the project is truly of major corporate priority, such financial gymnastics should not be necessary, since the highest probability of success should govern the decision. In smaller firms with very limited available funds, a compromise might be necessary.

Prototyping and pilot projects often permit satisfactory interim solutions until more funds are available. Prototypes can be especially beneficial to small companies that are growing rapidly. Fully structured systems might be delivered too late and may no longer be relevant for such a company.

- Do you have the internal staying power to see this project through to completion? Are there so many projects to be done that you might allocate your resources more effectively in a vendor project management mode rather than in a "doing" mode?

In an era of downsizing and leanness, more firms are favoring a philosophy of developing project management expertise and contracting out the projects. The risk comes later in maintenance and service provisioning.

- Do you have the maintenance and service capability to support the system when it's finished? If not, why not let the vendor do it all?

- If you are a governmental function, will the completed system be operated in a facilities management mode by the same vendor or a third party? If so, why develop the system internally at all?

BUILD OR BUY ETHICS

A build or buy decision should be made before any formal vendor solicitation. A build decision includes the situation where another division or department of your firm could be tasked to develop the system. In our thinking, tasked, subcontracted, co-opted or teamed are synonymous.

It is very difficult for a vendor to compete head-to-head in a selection process against an internal proposal team. No matter how well the specifications are written, there are always countless items of internal procedures, experience and relationships that give the internal proposer a formidable advantage. Therefore, if any internal team is to be considered, they should be evaluated and accepted or rejected before soliciting proposals from external vendors.

However, some companies are so decentralized that a subsidiary might legitimately be considered a qualifying external vendor. They must be separated from the buyer by the same restrictions that apply to all vendors. A company should take extra care that it shows no favoritism to such a subsidiary, by informing outside vendors that procedures have been established to ensure that all vendors are competing on a fair and equitable basis. Following the procedures in this manual will offer that assurance.

Once the decision to purchase a system is made, proposals are requested, received and evaluated. It is unethical to solicit proposals from vendors, read them, and then decide to do the project internally, based on what you learned from the proposals. This is outright plagiarism. The information is submitted in good faith by the vendors, (and may be proprietary as well), in the expectation that their proposal would get serious and fair consideration for the effort they have expended in preparing the proposal. You can be sure you will not have many vendors enthusiastically responding to your future requests for proposals. Word gets around quickly concerning companies that behave like this.

There is a circumstance where cancellation of a vendor selection might be indicated. Suppose that after reading the proposals you discovered that few or none of the vendors responded in a way you expected. You find that the prices are too high, the capability too low, the schedule too long, or any number of combinations. Invariably in such a circumstance, the requirements specifications were insufficiently developed to provide the vendors with a definitive understanding of what you wanted, therefore the unsatisfactory responses. As embarrassing as it is, you have no recourse but to retract the buy decision for the moment, and redevelop the requirements properly. An explanation of your mistake should be made and an apology given to each vendor.

After redeveloping the requirements, you may now find that the reason for your original buy decision is no longer valid. You may proceed to develop the system internally. Since the vendors really didn't help you in their original proposal, the build decision is acceptable now. You should explain the reason for the build decision now to the vendors. It will retain their respect for you, and make them eager to propose on a later system. Just don't make the retraction a second time.

Sometimes receiving unresponsive proposals allows you to recognize that you may not even have the expertise to ask the appropriate questions to write the requirements specifications. You may want to engage a vendor to help you in writing the specifications.

This is a common occurrence in government procurements, civil and military. For example, the County of Los Angeles frequently contracts for systems in two phases: a requirements phase and an implementation phase. The vendor that obtains the contract for the requirements phase is barred from subsequent phases.

The Department of Defense contracts with multiple vendors to contribute to a program definition phase, with all eligible to compete for the development and production phases. The objective is to obtain the best input the government can get to define the system requirements. This latter methodology is more applicable to advanced research and development programs than to applications systems projects.

VENDOR RELATIONSHIPS

In some firms you find vendor personnel ubiquitous. They have you covered like a blanket. They know every plan, project and internal screw-up before you do. You sometimes wonder how their employer can afford such obvious marketing overkill. The answer of course, comes from the necessity to control the account. The effort required to preserve one account (even at such expense) is one tenth the effort to find a new customer. (We'll examine vendor strategies in greater detail in Chapter 6.) You should be concerned that vendors have free access to your premises. Not only do they become privy to proprietary information, but they take up time of your personnel, decreasing their productivity and independence of thought.

But, your staff needs access to vendors for information about products, service, malfunction and performance issues and the like, and no one would want to hamper that discussion, but there are limits.

The description above applies for an existing contractual relationship. Is there really such a thing as a relationship with a vendor? Yes and no. The Japanese Keiretsu maintain corporate relationships that tightly bind each other with obligations. To a lesser extent, where formal contracts exist between companies in the United States, a corporation can have a formal relationship with another. Senior managers often have social and business relationships with their counterparts. Top executives share country clubs, interlocking boards, and civic and cultural contributions with their business associates. However, once a person changes jobs, he does not have that business relationship any more. The relationship belongs to the corporations.

A relationship can be more than contractual. The customer depends upon the vendor for free consulting on occasion, non-disclosure information about new products that allow for future planning, participation in *alpha* or *beta* testing to facilitate installation and customized tweaking of new products. The vendor relies on the client for strong sales, favorable testimony at national and international forums, and avoidance of unfavorable publicity when products may not meet performance expectations. Thus, both benefit from the relationship.

The customer may get lower costs, better technology and even more leverage if it maintains a multiple vendor strategy with a degree of distance between it and all vendors. It's not an easy choice. Some companies like the security of very close ties to their vendors. Others prefer strategies where they leverage all vendors to their self interest alone.

> One large company was noted for this. It played off vendors against each other, jockeying for extraordinary discounts, loans of free equipment for extended evaluation and testing and free design consulting. Finally, after all vendors were exhausted from this bashing, it would procure modest investments of equipment, far short of the scope originally discussed with the vendors.

> After a few cycles, most vendors became wiser about dealing with this client. Whenever they received a proposal, they gave it perfunctory attention, knowing that the company would come back to them again. Therefore, they conserved their energy for those times when it was obvious by the behavior of top management that the firm was serious. The firm was a loser. It had a poor reputation with the vendor community, and no longer gained access to the best talent that the vendors could provide in proposing solutions to problems.

But only very large firms have the option of choosing close or loose relationships. Small companies are much more limited in their ability to influence or leverage the vendor. They simply do not spend enough money to warrant special attention. Therefore, if you represent a small firm, you don't have a relationship or leverage with a large vendor. Your best leverage may come from contracting with small vendor firms (at some increase in risk).

Middle managers and technicians in the buyer's organization may develop strong personal and professional relationships with vendor's personnel. To the extent that professionals from two different companies can work together to exchange information, further their personal goals and their respective companies' goals this relationship is useful. In the context of corporate relationships this counts for nothing, and may even prejudice decisions. If the client abandons the vendor, the personal relationship will likely disappear as well.

The most important point is that relationships can be formed and they can be transient. "What have you done for me today?" may be more the current rule than the exception. The degree of formality or partnership you have with your vendors probably should mirror the behavior of your company in the execution of its business strategies. If it is intense, you may need to distance yourself from your vendors.

WHO TALKS TO THE VENDOR?

What about the case where a new vendor would like to gain access to your company? Should you have some formal means of controlling that vendor? All vendors?

There are several reasons why the answer should be yes. A formal access path allows for official representation of the vendor's personnel to your firm. A formal process allows you to direct the vendor to the appropriate qualified and responsible personnel within your firm to consider the vendor's offering. If you direct the vendor's representative to those who will listen to the marketing presentation, time and energy won't be wasted trying to penetrate any and every function in your company that might have the slightest interest in his product. Distractions and productivity loss caused by the vendor's pursuit of a listener will be avoided.

Productivity may be saved at the engineering level, but the story may not be the same at executive level. On one occasion, having assumed the top position in a function, over seventy-five different vendors requested meetings with me within two weeks of entry. Ceremonial protocol required meeting with our most important vendors and those with whom we might do business. The time demands were enormous. I calculated that politically correct vendor meetings consumed over twenty-five percent of my time.

The same drain on resources can occur throughout your organization if you let it. Therefore, we advocate a disciplined method of giving vendors access to your employees.

A formal channel, usually through the systems contract administration function (discussed in the last section of this chapter), allows the vendor to deliver corporate, management and financial information with product data and pricing, to a central repository. Since this is the point of convergence where a contract must be negotiated anyway, directing the vendor initially through this front door will be efficient.

The formal access also allows your company to tell the vendor, from the top down, who are the decision makers, the reviewers, the influencers and the doers. You have an opportunity to specify to the vendor what product lines will not be considered, and what areas of your company are off limits should that be necessary for proprietary or other reasons.

In this way you represent your company as the official point of contact. Since you define the rules of behavior from a policy viewpoint, the vendor is more likely to comply with your approach than scatter his marketing everywhere.

Does it surprise you that countless tales of corruption, bribery and scandal in federal, state and city procurements occur? Does it occur because the vendor has too much opportunity to talk to, influence and bribe civil servants? We think it does.

The first step in controlling your processes, including proprietary decisions on why you choose one vendor over another, is to control the access of vendor personnel to your employees. The second step is to make certain that your personnel have policy direction on their conduct with vendors. Most controversies surrounding procurements would disappear if management adopted the disciplined approach we advocate.

If the vendor does business with your firm, informal contacts with lower level technical staff will occur inevitably over time. Human nature requires information transmission at the lowest, directly useful level. You couldn't stop this from occurring even if you wanted to. Which you don't. Your goals are satisfied by the channeling process.

Most of that discussed so far pertains to equipment sales and standard package offerings of software. When you need to buy special application software, or need software to be customized, the number of candidate vendors decreases. You may need to seek them out, rather than the inverse.

Fred Everet has this problem. Since BB&T has been a wholesale bank for so long, there is no record of retail banking vendor contacts available. His predecessor should have discovered them, but didn't.

A PREFERRED VENDOR POLICY?

Should you limit the vendors you wish to consider? The question is controversial. Proponents of free enterprise, market driven choices and advocates for finding the best technical solution would say no. Those who think standardization is necessary to reduce inventory, limit interface complexity and reduce training costs would emphatically say yes. Most managers would affirm that equipment or software anarchy is unaccceptable to prudent management of a company's assets. Therefore most firms have a *de-facto* limitation on the number of vendors they use.

If your company chooses to limit the number of vendors it uses, should it make that decision formally with a *Preferred Vendor Policy*? A *Preferred Vendor Policy* is a deliberate management statement that defines its preferred vendor relationships and the results it expects to get from those relationships usually expressed in financial terms, strategic positioning or technological superiority. The policy includes a need to control employee conduct. In all cases the policy will reflect an enlightened self-interest by the company to increase its leverage over vendors through volume discounts, reduced inventory of spares and operational simplification.

Usually the preferred vendor policy would be expressed as a statement: "We are dedicated to vendor XX"; or: "We use primarily vendor YY and vendor ZZ, but we reconsider that decision every N years." Other statements might be: "We have standardized on Type GG computing, but we will consider any compatible OEM (other equipment manufacturer)" or, "We always choose the lowest cost compatible product."

This policy can be articulated as a verbal preference by management, or it can be documented. Sometimes the company will have business dealings of another nature with a vendor company. A preferred vendor policy might exclude that vendor from selling to your firm. Thus, to avoid potential embarrassment, management would not want a document excluding this vendor to be published. We think such a position is naive. If the vendor to be excluded had a product good enough, he would be a preferred vendor. Why should you build up his hopes that maybe he will get a sale in the future by keeping the door open? Why not stimulate that vendor to do better by directly informing him that his products are not competitive. Most firms understand the reality of complex business relationships in which your customer is also your competitor, and can simultaneously be a vendor to you in its line of business.

A primary example is the banking industry, which is a significant user of data processing and telecommunications equipment. Banks provide financial services to the firms they buy from, and those they don't buy from as well. In some cases, banks compete against leasing companies owned by the vendors, and also compete in the money market for funds.

In our view, the technical people should mind their part of the vendor relationship and not worry about the ramifications elsewhere in the company. Other lines of business should do the same with respect to their relationships with firms that might be vendors. Fortunately, our experience suggests that this is exactly how most businesses operate. In contrast to the Japanese approach of captive relationships, a practice of reciprocity with formal procurement tie-ins is against the law in the United States, i.e. restraint of trade.

One way of resolving these issues is to have a preferred vendor policy that includes an open practice of evaluating any new technology for inclusion in the preferred vendor category. By that, the door is open. The vendors should know that the timing of any deal will depend on natural life-cycle replacement, when technical obsolescence requires upgrade, or when it is financially or operationally compelling to consider replacement of one vendor by another.

We believe that a preferred vendor policy is not only important, but should be documented. The chief benefits for a documented preferred vendor policy are better control of your vendors and better understanding by employees of management's priorities. The policy should contain the following provisions:

- Policy objectives in dealing with vendors: 1) maximize available discounts and other leverage; 2) optimize investment by getting the highest possible performance from the products; 3) ensure equitable and cordial relationships with all preferred vendors; 4) specify the ethical behavior of company employees in dealing with vendors.

- Identification of currently preferred vendors and their product lines with an explanation for the corporate rationale for using these preferred vendors.

- A process by which a vendor can be evaluated for membership in the preferred vendor list.

- Criteria for determining how a build or buy decision is to be made.

- A standard process by which vendors are selected when proposals are evaluated (Chapter 4).

- A senior executive with accountability for vendor relationships and for decisions on vendor selections.

- Description of the roles, responsibilities and authority of various company functions in dealing with vendors. These would include: project managers, quality assurance, accounts payable, systems contract administration, etc. This would include an escalation path for disagreements with vendors.

Now, how does a company buy customized technology from a vendor?

EVOLUTION OF THE SYSTEMS PROCUREMENT FUNCTION

The discussion that follows illustrates how large companies manage their systems procurements. The process has evolved as a formidable protection against serious contractual mistakes. One key function has emerged because of the complexities of systems purchases: the *Systems Contract Administrator*.

A four person real estate office might use petty cash to purchase its supplies from a local store, including a supermarket or drugstore. A twenty person travel agency might obtain its supplies from the local stationer using a house account, with each purchaser signing for individual purchases. The stationer sends a consolidated invoice at the end of each month.

A mid-sized firm will buy from wholesalers, obtaining a better price because of the increased volume of the purchases. A much larger firm (e.g., Fortune 1000), operates on a totally different scale. It solicits bids from the manufacturers, not just from wholesalers. Competitive quotations are received. Prices, delivery schedules and service agreements are negotiated. Size is a very powerful influence in obtaining the best possible deal.

As commerce changed over the centuries from barter to currency and its equivalents, different methods of legally specifying, ordering and accepting goods were established. In the United States, the Common Commercial Code–a set of laws, usually enacted by each state– to govern routine purchase orders provides a standard contractual definition for commercial transactions. Under the code, purchase orders, when signed by an authorized person, are legal obligations. A *Purchase Order* is a document issued by an entity (business, school, government, church, institution) conveying authority to vendors to ship specified materials in specified quantities within a specified time for a mutually agreed price.

A high degree of expertise in finding vendors, specifying materials, negotiating prices and discounts and verifying quality is required. The personnel engaged in this activity have established careers for themselves as *Purchasing Agents*. Purchasing agents can save their firms many times their salaries each year by their expertise. Their contribution is so important that most firms require every purchase to be made by the purchasing department. This works very well as long as the materials are limited to piece parts for manufacturing, supplies for the back office and furnishings for the building.

When management decides to relocate, acquire another company, or engage new distributorships, the legal department (or external law firms) is engaged to add its expertise to the transactions. Since these transactions are beyond the commercial code and involve more complex issues including tax, environmental and zoning regulations among others, the terms are written into contracts agreed to by both parties. This area of contract law of necessity requires attorneys with their specialized terminology and knowledge. As long as the subject of the contract has some historic precedence, tangibleness and enough clarity for competent businesspersons, management and the lawyers can structure a favorable deal.

The computer introduces a perturbation in the processes described above. On the one hand, computers are machines that conform to rigid specifications. On the other hand, they are operated by software, which is semi-intangible. Both operating system software and application systems fall into the realm of intellectual property. They are ephemeral within the machine, becoming tangible only as source code instructions on paper or other media. The opportunities to modify the software, and its infinite permutations are additional complexities.

The systems staff has to become heavily involved in the data processing purchasing process. They understand the business issues the technology has to solve, as well as, the technical parameters of performance and service. Systems personnel could estimate what risk non-compliance with specifications would have on the firm. Consequently, since the late 1960s, a specialized expertise in purchasing data processing and telecommunications has evolved. This expertise has become a dedicated function supporting the systems organization. It reports within the systems organization in most firms, though in a few it resides within the legal department. The function can have several descriptions or titles. We call it *Systems Contract Administration* (SCA).

As the process evolved, purchasing eventually dropped out of participation in this activity. These days, most purchasing activity is focused toward repetitive procurements of standard items, and is not equipped to handle highly technical and complex issues. In the data processing world, nearly every procurement requires a special and unique contract or set of terms.

Systems contract administration and the legal staff work out a division of responsibility to cope with technological procurement. Contract terms and conditions related to protection of proprietary information, compensation, damages, contract change procedures and the like, are prepared by the legal staff and form the standard terms and conditions of nearly all contracts.

Standard terms and conditions are discussed in the Request for Proposal in Chapters 8 & 9 and examples of BB&T's standard terms and conditions are found in Appendix A.

If the firm is big enough, the purchaser has the set of standard terms and conditions codified for protecting himself, with the vendor having its own set. The attorneys for both parties negotiate the wording to mutual satisfaction. A smaller company would try to renegotiate objectionable terms and conditions in the vendor's contract, rather than insisting on its own version. Once a set of standard terms and conditions are approved by the legal staff, the actual technical issues and price are negotiated by the SCA, assisted by project management. Attorneys are required only for new or special situations.

As buyers and sellers gained more experience in these negotiations, *Master Agreements* were formulated for situations where there would likely be multiple procurements from the same vendor, as happens in the upgrade of data processing hardware. Since SCA's had the leverage to extract discounts, they soon began to use that leverage to negotiate for multiple sites, and multiple divisions and subsidiaries. These master agreements take the form of national and international corporate master agreements. Hardware vendors like these agreements because they allow better account control over their customers, despite the higher discounts and the need to share commissions between the head office account team and the remote branch.

As required by the situation, the issues related to each follow-on procurement are negotiated and incorporated into the master agreement as annexes or attachments. In this way, you have a long term relationship with the vendor, and future purchases can be handled by an established process. These annexes frequently include such subjects as: volume purchase agreements and discounts, special maintenance provisions, training, national or international account agreements, and even distributor or other equipment manufacturer (OEM) resale agreements.

The role of the systems contract administration staff can be extensive. Though differing slightly from company to company, the SCA role includes:

- Participation in proposal preparation (particularly the statement of work), vendor evaluation, negotiation and contract award.

- Advisement in evaluating the business, schedule, and financial risks associated with the proposed contract.

- Leading negotiations of the contract's terms and conditions, including the technical, performance and pricing issues. It is assisted and advised by the project manager and technical personnel.

- Acting as agent for the company to administer the contract. The SCA serves as the delivery point for documentation and invoices, analyzing them for compliance with the statement of work items, and initiating payment action to the vendor following the project manager's approval.

- Support to the legal staff in negotiating master agreements with the vendor.

- Monitoring existing contracts and intervening in problem situations, particularly where renegotiation is required. Renegotiation is necessary when there is a change in specifications, or a slip in schedule beyond the boundary limits originally established.

- Terminating and closing out contracts when completed, or when the purchaser invokes termination clauses for cause, for lack of performance, or for convenience because the procurement may no longer be necessary.

- Preparation of summaries, status reports and financial statements on contracts in progress, completion and terminations when requested. The SCA reports on the financial commitments and outflow for the contracts it maintains to give top management an accurate picture of obligations.

- Maintenance of operating contacts with the legal department, the personnel department and the finance department to ensure that changes in laws (e.g., EEO, OSHA or tax laws) or reporting requirements are observed.

- Maintaining a background on vendors, particularly concerning financial stability and management strengths and weaknesses. The SCA keeps a profile of the vendor's prior performance history with your company.

- Providing lists of other qualified vendors, products and services that might be of interest to your firm (Chapter 5).

- Helping vendors find the proper person within your company to discuss a new product or service.

Of the roles described above, two roles predominate: formulating a strong statement of work and negotiations. The statement of work governs what you buy, and the negotiation governs how much you will pay and the risk you will accept.

An experienced contracts administrator is essential in negotiating every contract, and you should never attempt to negotiate a systems contract without one. Furthermore, they relieve technical managers from having to worry about much of the paperwork required to facilitate the contract after it's signed.

A small firm could hire a consultant to fill this role for the infrequent times it does a major procurement. The expense incurred is the best insurance one can buy.

On Wednesday, Fred called on Monk Eternic, the Systems Contract Administrator (reporting to Anita Emerson, VP, Director of Technical Services) to review BB&T policy on vendors. They discovered that BB&T had not purchased any major hardware or software system in the past three years. Although KRV computers were pretty much a standard, there was no defined preferred vendor policy. Relations with the hardware vendor were cordial but distant because of the low procurement level.

Application systems were always developed internally, so a decision to buy was culturally new. It was unlikely anyone would have thought of criteria for build or buy if Fred hadn't raised the issue. Besides, Monk only worked at his SCA assignment on a part time basis of about 10%, and that primarily to review invoices. At least BB&T had a few standard terms and conditions that it had adopted from vendors and other sources over the years. Fred asked if the systems organization had ever sent out Requests for Proposals and evaluated them competitively? Monk answered "Not in my memory."

"Wow," thought Fred: "no vendor policy, no vendor relationship to speak of, no history of build or buy proposals, a part time contracts function, and no formal process to select a vendor in the systems organization. That's zero for five!" Not only did he have to deliver the system, Fred was going to have to build the entire infra-structure to do it from the ground up.

Fred next scheduled a meeting with Higby Wallace, EVP, the Chief Financial Officer, to see if there were other processes in existence he wasn't aware of.

Exhibit 3-1 summarizes the critical issues covered in this chapter.

EXHIBIT 3-1

ACTION ITEMS FOR MANAGEMENT ON PROCUREMENT ISSUES

1. Establish criteria to determine when to develop systems internally and when to procure them externally.

2. Establish a code of ethics on build versus buy decisions.

3. Determine what kind of relationship you wish to have with your vendors.

4. Document a Preferred Vendor Policy.

5. Implement a standard approval and evaluation process to select vendors in competitive procurements.

6. Implement a vigorous Systems Contract Administration Function.

## Chapter Four

VENDOR EVALUATION POLICY

PERSPECTIVE

When you go through the effort to find the best vendor, you want a high level of confidence that top management will agree with your selection. Therefore, it's advantageous to you to know what you must do to get management's approval. The very evaluation and selection process should be structured to achieve this goal.

This is accomplished by having a definite process to obtain management's approval for a project by having a standard method of evaluating and selecting the best vendor; and by choosing the best options available (among many) to obtain good proposals for that project.

> Plan, so you can be successful!

Vendor Evaluation is the process of reading, scoring and documenting a vendor's proposal against your requirements. *Vendor Selection* is the process of further analysis of the evaluation information and determination of the best vendor. One cannot be done without the other, though they are separate stages. *Solicitation* is that part of the process in which you invite input or proposals from vendors. Consider the evaluation process as a pyramid as shown in Exhibit 4-1.

At the top of the pyramid is approval by top management and the go-ahead for the next phase. Below that is a review and concurrence by senior advisors and peers, so you can obtain the best business input about your recommendation. Below that is the vendor evaluation analysis conducted by the team that evaluates the proposals.

This chapter discusses the first three levels of the pyramid. On the fourth level consider that there are many ways you can obtain input from vendors, and you need to choose

EXHIBIT 4-1

VENDOR EVALUATION PROCESS PYRAMID

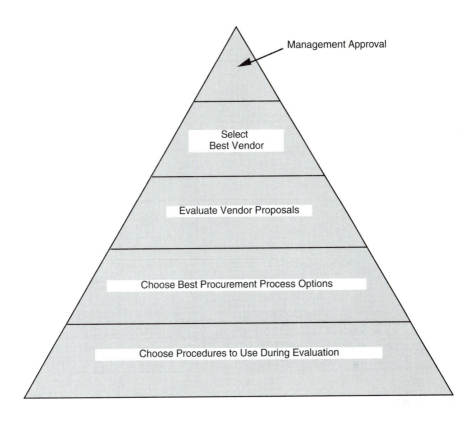

from among the options available to you even before the vendor solicitation process begins. These options are covered in Chapter 7. The lowest level contains the detailed evaluation procedures used by the evaluation teams. Chapter 10 covers this information.

PROJECT AND VENDOR APPROVAL HIERARCHY

Every company has a procedure by which management exercises its prerogatives to review recommendations for expenditures. The exercise of that prerogative depends on the culture of the company, and the degree of decentralization and autonomy that departments possess. Exhibit 1-2 highlighted a structure in which the Board of Directors was a participant in the project decision. But the approval can be delegated to the lowest practical level consistent with the expenditure required and the company's policy on who can spend what.

EXHIBIT 4-2

THE VENDOR EVALUATION HIERARCHY

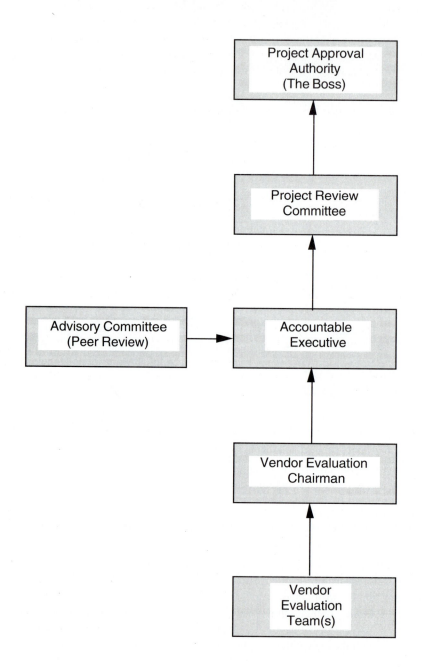

We use the term "project" because selecting a vendor to implement a system is, by definition, a project: a specific activity with a beginning and a formal end. The difference from an internal project is that not only are you requesting funding for the project, you are also asking for management's approval that you have properly selected the best vendor to implement the project.

Since funds to pay the vendor will be an out-of-pocket incremental expenditure, management's scrutiny will be somewhat more intense. This is reasonable since the idea of a corporate relationship is now present. A binding contract must be signed. The potential for unfavorable publicity, litigation or failure is increased because of the vendor's participation. Therefore, management wants to be assured that the risk is manageable.

As we discussed in the Introduction, a smaller company might abbreviate the process and have fewer participants. The principles presented herein should still be observed.

We can draw a generic hierarchy of participants in the process to get top management's approval in a larger company. Exhibit 4-2 provides a recommended structure.

At the peak, of course, is top management with final approval authority. Below that, many companies have a senior level review committee. Their role is to bring the full benefit of their business experience and knowledge of the company's mission and strategies to evaluate the logic of the selection of the vendor, the appropriateness of the costs, and to assess the risks that project failure might bring. Note that their role is not to address the technology. Their focus is politics, business and risk. They will review and concur with the recommendation before it can be sent forward for approval. They also confirm that the evaluation process was conducted according to company policy.

You should consider this review committee to be a hard filter. If they disapprove of a project (often by requesting rework or deferral, rather than by outright disapproval), you can consider it dead. No one wants to spend all the effort required to conduct a vendor evaluation and have it canceled. Knowing how to package the evaluation results to get past this hurdle is the key to an effective vendor evaluation process.

In small firms this committee could be nothing more than the individuals who sit in on the big boss' staff meeting. In an informal environment, an actual committee might not even be formed. The responsible technical manager might just hold a one-on-one briefing with those persons to whom the boss would look to for an opinion about the project.

Most large companies have formal committees to evaluate projects. They could be called "Project Review Committees, Capital Projects Review Committees, Systems Review Committees, or Business Project Review Board." In banks, they might even be extensions of Loan Review Committees that review proposed loans to customers. Whatever the name, the purpose is the same: to provide senior management input on projects that have a material impact on the company.

The *Accountable Executive* is the senior level technical manager who will have ultimate responsibility and accountability for successful delivery of the project. In most situations he will not manage the project itself, but will be at least one level above the project manager. This individual, rather than the project manager, will be the sponsor and presenter of the evaluation results to the review committee and to management.

Although Lisa Moore might be the proper accountable executive, her operational responsibility will remove her too far from the project to directly guide it. She would more likely be a member of the senior review committee, ex officio. Therefore, Fred Everet will be the accountable executive. Ulrich Schmidt will be the project manager. He will also be the vendor evaluation committee chairman.

If the accountable executive has any political sense, he or she will want to involve in some way those executives who will be affected by the project. Most of these will be peers in systems and operations. The accountable executive can't possibly know all the technology that will be implemented, and may not recognize operational or user affects of the recommended solution. Therefore, a prudent executive will request that a group of his peers advise him in reviewing the results of the vendor evaluation conducted by the evaluation committee.

The role of the Advisory Committee is to assess the results of the evaluation process. They decide the validity of the technical solution proposed by the best vendor (considering other vendors' submissions), the cost effectiveness of the solution, and the quality of the team proposed by the vendor to implement the project. They assess whether the schedule is achievable and whether the resources required to manage the project are sufficient. They use their professional judgment to compare cost, schedule and technical risk to provide the accountable executive with a probability estimate on the success of the project, and a list of items requiring correction when the project proceeds.

Finally, they usually, but not always, concur with the recommendation of the vendor evaluation committee on the best vendor. A recommendation to consider an alternate vendor would require the evaluation committee to reevaluate the vendors' proposals to justify the original choice, or accept the alternate because of new insight provided by the advisory committee. A follow-up review would reconcile the differences.

Because advisory committee members are part of the technology component, they could be tarnished by a project failure. Their future projects might not be approved. They have a vested as well as professional interest in making certain that the project proceeds only if the risks are low. The accountable executive needs that input, not as an adversarial activity, but as a professional assessment by colleagues with whom work and risk must be shared.

The accountable executive, being accountable, can and sometimes does refute the opinions expressed by the advisory committee. There is of course room for divided opinion whenever there is technological uncertainty. If determined and persuasive, the accountable executive will prevail in the end. At least the peer review will have highlighted the dangers and provided the accountable executive with the indicators to monitor a higher risk project more closely.

We recall one peer review held on a major system to be developed by an overseas division. Our role was more as headquarters technology reviewer in a matrix organization than as a directly accountable executive. The division operations manager was directly accountable. Because of concern about the proposed project, we assembled a review team and conducted a three day review. The review team's assessment was that the project would cost over four million dollars, not one and a half million, as suggested by the project manager; that the schedule could not be done in less than thirty-six months and more likely forty-eight (the proposed schedule was eighteen months); and that the operating system chosen was inappropriate because it lacked growth potential.

The accountable executive, citing the extreme urgency of the need, prevailed upon management to approve the project in spite of the objections. Still, top management did note the objections. The project ultimately was declared a success, after over four years of development, more than four million dollars, and a system that required rewriting three years after that. The accountable executive found other employment.

On another occasion, as accountable executive for a telecommunications network project, a peer review panel argued vehemently that the technology chosen was insufficiently elegant, had intrinsic limitations in theoretical reliability, and the proposed schedule was impossible. In this case we prevailed upon management to approve our approach on the basis that the technology was adequate to do the job, that this was the only vendor positioned to deliver to many overseas locations, that the schedule could be met, and that other options would be costlier without compensating benefits.

The implementation was successfully completed three months ahead of schedule. The equipment was still operating reliably eight years after cutover. An independent audit confirmed that the solution was cost effective over that period. Ultimately, as new technology became available and as international leased line costs decreased, the network solution was reengineered with newer technology.

The lesson is not that we were good, or that the other people weren't good project managers, but that peer review is a valuable resource to be used. If you override their opinions, you are on your own. With acceptance of the risk and subsequent successful delivery, hopefully, you also receive the rewards.

The true benefits of a peer review occur when a project that is destined for disaster is aborted because all can agree that the peer review considered issues that had not been addressed before, and were now show-stoppers. We would want to have the benefit of such counsel, as you would too.

VENDOR EVALUATION TEAM STRUCTURE

A committee chairman is appointed to conduct the evaluation of the vendor proposals. In many, if not most cases, this will be the individual who will have direct responsibility to manage the vendor and the project for the company. Supporting the accountable executive, the committee chairman assembles individuals from the designated project team staff as well as from other departments who can contribute special technical, operations or management expertise.

EXHIBIT 4-3

VENDOR EVALUATION TEAM STRUCTURE

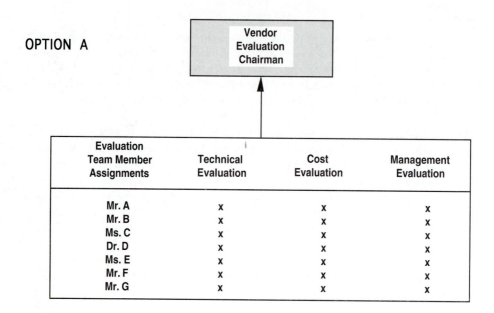

OPTION A

Evaluation Team Member Assignments	Technical Evaluation	Cost Evaluation	Management Evaluation
Mr. A	x	x	x
Mr. B	x	x	x
Ms. C	x	x	x
Dr. D	x	x	x
Ms. E	x	x	x
Mr. F	x	x	x
Mr. G	x	x	x

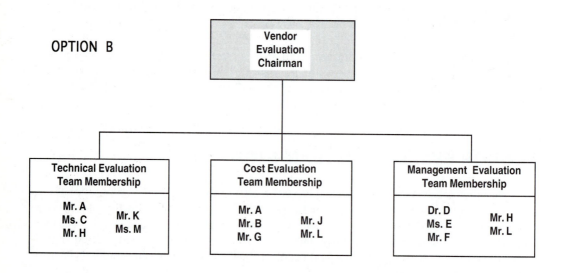

OPTION B

Vendor Evaluation Chairman

Technical Evaluation Team Membership

Mr. A
Ms. C   Mr. K
Mr. H   Ms. M

Cost Evaluation Team Membership

Mr. A
Mr. B   Mr. J
Mr. G   Mr. L

Management Evaluation Team Membership

Dr. D
Ms. E   Mr. H
Mr. F   Mr. L

The Vendor Evaluation Committee can be combined into one team, or subdivided into separate groups. These teams will review each vendor's proposal from three different perspectives: the adequacy of the technical solution; the cost veracity (and cost effectiveness) of the technical solution proposed; and, the adequacy of the vendor's staffing and management plan to implement the technical solution.

Exhibit 4-3 provides a graphic portrayal of the committee assignment options. In Option A, one team evaluates the proposals from three different contexts: technical, management and cost. In Option B, three separate teams evaluate the proposals according to the charter of that team.

We recommend that you use three separate teams. For example, the technical team could include database experts, operating system specialists, the application system specialists and manual operations supervisors. User participation is also desirable. Highly skilled technical application specialists can evaluate technical proposals without needing to cope with cost, schedule or management details.

A special expertise (e.g., project management experience) can focus on how the vendor will manage the project. The technology can be treated as a "black box." Similarly, quality assurance, project control, and experienced operating managers can evaluate the adequacy of the management proposals. Systems contract administration will assist in cost and management assessments. Financial analysts could contribute their skills to the cost proposal analysis.

Of course some persons may be members of every committee, if their experience warrants. Option B in Exhibit 4-3, shows that several persons are members of more than one committee.

This approach not only allows you to find the best persons to contribute their specialized expertise where it can provide the best benefit, but it also spreads the effort around more contributors. It allows for some confidentiality by compartmentalization of information (e.g., proprietary vendor cost data), if that is desirable. It can speed up the evaluation somewhat because not everyone has to read or evaluate every part of every proposal. On the negative side, establishing three committees requires a more expanded evaluation methodology and more coordination by the chairman. The approach we have selected uses Option B, the three team approach, because we believe the quality of the analysis is better.

We generally frown on committees, but we believe exceptions exist where a variety of input is not only desirable, but necessary. One example is in the recruitment of personnel, the other applies to vendor evaluations.

You may ask, why have three teams at all? Why evaluate according to three criteria: technical, cost and management? The rationale is as follows. If the technical solution is unacceptable, there cannot be a successful project. No matter how elegant the technical solution, if the costs are excessive you won't buy that solution. If the costs are underestimated, you will either have an overrun, or the vendor will lose money and may not be able to finish the project. Therefore, there must be conformity between the technical solution proposed, and the costs to deliver the technical solution. Finally, if the qualifications, experience and commitment of vendor management to implement the project are unacceptable, the project has infinite risk. Without quality of management, it can't be delivered on schedule or within proposed costs. Therefore, if any of these criteria do not meet the satisfactory level of assessment, that vendor cannot be selected.

Exhibit 4-4 contains three diagrams that graphically depict this concept. In diagram 4-4-A there is no congruence between the acceptable technical solution and the unacceptable cost and management proposals from that vendor. In diagram 4-4-B technical and cost solutions are acceptable, but management is not.

EXHIBIT 4-4

GRAPHIC REPRESENTATION OF VENDOR EVALUATION RESULTS

4-4-A Low Correlation Among A Vendor's Technical, Cost & Management Proposals

4-4-B High Correlation Among Technical & Cost Proposals, Low Correlation on Management

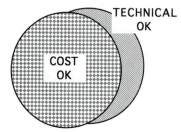 

4-4-C High Correlation Among Technical, Cost and Management Proposals

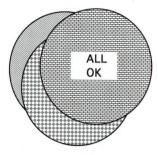

A better management solution or a better price can sometimes be negotiated with the vendor, thus making the project acceptable. But, you must know about the unacceptability of the management or cost proposal before you even know enough to renegotiate.

In diagram 4-4-C there is harmony among the acceptable technical, cost and management solutions proposed, so the graphic shows a high overlap among the evaluation categories.

We are not suggesting that each of these criteria must have the same weight in determining which vendor to select. After all, the reason you are doing the project is the technical need, and that will have the most emphasis. We are suggesting, however, that both the cost and management solutions proposed must be acceptable.

> No vendor can be an acceptable vendor,
> unless he provides a satisfactory and acceptable
> technical and cost and management proposal.

WHY HAVE A VENDOR EVALUATION POLICY?

Unfortunately very few companies have formally and rigorously codified the hierarchy, the review process, or the nature of the vendor selection teams into a Vendor Evaluation Policy. Some companies have policies on the higher levels of the hierarchy, but few, to our knowledge, go so far as to direct the specific conduct of the evaluation process. We believe that such a policy is imperative for successful selection and management of vendors, and is the cornerstone of the vendor relations principles of this manual.

The Department of Defense (DOD) has elaborate regulations on the conduct of vendor evaluations. Recent scandals point to the inadequacy of these regulations. We have participated in DOD vendor evaluations and have found them wanting, because they do not adequately establish standards for the procedural conduct of the evaluation committees. When the committees cannot furnish completed, compelling, documented justification for their recommendations, upper strata of the DOD can be influenced in the decision by external factors, namely politics, rather than technical merits.

A two page memorandum might be sufficient in a small company. An extensive document might be required for a large company. The small company has a flatter chain of command, so verbal guidance can substitute for some procedural documentation. A large company with a much deeper hierarchy cannot afford to have guidance misinterpreted, and so must document the policy and procedures thoroughly, so everyone gets the same message.

> A formal *Vendor Evaluation Policy* that specifies the conduct of vendor evaluations and, which mandates review, reporting and approval requirements, should be established in every company.

Who benefits from such a policy? Two constituencies benefit primarily. Top management benefits because they will have confidence that standard processes will deliver consistent and reliable recommendations for their consideration. Management can address the business issues of the decision without having to question the methodology. They are confident that the vendor evaluation process is so rigorously and fairly structured that the recommended vendor can be defended against any claim by any party.

If the FTS-2000 (The Federal Telephone Network) project had been conducted under such a strict policy, the project might have been implemented two years earlier, and with much less litigation.

Large projects get a lot of attention. In one project for an international T-1 circuit, we identified six eligible vendors, and were prepared to issue an RFP to them. Somehow, the nature of our project became known, and before we knew it, fourteen vendors had invited themselves to participate. Given the influential nature of some of them, and the top down leveraging style of others, we naturally included them in the RFP.

The evaluation committee used the process described in this manual. The strengths and weaknesses of all competing vendors were noted, and elaborate comparison charts showed the differences. The recommended vendor was approved by management.

But that did not prevent some vendors from approaching senior levels in the company to exert pressure for a reconsideration of the decision. Fortunately, we had the backup information from the very beginning of the evaluation, and could, and did, show top management that the vendors that were appealing, had no claim at all to the contract award.

Isn't this exactly the way you and your management want to operate? It removes a lot of pressure on everyone to have the vendor decision made solely on the merits of the vendor's proposal.

The vendor evaluation committee will benefit because they have a cookbook approach (which has management's a-priori approval) to follow. This will allow them to concentrate on the quality of the proposals, and not on how to organize themselves to create a process to evaluate vendors. The presence of a vendor evaluation policy is their <u>guarantee</u> that if they follow the process properly, and the project still is a bummer, they cannot be blamed for the results.

> The *Vendor Evaluation Policy* is a management statement that establishes the framework by which vendor proposals are evaluated fairly, consistently, and that all technical, cost, management and business issues, both tactical and strategic, are considered in the recommendation of the best vendor.

This policy includes requirements for documentation of the Vendor Evaluation Report, conduct of the vendor evaluation reviews, confidentiality procedures, and policy on debriefing vendors who were not selected. It includes details on guidance to participants on requirements for the selection of evaluation committee members, briefing of members, and standards for evaluation procedures. The actual conduct of the evaluation of vendors' proposals is discussed in Chapter 10.

Before we continue with elaboration of those issues, Exhibit 4-5 provides a summary of the roles and responsibilities of the evaluation hierarchy for your reference.

THE VENDOR EVALUATION REPORT

Action people want to do, not write! Unfortunately, you have to document the results of the vendor evaluation. This written justification is essential. The *Vendor Evaluation Report* is your official documented request to top management to approve the recommended vendor.

It is important for other reasons as well. Should you fail to negotiate a favorable contract with the best vendor, you will have materials on hand to select the next best vendor. The comparisons you make between the best vendors and the other competing vendors also will provide information to help you in negotiating a better price or obtaining a better design feature. The comparative matrices will aid you in debriefing the losing vendors on the strengths and weaknesses of their proposals.

The vendor evaluation report provides valuable historic information that will be of use to others in your company should they wish to issue an RFP to the same vendor in the future. It might allow them to evaluate the vendor's competitiveness before-hand, or provide additional information on how to package their RFP for a more effective response.

The vendor evaluation report is usually prepared by the evaluation chairman with the assistance of the evaluation committees. It is submitted to the accountable executive for use as his or her basic tool in advocating the recommended vendor to management. It is prepared after the advisory committee has conducted their review, and before the project review committee has convened. The report will include any major issues raised by the advisory committee, and will reflect any rework necessitated by that review.

The completed report will usually be presented to the project review committee for reading prior to their review meeting. In fact, the review meeting with the committee will be an extraction of the major points of the report.

EXHIBIT 4-5

VENDOR EVALUATION HIERARCHY:
ROLES & RESPONSIBILITIES

- **The Project Approval Authority**
  - Reviews the recommendations of the Project Review Committee.
  - Conducts the final vendor review meeting.
  - Approves or disapproves the vendor and the project.

- **Project Review Committee**
  - Reads the Vendor Selection Report.
  - Validates that the evaluation was conducted according to company policy.
  - Conducts the project review and assesses the quality of the evaluation results.
  - Considers the project and vendor recommendation in relevance to company plans, financial resources and other business issues.
  - Recommends approval to the Project Approval Authority or rejects the recommendation and requires rework, or discontinuation of the project.

- **Accountable Executive**
  - Selects the chairman of the Vendor Evaluation Committee.
  - Advises the chairman on the selection of committee members.
  - Conducts an orientation briefing for committee members on company Vendor Evaluation Policy.
  - Oversees the vendor evaluation process.
  - Assembles the Advisory Committee and chairs the advisory committee review.
  - Oversees re-work of evaluation results if required and coordinates compromises in assessment.
  - Reviews and approves the Vendor Evaluation Report.
  - Makes presentations to Project Review Committee and to Approval Authority.
  - Makes the vendor recommendation.
  - Conducts debriefing of vendors that were not selected.

- **Advisory Committee**
  - Reviews the results of the vendor evaluation process.
  - Determines whether the recommended vendor's technology, management and costs are acceptable.
  - Assesses the risk of the project and the chosen vendor.
  - Verifies that small changes in evaluation criteria, weightings or priorities would not cause another vendor to be chosen, or if that is so, reconciles the issue.
  - Advises the Accountable Executive on the above items and recommends corrective action on deficiencies in the vendor's proposal.

- **Vendor Evaluation Committee Chairman**
  - Selects evaluation committee members.
  - Manages the conduct of the evaluation process.
  - Participates in all evaluation activities.
  - Prepares evaluation results, summaries and conclusions.
  - Coordinates the preparation of the Vendor Evaluation Report.
  - Ensures that all company policies on vendor evaluation and confidentiality are observed.
  - Supports the Accountable Executive.

- **Evaluation Committee**
  - Reads, analyzes and evaluates vendor proposals in relevance to the RFP and the Requirements Specifications.
  - Adheres to company policy on evaluation proceedings and confidentiality.

Exhibit 4-6 contains an outline and description of the minimal contents of a vendor evaluation report. Although the emphasis of the report must be on the virtues of the recommended vendor, you should provide management with sufficient information about the other close competitors so they can make their affirmation about your wisdom in selecting the vendor. You must give management an opportunity to be more than a rubber stamp. If you've conducted the evaluation process properly, and presented enough facts and analysis to management, you will get the approval anyway.

VENDOR EVALUATION REVIEWS

Although some will read the vendor evaluation report in detail, most senior managers prefer to receive an oral presentation supported by visual aids, instead of reading documents. We would expect that the project review committee would operate in the same fashion in your company, though several would scan the vendor evaluation report before the review meeting.

We prefer to use overhead projection transparencies for briefings rather than slides. The primary reason is that overheads are easier and faster to prepare. With today's presentation graphics on microcomputers, content is no longer confined to word and number charts, and graphics can more easily present complex information, particularly comparisons among vendors. The second reason is that overheads give the presenter greater control over the sequence and timing of the presentation. Back-up information can be inserted where questions require an expanded presentation, while some overheads can be removed from the presentation if interest in that topic is limited, or if greater time is required elsewhere.

A third reason is that some senior managers still think slides require graphic artists and cost $200 each. They may be PC presentation graphics illiterates. They might regard the presentation as too polished and expensive if slides are used.

The presentation to top management will depend upon the particular style that management prefers. It could be a formal stand-up presentation before a large audience, a chat around his desk, or a two page memo recommendation. You'll have to decide how the same information gets communicated under these differing scenarios.

VENDOR DEBRIEFINGS

Although bearing bad news to vendors is never pleasant for either party, we believe that a meeting with each losing vendor is desirable.

The meeting should be scheduled when management has formally approved the recommended vendor because until then, all satisfactory vendors still might be eligible for the award. The objective of the meeting is to communicate the company's decision concerning the recommended vendor, and to highlight areas in the proposal where improvement is required, so that in future proposals this vendor can be more competitive and responsive. The more you can help the vendor understand his deficiencies, the more likely the vendor will want to show improvement in future proposals.

The accountable executive should conduct the meeting because then the vendor

EXHIBIT 4-6

VENDOR EVALUATION REPORT FORMAT

#	TITLE	SECTION CONTENTS	DESCRIPTION OF CONTENTS
1.0	**EXECUTIVE SUMMARY**		
1.1	**Project Description**	What the project is about.
1.2	**Business Requirements**	The business issues it supports.
1.3	**Recommended Vendor**	Identify the vendor.
1.4	**Recommendation Summary**	Identify vendor selected, total cost, schedule to negotiate and schedule to complete, and a short summary on the qualities of the vendor's proposal which led to the recommendation.
1.5	**Concurrence**	Statement indicating that the Advisory Panel and the Project Review Committee concur with the recommendation. Include their pertinent comments or reservations.
2.0	**RFP PROCESS**		
2.1	**Evaluation Process**	Describe the vendor evaluation process, including solicitation options selected. Include explanations for any deviation from the company's vendor evaluation policy. If none, merely state that the policy was fully complied with.
2.2	**Invited Vendors**	Identify all vendors to whom RFPs were sent. If a notable vendor was excluded from the RFP, you might comment as to why.
2.3	**Bid/No Bid Response**	Identify all vendors which responded and those which declined to propose.
2.4	**Conforming/ Non-conforming Proposals**	Identify those vendors which submitted unresponsive proposals and which were rejected for cause, and why. Identify qualifying vendors.
3.0	**EVALUATION PROCESS**		
3.1	**Evaluation Committee**	Identify the evaluation participants. The purpose is to give management awareness of the scope of the evaluation, and the quality of talent deployed.
3.2	**Evaluation Process**	Describe the process used, the scoring methodology, weight assignments to requirements, and the weight distribution among technical, management and cost facstors. If a company standard process was used, simply state the fact.
3.3	**Major Evaluation Factors**	Identifying what factors were most important enables management to make their own judgment about the appropriateness of the choice.

EXHIBIT 4-6 (continued)

VENDOR EVALUATION REPORT FORMAT

4.0	**VENDOR COMPARISON**		
	4.1	**Technical Proposals**	Compares each vendor against all others to illustrate (in condensed format) where one vendor excelled, and where any other was deficient.
	4.2	**Cost Proposals**	Same as above for proposed costs.
	4.3	**Management Proposals**	Same as above for management issues.
	4.4	**Summary Comparisons**	Include summary scoring sheets comparing vendors. Include a page showing scoring sensitivity to results.
	4.5	**Strengths and Weaknesses**	Provides two-three pages of analysis for each vendor describing that vendor's strengths and weaknesses, with particular attention on factors which were major deficiencies. This information will also be used to de-brief the vendor.
5.0	**RECOMMENDED VENDOR**		
	5.1	**Rationale**	Detailed presentation on why the vendor was the best.
	5.2	**Summary Design**	A brief technical description of the design you are buying. Include detailed cost profiles per task.
	5.3	**Rework**	Describes deficiencies in the recommended vendor's design which will need to be corrected.
	5.4	**To Be Excluded**	Describes elements in the vendor's proposal that will be descoped, or eliminated entirely (i.e., not purchased).
	5.5	**Risk Assessment**	A detailed analysis of the risks to cost, schedule and technical performance if this vendor is awarded the contract.
6.0	**COST AND SCHEDULE**		
	6.1	**Negotiation Position**	Approach to be taken in vendor negotiations.
	6.2	**Project Cost**	Describes not only what you will pay the vendor, but the expected total cost of the project, including internal labor costs.
	6.3	**Proposed Schedule**	A view of the major milestones and other critical dates in the schedule to completion.
7.0	**BENEFITS**		
	7.1	**Quantitative Benefits**	A financial statement of the benefits of the project to the company, including cash flow, break even analysis, net present value, and internal rate of return.
	7.2	**Qualitative Benefits**	A description of the non-quantifiable benefits which the project may bring: staff retention, improved morale, customer satisfaction, etc.

knows that senior management was involved in the evaluation, and that business issues as well as technical have been addressed. At the very minimum, the vendor evaluation committee chairman could debrief each vendor.

Letting a lower level employee brief the vendor can only lead to difficulty. They will not have the full perspective of the project; will not have been privy to the advisory and project reviews; and may bias the conversation with personal views instead of the company's position.

The accountable executive should open the meeting by thanking the vendor for the time and effort expended on the project, and might explain how the evaluation process was conducted, so that the fairness of the approach can be understood. Details of the weighting, scoring and comparative numerical scores, or identity of the evaluation committees should never be revealed, since they are company confidential. The recommended vendor should be identified. Characteristics of the winning proposal, except where it clearly and unambiguously distinguished that vendor from the one being debriefed, should not be communicated. You don't want to divulge anything that might be proprietary. Technical superiority and major pricing differences are obvious comparison issues.

Next, the accountable executive will address those areas where this vendor just didn't do well. The strengths and weaknesses that were compiled provide the basis for this part of the debriefing. Where the vendor did have areas of excellence in the proposal, congratulations should be extended. Deficiencies should be discussed to no more degree of detail than the extent discussed with the review committees. In this way, everyone in the purchaser's company has an identical understanding of the results. If the vendor inquires elsewhere, he will receive one consistent story. Finally, thank the vendor again, and encourage their effort on the next occasion. The elapsed time of meeting should be no more than thirty minutes.

The debriefing should convince the vendor that the decision was fair and final, and the vendor has no right of appeal. Nevertheless, reality dictates that some vendors will attempt to pursue higher level consideration of their cause. If the accountable executive feels that a "sour grapes" issue is about to commence, he might as well direct the vendor to a member of top management who will entertain a call or appeal. When you have taken the effort to involve your top management in the process, you can be confident that they will support the decision. After all, it's their decision too that is being challenged. How dare a vendor impugn the fairness of _our_ process?

It would be totally counterproductive to allow any vendor to obtain actual evaluation documentation, reports or internal recommendations, including any written data used for the debriefing. If the vendor wishes a formal letter informing them they did not have the best proposal, that can be done to satisfy vendor management.

To restate the debriefing objectives: you want the vendor to seek your business in the future, and you want the vendor to be more competitive next time. If you can avoid sour grapes as well, that's good. If you can't, at least the integrity of your evaluation process cannot be challenged, and any vendor will soon know that.

Exhibit 4-7 provides a check list to use in conducting the vendor debriefing.

EXHIBIT 4-7

PRESENTATION OUTLINE FOR A VENDOR DEBRIEFING

1. Accountable executive greetings and introduction of attendees. [3 min.]

2. Expression of appreciation for vendor's participation. [2 min.]

3. Discussion of evaluation process: [10 min.]
   - Decision made by Approval Authority
   - On basis of recommendation by Senior Project Review Committee
   - Technical Review also conducted
   - Proprietary evaluation standards were employed
   - Confidentiality was, and will be maintained
   - Evaluation was conducted with consideration of three components: technical, management and cost, with the highest weighting given to
   _____ .

4. The winning vendor was _____. The vendor won on the basis of a superior proposal in (all) (some) (technical) (cost) (management) categories. Amplify only if it was so superior that the competition was really not that competitive. [1 min.]

5. Relative position of this vendors submission was: (unacceptable) (near the bottom) (in the middle) (good, but not close) (close to the winner). [1 min.]

6. Strengths of this vendor's proposal: (Enumerate a half dozen). [2 min.]

7. Areas of gross weakness in the proposal. [1 min.]

8. General weaknesses of this vendor's proposal: (Identify ten or so). [9 min.]

9. Appreciation for effort and close out of meeting. (Identify appeal contact only if vendor reaction is extremely negative and unpleasant.) [1 min.]

[Total Suggested Elapsed Time: 30 min.]

CONFIDENTIALITY IN VENDOR EVALUATIONS

A vendor evaluation process should be company confidential. However, we wouldn't have written a manual about how to conduct such a process if everything about it were a secret. Confidentiality is needed to protect two parties: the vendors who submit proposals and the company itself. Let's examine each in turn.

The vendor has every right to expect that all information provided in the proposal will be protected from the competition. The vendor should have confidence that the persons with access to that information are motivated to maintain the highest levels of confidentiality about the proposal's contents.

Fortunately, most RFPs require the vendor to label every page of a proposal that contains proprietary information. That information is protected by law. Even with labeling it's difficult to separate proprietary from non-proprietary information. If you reveal nothing publicly, no damage can occur. Companies must take serious efforts to insure that this information is protected. But, protection of proprietary information is not sufficient. The total scope of the submission by the vendor may reveal more about the vendor than the vendor ever anticipated. This can bring another issue into consideration.

A company that receives several proposals for a project has a unique opportunity to compare one vendor's technical, cost, and management performance against the other vendors. This information is extremely powerful, in that it is information that the vendors do not have about each other. Sometimes, the information about strengths and weaknesses may not even be apparent to the vendor itself.

It would seriously endanger your relationships with your vendors if you told each of them all about the other vendors' proposals, including costs and performance features. No one likes to have their deficiencies displayed for public view. Publicizing a really poor submission could not only embarrass a vendor, but might jeopardize its future earnings potential. If sufficient damage is done, your company might even be subject to a libel lawsuit.

In many procurements in the public sector (e.g., city or state governments) all proposals and data are in the public domain. Vendors can obtain copies of the non-proprietary parts of other proposals and compare their proposal against their competition. We just don't think it is proper for the client to do this for them.

Some managers object to this point. They believe that revealing all strengths and weaknesses in an open forum will make vendors improve their products, to everyone's benefit. Our view is that if the vendor is a major company, your evaluation will have little impact on that vendor's business strategy. Publicizing the deficiencies in the proposal will have an emotional impact upon the people who prepared the proposal. It is these people who service your account, and to whom you will look to for proposals in the future. Why make them feel uncomfortable?

The company also has internal reasons for ensuring that the evaluation is confidential. First, it should recognize that in the same way that vendors like to exercise account control, maintaining privacy of internal proceedings allows the company to deny that control to vendors. Thus it increases its leverage over all vendors as a group.

Secondly, there are circumstances in which senior management will choose a vendor other than the recommended vendor for business reasons not directly related to the proposal's quality. This could be related to new financial information concerning the vendor's viability. It could relate to forthcoming products of another vendor which are known on a nondisclosure basis only to top management. By maintaining confidentiality over the whole process, management guarantees that its decision reflects the corporate choice. The last thing management wants is some junior participant in the evaluation expressing personal views publicly that "the best vendor didn't get the contract."

Thirdly, controlling the anonymity of the individual participants in the evaluation process allows them to express their views freely without concern for vendor marketing pressure during or after the evaluation. Management controls who its spokesperson will be.

The following procedures should be taken to establish the appropriate levels of confidentiality:

• Physical Security

Vendor evaluations are intense activities with time and performance pressures. The evaluation process can be made more productive, and a spirit of teamwork better established, if a private area can be set aside for the evaluation teams during the evaluation. The special nature of the evaluation is emphasized by operating away from the normal job location. Intrusion by non-participants can be restricted and gossip about the deliberations avoided.

All documentation, both vendor and evaluation team working papers, should be secured in a locked file when the team is absent.

After the evaluation, all excess vendor proposals should be destroyed or returned to the vendors. One copy should be archived in the SCA vault, along with the working papers, analysis and reports of the evaluation committees, the advisors and the reviewers.

• Anonymity

Identity security is useful. We suggest that working papers use coded names or numbers for vendors' identities, and similarly for the identity of the evaluation participants. We have found that there is an interesting and beneficial psychological aspect to the use of coded identities in an evaluation. Every evaluation team will have an a-priori advocate of their favorite vendor. The name of the vendor elicits an emotional response, almost Pavlovian. When the vendor's name is coded (e.g., Vendor XX), analysis seems to become more objective, and based upon the merits of the proposal's wording, and less upon the name recognition and image of the vendor. A more balanced and logically supportable evaluation results.

Every company also has those individuals whom for whatever reason fail to express themselves candidly. Peer and management pressure intensify the basic insecurity manifested. (Perhaps with some validity?) When afforded a nom-de-plume, these individuals transcend that insecurity, and often provide enlightened (and sometimes trenchant) analysis, adding significant value to the evaluation.

To fortify the feeling of security, the opinions of individual committee members should not be revealed even during the reviews or approval process. There is no practical reason for management more than one level above the evaluation chairman to have knowledge of what position or view is attributed to whom. The only reason the accountable executive might need that information is to chair a meeting among disputing members of the three committees to reconcile logical inconsistencies in the analysis.

• Non-Disclosure

The above measures are ineffective without a company policy that establishes that participation in a vendor evaluation is a company confidential and proprietary activity. The policy must include a statement that: disclosure to anyone, not authorized by management, of the process, participants and results of the evaluation, by anyone directly or indirectly privy to the evaluation information, will result in that person's termination from employment, and potential legal action.

Many of the woes of various federal procurement scandals can be attributed to people who couldn't keep their mouths shut. There must be a penalty for disclosure of internal information.

In 1989 an individual was terminated by Apple Corporation for disclosure of company proprietary information. While the merits of the degree of proprietary information that was purportedly revealed can be debated, what cannot be debated is management's right to reserve to itself how, what, and when information can be disclosed. No individual without authorization can assume that right, no matter how they might disagree with management's position. To do other is anarchy, and no entity can operate in such a circumstance.

CASE STUDY

Fred and Higby Wallace, CFO, met in the latter's office to discuss BB&T's needs for the BITS system. Fred outlined the vendor evaluation process he had in mind. He emphasized the need for a project review process to ensure that all BB&T's requirements would be met.

"Well Fred, its really been years since we had occasion to make a major decision on any purchase other than the acquisition of Mimosa Street Bank. And even that was done by Mr. Oldsin and the Board of Directors. We weren't involved until after the decision was made."

"What about the Loan Approval Committee?" Fred asked. "Oh yes, we meet once a month without Mr. Oldsin to approve any loan below $1 million. Any loan higher than that must also be approved by Mr. Oldsin."

"Why shouldn't we create a special version of the loan committee to review the proposal for the new retail system?" Fred asked. He continued: "My initial estimate is that our internal costs to collect the requirements, conduct the evaluation and complete the project will be over $500 thousand, and the vendor proposal could cost another half a million or more. But we'll also need to get some senior managers from the Mimosa Street Bank involved, since their knowledge of the retail business is necessary to keep us on track."

"Great idea, Fred. Why don't you proceed on that assumption. I'll bring up your proposal at Mr. Oldsin's staff meeting tomorrow, and if there are any modifications, I'll let you know. Assuming everything is as you've suggested, I'll also take it upon myself to enlist George Zecker to join the review committee. I'll get names from him on whomever he would like to support your evaluation and reviews. I'll get back to you on that within a day," promised Higby.

Higby Wallace called Friday morning and confirmed Oldsin's enthusiastic approval for the review process. He confirmed also that George Zecker himself would be

Chairman of the Project Review Committee, and that Carmine Zilva and Ed Zaraczyk of MSB would be members, with Lisa, Bill Carney, Mike Chan, Jon Willoughby and himself from BB&T. Wallace also said that Zecker had offered any of the resources of MSB to serve on the evaluation committee, and that Ziggy Zablonski and Phil Zownes would like to participate on the advisory team.

So with the stage set for management's involvement in the crucial decision, Fred now sat down to plan the effort required. The staff worked all weekend to identify the critical tasks necessary to try to achieve Mr. Oldsin's target date. With a mandated system, and an approval process in place, Fred could make some assumptions about the time it would take to conduct an evaluation and obtain approvals. (His experience had been that the elapsed time could be as long as eight months.) Activities of the evaluation committees were not on the critical path, and further planning could be deferred for a while. Fred allocated only about forty working days to that activity. Since the evaluation committees would be drawn from his dedicated staff, Lisa's direct reports and MSB personnel who would be spending time on the project, Fred thought that his time estimate was reasonable. The learning curve on the project would be absorbed in the requirements process.

The team then assessed the time it would take to collect and document requirements. They agreed that at least ninety working days were required. Although parts of the request for proposal could be prepared in advance, key elements would have to wait until the specifications were complete. Fred wanted to give the vendors as much time as possible to respond to the RFP, so he allocated 25 working days for their response.

With these assumptions completed, the final question was: "What time is left for the vendor to do the project?" The model indicated that if the vendor started work on November 15, the system would be operational on April 2nd. Was this reasonable?

Peyton responded that he thought it could be done because of the way they had decided to specify requirements, and through allowing the vendor flexibility in the retail software. It would be risky. Fred thought that he could squeeze a little more time out of the RFP preparation phase. But, what they had now was the best they could plan for the present. So they agreed that Fred would present the schedule shown in Exhibit 4-8 at Lisa's Monday meeting.

The critical path is shown in bold on the schedule in Exhibit 4-8.

Lisa's staff greeted Fred's presentation with a great deal of skepticism. But, they agreed that the schedule would be the baseline until new information and more detailed planning could be done. The consensus was, that in the eleven days since Mr. Oldsin's announcement, a lot of planning had been accomplished, and there was a faint glimmer of hope that they could meet management's expectations.

They also agreed that the most significant current problem was to find vendors who would qualify for consideration to receive the BB&T Request for Proposal. After the meeting, Fred met with Walter and Peyton to see how finding vendors could be done.

EXHIBIT 4-8

INITIAL SCHEDULE FOR BITS PROJECT

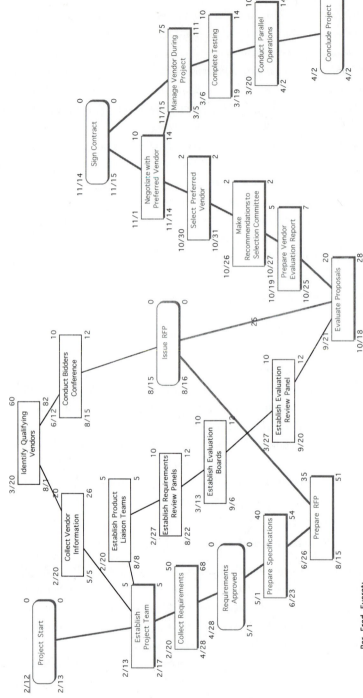

Per Fred Everet:

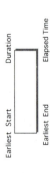

Earliest Start   Duration

Earliest End   Elapsed Time

After that, Fred began assembling the outline and membership of the evaluation teams and hierarchy. Table 4-1 contains his preliminary list of participants.

TABLE 4-1
BB&T VENDOR SELECTION HIERARCHY

- **Project Approval Authority:**   Hampton Oldsin, CEO BB&T

- **Project Review Committee:**   George Zecker, Chmn. & CEO, MSB

Carmine Zilva	MSB
Ed Zaraczyk	MSB
Lisa Moore	BB&T
Bill Carney	BB&T
Mike Chan	BB&T
Jon Willoughby	BB&T
Higby Wallace	CFO, BB&T

- **Advisory Committee:**   Fred Everet, Chairman

Ziggy Zablonski	MSB
Phil Zownes	MSB
Brian Ericson	BB&T
Diane Evens	BB&T
George Elias	BB&T
Anita Emerson	BB&T
Sung How Kim	Auditor

- **Accountable Executive:**   Fred Everet, SVP

- **Vendor Evaluation Chmn:**   Ulrich Schmidt, BITS Manager

- **Vendor Evaluation Teams:**

Monk Eternic	SCA
Peyton Somers	Consultant
Rip Scali	Requirements
Walt Smerski	Technology
Tony Scerbo	Interfaces
Alvin Eberhardt	Systems Engineer
Dwayne Eber	Ind. Engineer
Roger Eillinger	Quality Assurance
Toshio Sumizaki	Financial Controls
Dmitri Sorjak	Interface Systems
Peijun Shun	Budgeting

## Chapter Five

FINDING AND QUALIFYING VENDORS

THE CONCEPT OF A VENDOR INVENTORY

It's hard to imagine that Fred Everet lacks a viable reference source to identify vendors to bid on the BITS system. Yet, consider your situation. If you are a professional who is frequently relocated by your company, or who changes jobs often, you know what a task it is to find your personal vendors in a new location. Finding a pediatrician, dentist, electrician, plumber, gardener and attorney can be a time consuming task. Yet we all go through that process, almost unthinking about whether we are finding the best, or only an adequate personal services practitioner.

We often rely on *Welcome Wagon* or new neighbors in relocation situations to provide an initial list. We have no idea whether they are reliable sources of reference information.

The search for vendors to support your company's technological requirements is an equivalent exercise. Many companies, even the largest, find vendors using the same ad-hoc methods we use in personal life: we ask someone. Although this approach is a valid starting point, a more rigorous and sophisticated methodology to find vendors is necessary.

Finding a vendor isn't enough. Since time is at a premium precisely when you need a vendor, you will benefit by finding, cataloging and validating vendors earlier than the requirement. Long term, the effort expended will result in more qualified vendors to support you, at a better price and with consistently better performance.

We believe most firms, large or small, consistently make a mistake of not obtaining enough competitive bids. They deprive themselves of knowledge of the current state of the art, competitive pricing, and bargaining leverage. To ensure enough qualified vendors, establish a vendor physical repository or inventory of information.

We all do this to a greater or less extent. As we read a journal article about a new product, we'll tear out the article and put it on a pile for future reference. We'll even obtain more information about the product using the product inquiry cards found in most magazines. After a while the information piles up and becomes obsolescent. We throw it away only to start anew.

If you are going to be technologically current, you must do this. But companies need to do this even more because the company's needs are more than the combined sum of its employees' filing cabinets.

The repository for vendor information; can be in the technical library. The systems contract administrator could establish the repository as part of his or her vendor tracking responsibilities. Some companies have their marketing research function do this task as part of competitive analysis, business trends and customer satisfaction analyses. Others might collect the information in their strategic planning unit, if they are looking for acquisitions.

Wherever it resides, one factor must be recognized. There must be an accountable person who will maintain and control the data. There are two reasons for this: the data must be selective and non-redundant; and the information is perishable and must be purged. You don't want just any kind of data in the files. Relying on employees to contribute their personal vendor files won't do, because their files will not be targeted toward the information the company needs.

We discovered the following paradigm: "The half life of information is less than six months." This means that information you collect today, loses 50% of its value (timeliness, appropriateness, accuracy) in less than six months. After the second year, only 6% of the information is useful. Therefore, someone has to purge old data and insert new data. Because of a vested interest in vendor information, the systems contract administrator is the most logical caretaker of the vendor inventory.

Consider the volatility of software upgrades for the most popular personal computer programs. It seems that we're paying another hundred dollars every eighteen months or so for a new version. Telecommunications product upgrades and new features are similarly prolific in the rate of change, particularly related to local area networking and file servers.

If your company buys systems as seldom as Baccarat Bank & Trust, perhaps you can rely on a one-time vendor data collection effort to build your inventory. Crash efforts seldom identify all the potential candidates.

Therefore, an inventory of vendors and their capabilities should be a resident file. This is analogous to the information about marketing prospects that vendors collect. There are two features to this inventory. First, you have to know the right sources to collect the information, and second, you need to make a knowledgeable judgment about the information collected. The remainder of the chapter develops these themes.

Establishing a vendor capabilities inventory is an intelligence collection process. You need to know everything you can about a vendor: management, products, financial status and personnel, including what others think about the firm. The best place to start that intelligence collection is from your employees. As suggested above, each will have a file of vendors (perhaps future employers?). The raw data they provide forms the basis for obtaining the objective information you require. Don't ignore the subjective opinions about the vendor from associates, competitors and clients. Separating the vendor's self-image from the perceived image of the marketplace ensures you have a "reality check" on the vendor.

TECHNICAL INFORMATION SOURCES

No matter how current, it is impossible to keep up with the pace of changes in specifications; the merger, acquisition or demise of companies; trade and user associations; and trade publications in a book like this. All these things come and go. Furthermore, you should consider the examples in this chapter to be illustrative, rather than an exact formula for collecting vendor information, since it reflects the author's interests and needs, and not necessarily yours.

Let's examine some means by which you will collect technical information about the vendor's products.

• Vendor Literature

The most obvious source to collect technical information is from the vendor directly. The vendor's name usually comes from your employees, your associates, or trade magazines that carry the vendor's ads, product evaluations, or articles by the magazine's staff.

A software publisher's trade association was formed some years ago, and over four hundred members are listed in the directory. The directory includes extensive listings of IBM personnel to contact, as well as small firms with less than $1 million in revenue. The Software Publishers Association is in Washington, DC. Other associations offer lists of their industry members.

Once your list of names and addresses is complete, the vendor literature you obtain by direct contact is classified as promotional, explanatory, specifications or detailed operational materials. Promotional materials are the high-gloss marketing brochures that explain the high level functionality of the products. They are used to figure out if the product line is worth further exploration. Explanatory materials are product specific, provide better insight into product features and performance, but do not permit understanding of processing logic. Specifications are the meat and potatoes of a vendor's offerings. Some of these are readily obtainable (e.g., IBM publications) for a fee or obtained from the account executive. The most difficult materials to obtain, for some unknown reason, seem to be the operating manuals.

The level of sophistication you require will depend upon the product you are assessing. However difficult it may be to obtain, without a sufficient level of technical information to satisfy your staff, the vendor cannot be considered useful to your company. Since vendors usually update their products about once a year, you'll have to update your files accordingly.

• Vendor Demonstrations

Vendor exhibits at trade shows, and vendor demonstrations in their offices are excellent ways to obtain an appreciation of vendors' products. Trade shows (mostly for hardware, but some software as well) are also prime situations to conduct casual competitive analyses of vendors. The National Computer Conference, INFO 199X and COMDEX are all good places to get an initial familiarity with a vendor's data processing products. In telecommunications, the ICA convention, TCA and COMNET are leading shows that target the user. These shows, and others not mentioned, vary in quality and attendance from year to year. New trade shows arise, while others disappear. It's as trendy as the latest Beverly Hills restaurant.

You should not expect to obtain the detailed information you require at a trade show. It's the place to exchange business cards and set up a future call by the vendor's marketing representative. Alternatively, you can meet off the exhibit floor with the vendor's senior representatives.

If you attend the same trade show every year, you find interesting changes in emphasis over time. For example, at ICA, the shift in vendor exhibits has moved from PBXs, to Data Communications Multiplexers, to ACDs, to Voice Mail, to T-1 multiplexers, to Network Management Systems, to ISDN and so on. In the case of Network Management Systems, the fashion was to use Sun Microstations as the network management capabilities display. Each vendor tried to outdo the next in the number of windows, colors and icons he presented. You could obtain a good appreciation of the pace of evolution of products, the ability of vendors to respond to the market, and an impression of what the product should feature in this venue. For network management, no vendor has yet shown what the sophisticated telecommunications manager really needs, a totally integrated database system. So, all the glossy displays are irrelevant if the substance still isn't there.

A vendor's demonstration facility is a good place to obtain a real feel for the product. You have the opportunity to have a dedicated demonstration in privacy. You can ask as many questions as you like, and can direct the demonstration to areas of interest to you. To obtain the best benefit from the demonstration, we suggest that you show an avid interest in the product to stimulate the vendor to do well. It is a good idea to provide the vendor with a list of topics you want covered before the demonstration. The personnel providing the demonstration will otherwise try to show you what they are familiar with, and what part of the system functions the most completely and powerfully. Therefore, it may be difficult to steer the demo in the direction you want if you haven't provided a subject agenda in advance. Bringing a checklist of important features to be seen in the demo will also help your questioning. Though it slows the demonstration down, we particularly like to operate the terminal ourselves during an on-line demo. It provides an immediate feedback on the user friendliness of the product.

Local chapters of professional organizations (Association of Computing Machinery [ACM], Data Processing Manufacturers Association [DPMA], Institute of Electrical and Electronic Engineers [IEEE]) sometimes have vendor nights at their regional chapter meetings. These are of interest, for besides the product discussion, they highlight the local vendor team, which is not necessarily the national capability.

Major vendors have press conference shows to announce their latest product offerings. These "Roman circuses" aren't worth your time. It will be a few weeks before the knowledgeable consultants and industry observers will have views on the product. It's best to wait for their analyses to be published.

• Industry Publications

The number of industry publications is enormous, and the redundancy in reporting the same information is equally enormous. With the coalescence of telecommunications and data processing, the overlap in reporting is increasing further. Only a few publications manage to differentiate themselves from the others entirely, unless they are highly specialized services to a segment of the industry. So subscribing to a few representative publications is sufficient. It will take a while to find those that market to your needs.

Other information technology and telecommunications industry publications that provide summary lists of vendor product comparisons include: *Computerworld, Datamation, MIS Week, Modern Office Technology, Communications News, Teleconnect, Telecommunications, Telephony* and *Satellite Communications*, to name a few. The personal computer user has a host of magazines that feature extensive reviews and comparisons of hardware and software: *Info Week, Personal Computing, PC World, MacUser* and *MacWorld*. Many of these magazines publish annual or semi-annual buyer's guides that are useful.

It is impossible to identify all the sources for software that might be applicable to each industry sector. Retail and commercial banks, savings and loan associations, and insurance companies all have individual peculiarities in software applications that might also be commonly applicable. The same applies to the transportation, automobile and consumer durable industries. Retailers, both food and garment, have systems (point of sale) that are quite similar. Find those systems trade magazines applicable to your industry for the best leads on vendors capable of supporting you.

• Evaluation Services

This category includes those firms that specialize in definitive technical analysis of vendors' products (with the emphasis on hardware and operating systems software), and others that do market research on industry segments. Representing the technical evaluation category are: *ACM Transaction Series, Datapro Directories, IEEE Transactions, Advances in ... by JAI Press* and *Auerbach's Services*.

Included in the market research firms are: International Data Corp. [IDC]; the Gartner Group; the Yankee Group; Dataquest; Frost and Sullivan, Inc.; INPUT; G-2 Research; the Ledgeway Group, Computer Intelligence and International Resource Development, Inc. Services will vary, but these companies conduct detailed market surveys and analysis of industry trends, technology trends, market size and growth, and technology niches. Their principal clients are the vendors who use their analyses to decide product development strategies. Some of these firms provide end user consulting, though usually not as a project manager or service provider.

• Management Consultants

You can collect vendor information from more than 100 thousand independent consultants. Every reader will know a half dozen who will provide leads and information on vendor capabilities. A key advantage of polling a smaller consulting company or an independent consultant is that they are more likely to have hands-on knowledge of software systems than larger consulting firms that primarily address management issues, though not exclusively.

The larger consulting firms include the prestigious accounting/tax behemoths of KPMG, Arthur Andersen, Ernst & Young, Coopers and Lybrand and Price Waterhouse among others. Their systems and telecommunications practices ebb and flow over time, so selection of the right source may require some inquiries. Professional ethics would restrict these firms from providing information about their clients, but they might be willing to discuss hardware and software offerings. They will have good understanding of the technology, and through their cross-industry practices, excellent knowledge of systems applicable to your industry. Since these firms maintain extensive alumni contacts, an inquiry from an alumnus within your company may be more effective than a formal request.

Systems integration companies like EDS, Computer Sciences, PA Associates, Cap Gemini and Computer Task Group are less likely sources of information on vendors because they prefer to be the vendor of choice themselves.

• User and Professional Organizations

Your contacts in user organizations such as SHARE, GUIDE, DECUS, ADCU, ICA, TCA and the multitudinous microcomputer electronic billboard users groups are important sources of information on vendors and software packages. Although the formal users groups like SHARE are single vendor oriented, the intermissions will provide enough time to poll the participants for vendor leads.

> During the years of rapid growth in international banking (before third world debt was an issue), finding qualified vendors who developed international banking systems was difficult. There were only a few US banks with extensive offshore branches in the mid-nineteen seventies.

> Through a consultant moderator, a group of sixteen banks met on an informal basis twice a year to exchange experiences in dealing with overseas cultures, regulatory reporting and the quality of available systems. Proprietary activities were closely guarded. Nevertheless, the information that affected all banks was freely exchanged. It helped many institutions to avoid selecting incompetent vendors, or packages that didn't meet their needs. The value of this exchange is illustrated by the fact that the group still meets after many years in existence, although the roster of participants has changed.

> You should be able to find an equivalent group (or form one) in your industry.

• Installed Customer Visits

When you are seriously considering a vendor, a visit to an installed customer site is the best possible source of technical and operational information. Try to arrange a visit to the site without the vendor's presence. The user can then provide a candid commentary about the product and sales and service support. Alternatively, if a visit can't be arranged, a well-scripted telephone conversation with the customer can provide the needed information.

> After installation and successful operation of a global packet network, we found ourselves continuously bombarded by calls and requests for visits by potential clients of our vendor. Although burdensome, we responded to those requests for three reasons: we were proud of the quality and operational excellence of our installation and wanted to publicize our prowess; the vendor was responsive (though we had extended his resources) and we wanted to acknowledge that fact; and we wanted other companies

to purchase the equipment so that the international presence of the vendor could be expanded, thereby improving the quality and timeliness of service to us as well as the other clients.

Furthermore, once we established these contacts, and if they bought the equipment, we could jointly lobby the vendor to provide enhancements and improvements. Site visits thus increased our leverage by making the vendor even more dependent upon us.

Unless the vendor has a troubled relationship with a client, he will be pleased to provide you with a client contact list. Insist on it, including a list of those clients who may not be totally pleased with the product. During a client site visit, ask the persons you are visiting if they know of any other clients who are unhappy with the vendor's products. Then, follow up.

FINANCIAL AND MANAGEMENT INFORMATION SOURCES

Once you've found a potentially qualifying vendor, you need to determine if it has a reasonable probability of survival. Survivability is always traceable to financial viability and quality of management, and seldom to product efficacy. We believe this holds for a two person firm as well as a billion dollar firm. The degree of risk is highly different for a small company, and the time scale to bankruptcy may be quicker. But inadequate financial and managerial strength exists in huge companies as well.

It is said that you should never consider a vendor unless you behave like a banker, and are willing to make that company a loan. If so, the world would still be looking for the personal computer to be useful. You cannot afford to behave like a banker in assessing the quality of a vendor's financial stability or management skills. Bankers are too, too conservative. You cannot afford to give up needed technology because there are financial and management risks in using that vendor. The smaller you are yourself, the more important it may be to consider smaller vendor firms to support you. But you cannot blindly believe in the vendor's longevity either. You need to collect enough financial and management information about the vendor to make a prudent business judgment about the degree of risk you are willing to accept.

It is an essential principle of this manual that once you make a risk assessment about a vendor, and you accept those risks for the benefit of superior technology, that vendor by definition is as qualified as any other vendor you have evaluated. Therefore, no additional risk assessment can be applied to the vendor during a vendor selection process. The corollary of this principle is that you cannot give a large vendor additional benefit of the doubt based on financial strength or image during a vendor selection process. Otherwise, only large vendors would ever be selected. Unfortunately, that is all too often the case.

There is no guarantee that selecting a large vendor will guarantee survivability of the product. An S&P 500 firm whose primary business is other than technology, decided to sell some software it had developed in-house. Over time, a number of systems were sold to other companies in the same industry.

When a change in strategic direction occurred, the firm decided to get out of the software business. Since it had committed to service contracts and version updates, it needed to find someone to buy the business. That was not easily done. The customers, fearing loss of support, sued for contract violation. Ultimately, a financial settlement was reached, but the buyers were faced with a software product that had a premature death.

The moral of the story is that technical, management and financial risk abound even when you choose large vendors. Pertinent to this manual, you better negotiate a good contract so you can get relief in some manner from the vendor, no matter how big, if they violate the contract.

> ## A vendor you have qualified is equal to any other qualified vendor, no matter the size or prestige.

You do want to know the size of any financial and management risk. Let's examine means of finding that information about your vendor.

• Regulatory Information

Every public company must file an Annual Report and 10K Form with the Securities and Exchange Commission. Both are available on request from the secretary or public affairs office of the corporation. These reports provide profiles of the firm's revenues and profits for the last year, and usually comparisons of performance for the last five years. If you are a qualified investor or financial analyst, you should be able to determine the quality of the earnings, stability of revenue and strategy of management. If not, have your accountant or someone in your financial department walk through such an analysis with you. Otherwise, enlist outside financial analysts to make an assessment.

Please notice that the assessment of a Wall Street analyst to recommend investment in a firm is not necessarily dependable for your purposes. For example, in the early 1980s, Wang Laboratories was very high on the recommended lists of analysts, and for some time, returned investors a good premium. Our analysis revealed that the firm was likely to grow from a $250 million firm to a $1 billion company in about three to four years. Personnel growth was increasing proportionately to the revenue increase.

If you have ever grown an organization, you know that 50% annual increases in professional staff cannot be managed without significant problems in assimilating, training and directing those personnel, even with abundant funds. We thereby predicted that when Wang would reach a $1 billion revenue level, it would begin to have serious quality control and servicing problems.

Our prediction was correct. That did not prevent us from buying Wang equipment. We bought a lot of it. However, we negotiated strong service agreements, required dedicated service personnel, established longer and more rigorous acceptance testing, and kept their feet to the fire. Not everything worked out perfectly, but much of the pain other buyers experienced was avoided. Then Wang's overhead got too high and new products failed to appear. Among other vendors, the PC revolution also blind-sided Wang.

The moral of this story is that you must understand the fundamental financial information and you need to correlate that information with the behavior it may imply. You need to read between the lines, as they say. Furthermore, you need to anticipate that no firm may be your vendor of choice for more than a few years. You need to constantly update your risk assessment of financial stability.

Just because a public firm publishes a glowing annual report, that doesn't make it financially viable either. The telecommunications equipment industry and the microcomputer industry have the consolidations, acquisitions and bankruptcies common to industries that are shaking out from the entrepreneurial class to a limited group of major players. In spite of the risks inherent in these industries, most companies will survive long enough for you to obtain a full life cycle of equipment usage. In a highly dynamic industry your risk assessment must consider a probable faster rate of product obsolescence and replacement reinvestment. This is true for equipment manufacturers, less so for software companies.

There is usually enough information available about large private companies that you can make similar judgments about them as for public companies. Lack of profit information won't be a liability if there is a good historic profile of revenue growth. Smaller public companies (fewer than 300 shareholders) have fewer disclosure requirements, so regulatory mandated information may be limited. A written request to the secretary of the company should provide you with the information you need.

The challenge of determining the financial viability of small private companies is more difficult. Every private corporation must file with the Secretary of State or the Bureau of Corporations within the state in which it does business. The articles of incorporation, officers and other required information must be updated annually. Other than validating the existence of a legal entity, there will be little else available in the required filings. For these firms, you need to find other sources, including the owners.

• Business Publications

There are two types of business publications: general audience and industry specific. Each has the dual purpose of reporting financial results for companies, and reporting management decisions, transactions and reorganizations. General audience publications include daily papers like: *The Investor's Daily, The Wall Street Journal and Crain's Business Review,* and the financial section of your local newspaper; weeklies include *Barron's,* and *Businessweek*; and semi-monthly or monthly magazines are: *Forbes, Fortune, Duns Review, Institutional Investor, Value Line Services* and *INC*. Nearly all publish quarterly comparative financial results of public companies. They provide extensive coverage of behind the scenes' activities at companies large and small. But, they can only provide a macroscopic picture of a firm. For a large firm, that might not be the granularity you require.

Special purpose publications (including those mentioned in technical information sources above) and higher level magazines devote less column space to technical issues, and more to management, industry analysis and corporate performance. Of particular note is *Information Week*, which concentrates on proactive managers in the information services field. There are at least thirty publications that provide management and financial information on the banking industry alone. Your local library will have a copy of *The Directory of Directories* that can start you on the way to finding the publications that will focus on your industry.

In each community the local newspaper will publish news of interest about local firms, public and private. Much of the information never gets published in national publications. For example, the *Los Angeles Times* publishes a regional business section on local businesses. A special weekly publication, *The Los Angeles Business Journal*, concentrates on the business community. It publishes fictitious business names (Doing Business As....), transfers, bankruptcies, and news of note about business in the Los Angeles area. Many cities have similar publications.

If you are curious about a small company, you might well call the research staff of a local newspaper in the headquarters city of the vendor. If they can't give you detailed information directly, the research staff may remember if records exist and direct you to do the archival search yourself.

• Credit Sources

Subscribers can see credit information about any company from Dun & Bradstreet, TRW Credit Services or Equifax among others. Proprietary companies will have the owner's credit rating substitute for the company's. Moody's Investor's Service, Inc. and the Standard & Poor's Corp. services provide credit ratings for larger firms.

You should not ignore your company's banker in your pursuit of financial and business information about a vendor. Your banker will be glad to help you in obtaining the information required. Since a banker does credit requests all the time as part of their job, this may be the most convenient approach for you to take.

Alternatively, if you are a good client, your securities dealer can obtain the data from the brokerage's research department or other industry newsletters and evaluations.

• Other Sources

You will be surprised what a simple telephone call can reveal. Competitors and suppliers are among the best sources of unfiltered (and subjective) information about a vendor. The credit standing can be quickly confirmed by contacting a the vendor's suppliers. An equipment maker will have many payables, and a sampling of creditors will help to understand whether cash flow is sufficient for continuing operations. Suppliers may know of a problem long before the firm's bankers or lenders.

Ask the vendor's customers if they know of any reason the firm is not viable. They will be the first to notice poor response, service deficiencies or multi-tasking of otherwise dedicated staff. Requests for advance payments above and beyond reasonable terms can indicate cash flow problems. A final source of subjective information would be the firm's current and recent employees.

The number of on-line services providing the above information is growing too fast to keep track of them. These services may be the most rapid means of obtaining the information you require.

PRICING INFORMATION

Vendor's quoted prices that you find in publications are worthless except as a general indicator of scale. Accurate pricing information is available from three sources:

1. From a Freedom of Information Act request when the vendor has sold the identical product to the U. S. Government. The public domain data will reveal the lowest possible price that the vendor can charge for his product. The Federal government, by law, is a "most favored nation," and must obtain all goods at the lowest price offered anyone. You will probably not be able to obtain the product at that price, but it is the best deal possible. Some very large commercial buyers can negotiate equivalent "most favored nation" clauses in their contracts because of their leverage.

2. From other purchasers of the vendor's products. Many companies would regard their ability to negotiate discounts from the vendor's quoted prices to be proprietary information, and of strategic importance. Others don't really care, or are proud to disclose how good they are in negotiations. You won't ever know unless you ask. Sometimes even a range of discounts could give you sufficient information to materially affect the price you pay. However, the vendor's contract with a client may prohibit price or discount disclosures.

   A negotiation for a national discount on modems was in progress, and we felt that a 30% discount from list price was a great price on a multi-million dollar purchase. A telephone call to an associate in another company revealed that a discount range of 40-50% was available, if we negotiated the contract to bypass certain distributors of the vendor. After reviewing the risks of not getting maintenance services from the distributor if we bought direct, we determined it was more cost effective and operationally viable to install redundant equipment and factory ship malfunctioning equipment. We saved a lot of money.

3. From the vendor's official published price lists and the discount schedules.

   Sometimes a used equipment market exists for the product. Specialists in the leased equipment market can frequently establish the real price the vendor is offering by the manner in which the used or leased equipment markets are quoting equivalent equipment. Unfortunately, this does not apply for software.

   Remember, there is no such thing as a firm fixed price if the vendor wants your business. All prices are negotiable, and if not, service, maintenance, training or additional software may substitute for a lower price.

OTHER ASSESSMENTS

You need to verify some other categories of information about a vendor that don't fall into the categories above.

• Production Capability

If this is an equipment manufacturer, can the factory respond to your order in the time frame you require. Does the vendor maintain an inventory of standard equipment, or is everything made to order? If the latter, and you are a small firm, what is the chance that your order will get bumped for a customer with more leverage? If the vendor has a history of doing this, you may want to extend your project schedule as a contingency, or find another vendor.

• Personnel Adequacy

If this is a software procurement, does the vendor have the right kind of expertise to give you confidence that the modifications you require can be done? It's too early in the process to investigate specific individuals who might work on your project. But you do want a feeling of confidence that there are enough quality personnel available to get the job done.

Find out, if you can, the rate of turnover of professional personnel and management. Entrepreneurial firms will have a bit of turnover. The risk comes if it is the wrong turnover. For a new small firm, it's critical that the original inventors (and their potential replacements) are still with the firm. You will be buying their brains as much as the product.

• Service

Can the vendor support the product in the field? Is there sufficient institutionalization within the vendor that you have reason to believe that quality documentation and version updates to the system will be provided? Can you expect that installation, training and maintenance will be available regularly? Will customer service for outages be prompt and effective? Can you expect that bugs will be fixed quickly?

It's not always a disadvantage to consider fewer vendors, or those with inferior service, but adequate products. Your expected use of the product may be short enough that it will serve your purposes. Furthermore, if you can service the product yourself (especially software maintenance), you will not be dependent upon the vendor's future stability. You may be able to get real savings in time, expense and risk by choosing such a vendor. The smaller vendor companies may be most representative of this possibility.

The best sources for this information are the vendor's current customers. Seek them out.

A VENDOR PROFILE

Now that we've examined where to look for information, let's examine what we collect and how we organize the data. You can consider a vendor profile to be a file folder containing two categories of information: a summary of the critical information analyses about vendors, and the raw information collected from information sources.

An outline for a summary vendor profile is found in Exhibit 5-1.

As you develop your lists and files, you may expand the contents of Exhibit 5-1 to fit your situation. The following discussion will follow the outline of Exhibit 5-1.

EXHIBIT 5-1

OUTLINE FORMAT FOR A VENDOR PROFILE

1. Technical Characteristics
- Product or Service List and Description
- Assessment of Product State-of-the-Art
- Production Capability
- Installation Support
- Customer Service and Maintenance
- Documentation & Training

2. Management Characteristics
- Management Organization (Organization Charts)
- Management Quality and Depth Assessment
- Stability of Management
- Quality of Controls and Procedures
- Coherence of Management Behavior to Products

3. Personnel
- List of Key Technical, Operational and Managerial Staff
- Assessment of Quality of Personnel in General
- Turnover and Morale
- Assessment of Skill Level Coherence to Products

4. Financial Characteristics
- Annual Report Assessment of Company
- Credit Situation by Independent Sources
- Improvement in Earnings/Revenues Over Time
- Financial Assessment

5. Position Within Industry
- Company Size in Comparison to Others ($, personnel, geographic reach)
- Technological Competitive Assessment
- Management Competitive Assessment
- Financial Competitive Assessment

6. Independent Evaluations
- Company Provided References
- Employee Assessments
- Competitor Assessments
- Supplier Assessments
- Client Assessments
- Assessments by Personnel Surveyed or Quoted

7. Historical Relationship
- References to Previous Contracts/Purchases
- References to Previous Contacts with Company & Management
- References to Previous Dealings with Company Management
- Estimated Knowledge of Us, and Commitment

• Technical Characteristics

List the products that are of interest to you and a brief description of each. Make references to the information in the folder, rather than repeating information. The purpose of the profile is to provide a quick summary, not an in-depth presentation.

Consider the age and maturity of the product line in comparison to the competition, if known. Evaluate the product in terms of its place in the evolution of technology.

A software system may be well designed and operate effectively, but may use a hierarchical database or sequential files. Although it is a system to consider, the lack of a relational database structure may require it to be excluded for some applications, while acceptable for others.

The purpose of the assessment is to be objective about technology and not make a judgment about your requirements. Remember, if you are following the recommendations herein, you will be making this review long before you have a requirement.

What is the timing of the vendor's fiscal year? Are there better discounts available at the end of fiscal quarters or the end of the year? Does the vendor typically have a "fire sale" of their products just before a new product announcement? This is usually true.

If an equipment manufacturer, does the vendor have sufficient capacity to produce the volume of product required by the market? Find any production scheduling problems.

If a software vendor, can the vendor support multiple clients simultaneously if the product requires customization for each client? Can the vendor produce updates and fixes in a timely manner?

Does the vendor unbundle the product and services? Can you buy just what you need? Are you large enough a buyer to force changes in the vendor's policy?

Assess the support characteristics for installation, problem resolution, maintenance (both planned and emergency) and quality of other product support like documentation and training.

• Management Characteristics

Compile a set of organization charts, either provided by the company, or constructed from the literature you've assembled. It can be useful to refer to any biographical information you have assembled.

Human nature is interesting. Individuals favor those who are like themselves, and are distant from those who are not. One of the strongest ties that can lead to access or relationships is when two individuals are alumni of the same college. Religious or ethnic ties are a more tenuous linkage.

Gather biographical information about management. Assess the quality of management as revealed particularly by personal comments. The vendor may not have the best product in the market, but deficiencies can be corrected quickly if management is capable.

If key members of management were to depart, is there sufficient management depth for the firm to carry on? If management has been without turnover of consequence, is there adequate quality at the next levels of management, or is there turnover here due to no upward growth? This will be more apparent in older more established firms than entrepreneurial ones. Establish the chain of command for marketing, development, production, services and maintenance.

Note, we are not determining the exact project manager who might work on our project here. The purpose is to look at the company as a whole, to see if it is structured as a viable organization. The smaller the vendor's size, the more important it is to do this analysis.

Examine the company's internal policies and procedures to determine if they are in control of their products, their processes and their personnel. Loose controls would imply they would not monitor their contract with you adequately, thereby increasing schedule and development risk.

Review the behavior of management in the industry. A series of acquisitions, new product lines unrelated to current products, or other new ventures would imply that management's attention is not on their current products, but on something else. If so, you may be contracting for an orphaned product.

• Personnel

A high technology company cannot survive for long if the quality of its technical personnel is mediocre. Create a list of key technical personnel in the company. Make a judgment about their relative competency within the industry. Software firms are particularly vulnerable to the loss of key designers and analysts. Are the personnel reasonably satisfied with their company? Is the turnover within industry standards for this type of firm? Are they filling open slots with equivalent or better qualified employees?

• Financial Characteristics

Is the company profitable? If it is a start-up, has there been noticeable progress in increased sales, revenue growth and a forecast for profits soon? Is there sufficient cash on hand to assure the firm's survivability until cash flow turns positive? Summarize the credit reports and any investment analyst review.

A small software firm is going to have some financial limitations. Your assessment must judge whether the product is so good that survivability is likely. Would your project make the vendor totally dependent upon you for survival? This can be beneficial and dangerous simultaneously. If you represent a major company and you really need the system, you might even consider outright acquisition of the vendor. If you are a small firm, would the vendor abandon you if a larger contract was available?

• Position Within Industry

List the objective measures of company performance and make a comparison with competitors. Use the comparative data provided by the evaluation services. Itemize to the extent you can comparative levels of personnel, production rates, financial strength, and technical prowess. Does this company provide products that are technically superior? What about products that are competitive, but less expensive than others? Are the products inferior?

Is the management of this firm competent in its own right, of comparable maturity and experience to the management in competing firms? Better? In what ways?

What are the vendor's relationships to your competitors? Does this matter at all to you, or is it a benefit?

• Independent Evaluations

What do others think of the vendor? Itemize comments provided by the following: references provided by the company; employee and previous employee comments; competitor assessments; supplier assessments; client comments; and finally, comments by your staff who know of the firm.

Test the credibility of the comments for personal or professional bias. Make a judgment about what aspects of a vendor's reputation are important to you, which are not. If there are characteristics that you don't like, will you have enough leverage to change them?

• Historical Relationship

In large companies it is entirely possible that one division may have had a relationship with a vendor unknown to the remainder of the firm. It is worthwhile to check archives, with purchasing, the contracts administration function, and the legal department for any references that show a previous relationship.

A wealth of data will be available about the vendor if the systems contract administrator in your company has maintained a vendor history. You should learn something about the vendor's negotiation strategy, pricing points and areas of flexibility and rigidity if a previous contract existed. How well does the vendor know our company? How enthusiastic was their marketing? Did the vendor market to us from management downward, or technical level upward? If the former, how was the relationship continued, if at all? What is the vendor's commitment to us? How did the vendor perform technically? Were cost and schedule within the scope of the contract?

If our company has changed a great deal since the last relationship, we will need to start the vendor contact and briefing process over (Chapter 3).

The vendor profile is an objective document with quite a bit of subjective analysis. Sometimes it is unflattering to a vendor, so it should be kept confidential.

WHAT IS A QUALIFIED VENDOR?

At the conclusion of this compilation and assessment, you have to make a summary judgment. Is this a vendor with whom you wish to do business? Is there a possibility that even if this vendor is not ideal in all respects, that corrective actions have been taken about which you are not aware? Can corrective action be initiated as part of a negotiation?

When you then conclude that this vendor has the minimum technology, the minimum management, and the minimum financial strength, although some risk may still exist, you have qualified the vendor.

> A qualified vendor is a vendor that meets minimum requirements in technology, management and finances to be eligible to receive an RFP.

Until you actually evaluate a vendor against other vendors in a vendor evaluation process, any vendor you have qualified is as qualified as any other vendor. You may not distinguish among qualified vendors. They are all equal.

A practice, more prevalent in Europe than in the United States, is to conduct two evaluations of vendors. The first evaluation is to effectively qualify a limited set of vendors who will then tender a subsequent more elaborate proposal. This is called short-listing.

This is a barely acceptable alternative to a qualified vendors list. The problem with the approach is that two evaluations will require more time, just when excess time is unavailable. We believe that important corporate information may be either ignored or overemphasized when collected under the time limitations of an evaluation. Vendor qualifications should be done deliberately.

One benefit of the short list approach is that the vendor list is current, and somewhat better targeted toward the specific product or system you need.

The identification of a qualified vendor does not make that vendor eligible, or capable to provide his product to you if you require product customization. At the time you solicit proposals, the vendor's personnel may be dedicated elsewhere, and may be incapable of supporting you. The local marketing organization may not be aware of a resource conflict.

A vendor that is under strategic change may be qualified today, but may not be eligible in the future. You usually won't know until you request a proposal, or find that the press has indicated a new strategic direction. The vendor may suddenly be no longer qualified.

What do you tell vendors whom you've qualified, or those you have not qualified? Since you do not devote the time and effort to qualifying vendors unless there is a reasonable probability that you may require their products, it seems reasonable that you communicate your assessment to the vendor. After all, the vendor needs to know you to help you.

Establishing the vendor contact at this time gives the benefit of allowing the vendor to assess what your needs may be without being under the pressure of responding to an RFP. You will receive company and product information directly, without having to request it. Qualified vendors who become aware of your interest in them can only be more eager to obtain your business when you issue the RFP. You want the competition to be very good, so an early alert works to your advantage.

What about the vendors that you have not qualified? If the product line is inappropriate to your needs, do nothing. However, if the vendor doesn't qualify because of some issues in management, financial strength or the like, it's a good idea to inform the vendor about your reservations concerning its competitiveness. If you are correct, maybe the vendor will correct those deficiencies. By the time you are ready to issue the RFP, the vendor may have made adjustments in order to qualify. This could be especially true of those small firms that can have tremendous bursts of positive change in a brief period. You have nothing to lose other than a few minutes of your time, and much to gain by holding the conversation.

THE QUALIFIED VENDORS LIST

Once you have qualified a number of vendors, you might maintain a list of them by technical category.

You will want to create your own list for this purpose, but Exhibit 5-2 provides an example of categories that you might consider for qualifying vendors if you are in the information systems business.

As an industry expert, Peyton identified seven companies that marketed retail banking systems software. His inquiries to other consulting associates resulted in six other smaller firms being identified. Walter used more conventional research methods, and was able to find sixteen firms, eight of which duplicated what Peyton had identified. As they reviewed preliminary data about the twenty-one unique companies, Fred, Peyton and Walter found four instances where the software was just not applicable for their requirements; two companies that were so small (five employees or less) that they would not have the resources to do the job; and two other companies whose software was on different mainframes, and could not be easily converted.

The remaining thirteen software companies were potential candidates as a result of this first screening. Fred requested Peyton and Walter to begin more deliberate collection of information about each to qualify them further. Fred asked that they jointly visit or request a marketing call from each vendor to establish a first-hand knowledge of the products and the vendors' capabilities.

After about a month the information was collected, and in the following four weeks, Fred's staff went through the Vendor Profiles prepared by Peyton and Walter. On completion of the discussions, nine vendors were qualified to receive the Request for Proposal when it was issued.

EXHIBIT 5-2

A TECHNOLOGY LIST FOR QUALIFYING VENDORS
(Illustrative Only)

- **Computer Systems**
  - Supercomputers
  - Mainframe Computers
  - Minicomputers
  - Workstations
  - Microcomputers
  - Special Purpose Computers (e.g., Process control, Pen based systems)

- **Computer Systems Peripherals**
  - Disks, DASD
  - Tape Drives
  - Controllers
  - Input/Output Devices
  - Displays, Terminals, Plotters, Scanners

- **Communications Systems**
  - Data Transmission (e.g., VSAT; CATV; Fiber Optics)
  - Data Concentration Equipment (e.g., Channel Banks; T-1, T-3 Muxes)
  - Packet Networks & Switches
  - WANs, MANs & LANs

- **Control Program and Analysis Software**
  - Operating Systems (e.g., OS/ESA; Unix; VMX; DOS)
  - Data Base Management Systems (e.g., DB2; Oracle; Adabas)
  - Performance Monitoring Systems (e.g., Netview; Omegamon)
  - 4GLs (e.g., FOCUS; SAS; NOMAD)

- **Application Systems**
  - Transaction Processing Systems
  - General Ledger
  - Accounts Payable/Receivable
  - Purchasing/Inventory Control Systems
  - CADCAM, CAE
  - Materials Management
  - Human Resources

- **Service Functions**
  - Service Bureaus
  - Contingency Sites
  - Facilities Management
  - Timesharing

- **Consulting Services**
  - Contract Programming
  - Systems Analysis
  - Outsourcing
  - Systems Integration

## Chapter Six

VENDOR CULTURES AND NEEDS

WHO CARES ABOUT A VENDOR'S CULTURE?

The information you've collected on qualified vendors in the last chapter is necessary, but may not be sufficient for your needs. If you want to go another step toward ensuring that vendors respond to your RFP, or maximizing your potential leverage over a vendor, you might consider analyzing the vendor from a different perspective. What does the vendor think of itself? What does the vendor think of its customers? Other relevant questions might be: What affects how vendor employees operate? What are the attitudes and cultural characteristics that govern the company?

The answers to these questions will reveal much about the organic metabolism of the company, as opposed to the more structural characteristics identified in Chapter Five. If you know how the organism operates under various situations, you might create situations where you can predict vendor behavior, and can mold that behavior to your benefit. Getting the most out of your vendors includes more than negotiating a good price for a good product. It includes obtaining the best possible commitment from the human part of the company and its employees.

In this chapter we'll examine vendor cultures to see what can be exploited for your benefit. In particular, if you are a small company, what should you know and do, to cause the vendor to want to respond to your request for proposal? After all, there are many no-bid responses to RFPs.

Contrary to macroeconomics theory, sales strategies of a product are not just an automatic recognition of a supply-demand equation. The vendor's strategy may require that a product or project would have to deliver a minimum gross revenue. Anything less would consume too many internal resources for the potential gain.

For example, small consulting firms can compete effectively against major consulting firms, because major firms' lavish quarters, fixed costs and high overhead require project sizes greater than $50,000 for even minor studies. The small firm can deliver an equivalent product at less cost because of lower overhead and greater flexibility.

How do you maximize your chances of getting good proposals from vendors, particularly when your size might preclude consideration by all but the hungriest of vendors? Are you sure that your company will meet the vendor's qualification criteria for customer sales, particularly if much pre-sale effort or proposal generation is required?

CLASSIFYING VENDOR CULTURES

In the same way that others characterize us as placid, deliberate, aggressive, excitable, organized, pompous, arrogant, cooperative or defensive, so too can organizations be described. They obtain their characteristics from top management, the nature of the industry, the community, the language, or their country.

This discussion of cultures is not comprehensive, nor does one characteristic culture preclude others. If a characterization of a company can be made, that characterization can be used as an indicator of an action plan for dealing with the company.

IBM has always been considered a great marketing company. Their products are seldom leading edge. It takes light-years to get application software out of the laboratories. Account representatives can be painfully uncooperative at times. Yet, IBM has historically been able to convince senior executives that they will always stand behind their customer and deliver value beyond mere hardware and systems performance.

Often that has proved to be precisely true, particularly in disaster recovery situations as fires or earthquakes. It's not that other vendors don't respond similarly. Many do. However, IBM exploits its responsiveness as a major element of its marketing.

THE MARKETING COMPANY

A marketing company views customers from a relationship perspective, rather than just a buyer. Marketing companies might be further characterized by the intensity of effort they place upon:

- Company image

- Customer caretaking

- Consistency of behavior

- Product line emphasis

• Company Image

Brand-name recognition was a major factor in the premium prices paid by merger and acquisition raiders to acquire firms like RJ Reynolds/Nabisco. When a product or company has instantaneous visual and oral recognition, it is said to have a "franchise." Some companies spend millions of dollars and years of effort to establish their image before the buying public. Those who have established such franchises can exploit it to their marketing and sales advantage. Which comes first, the marketing, the product, or the image?

Usually the product is successful first, marketing then exploits the product, and the image forms because of long term, consistent product quality. The image of the product then transfers to the company, making it synonymous with the product. Over time, the image of the company may replace the product. This is how many companies achieve the image they possesses.

> Images are perishable as well. Consider the disastrous fall in market share and prestige that befell DATSUN, when a name synonymous with sporty cars went through a seven year name change to NISSAN because the founder had an ego trip. Remember how Cadillac lost its image and its market by offering the smaller, lower priced Cimarron?

A firm that has a strong image might allocate more resources to marketing the company name or logo than it does to marketing specific products. It is saying to the customer: "Trust us." The plea has great receptivity at executive levels where the "big picture" may be more important than some narrower objective. More often, it's the lazy way out of analyzing risk and reward properly. You remember the saying that no one ever got fired for choosing IBM. These days, even that may no longer be true.

For most companies looking for support from vendors, there is probably not much leverage to be gained from a firm endowed with image. The very psychological impact of the prestigious name upon employee attitudes can lead to a culture in which compromise is not practiced. The prevailing attitude can be: "This is our product; The world knows it's good; So should you; Take it or leave it."

• Customer Caretaking

We are customer driven. We deliver solutions. These themes abound in marketing materials. The customer wants to hear these precious words. All needs will be satisfied by the vendor. The reality may be less probable.

A marketing organization's use of this concept may be more for maintaining customer control or account control, than in really intending to help the customer find the best solution. Often "the best solution" is that solution within the vendor's product line that comes closest to providing a minimally satisfactory solution. As long as the customer requires products or services within the product line, the vendor will marshal staff to support the sale. The staff will fade away if redesign or customization is required to solve the need in the best way. These personnel, after all, are supported by the high margins that a standard product line provides.

> For years one major computer firm espoused that it was solution oriented. As long as the solution was their solution and required few fixes, free consulting support and studies were available. Once the customer asked for software development assistance, or wanted another vendor's equipment, the support evaporated. Vendor managers escalated to customer management, sometimes subverting the plans of the technical personnel by questioning their capabilities and judgment. These tactics were successful for a while. Ultimately, the tactics backfired as other vendors provided advanced tech-

nology with improved reliability and service. It is gratifying that the vendor abandoned the tactics, and is now working with customers to find solutions that the customers want.

In the best sense, customer caretaking includes a continued relationship with the client, not just a visit to receive an order, but a constant research into client's needs that may translate into new products or future sales.

3M has built a marvelous culture of listening to customers to drive their incredibly creative output of solutions to the marketplace.

Caring for the customer includes monitoring the effectiveness of the vendor's products used by that customer, and marshaling the most responsive service restoral and maintenance efforts when problems occur. When this happens, the client has the confidence that the vendor has the resources and the commitment to help in time of need. Just like insurance, you pay a premium for this service. It is in this respect that IBM has built its well-founded reputation for "taking care of its customers."

What is the leverage one can exert over a vendor who markets customer caretaking? If the service is truly responsive, your public recognition of that responsiveness can be of help. Everyone likes to get praised for the good they do. Vendors find this testimonial of great importance in influencing new customers. Once praised, the vendor should want to expend extra care to continue to please the client. This pride can then be translated into extra features, additional technical support and perhaps lower costs. The vendor assuredly knows it takes ten times the effort to find a new customer than retain an old one.

Do you have vendors that are not performing up to their publicized level of customer responsiveness? If you have maintained records of vendor performance that objectively prove this inadequacy, then a good time to confront the vendor is just when you want its optimum commitment for your new project. Fear of loss of the account is a powerful motivator to change behavior and redirect the vendor's efforts to respond to your new requirements. The new situation allows the vendor to approach the challenge as a new page on the ledger, thereby saving "face." The rationale would be: "We know we weren't great before, but give us a new chance. We'll really prove ourselves this time." Whether they do improve remains to be determined. During the proposal period and negotiations, you should be able to constantly provoke fear of account loss as a tool to obtain improved performance on existing products, if not future concessions.

What about vendors with whom you don't do business? The vendor should want to go all out to capture your account. The firm should be saying: "Just give us a chance to show our capabilities and customer responsiveness. We'll show you how much better we are than your current vendors."

Your leverage in influencing this vendor may be less than you think. From the vendor's perspective, preparing a proposal in response to your RFP is a considerable cost. Without knowing a great deal about how you deal with vendors and evaluate proposals, there may be a reluctance to propose. Once a proposal has been submitted and negotiations begin, the vendor may still be reluctant to provide concessions because of the uncertainty of how the relationship will work out, not to mention the vendor's concern for being profitable in the venture.

In these cases the best approach is the one discussed at length in Chapter 3. Have a senior executive brief vendor management to highlight the openness of the competition, the fairness of the evaluation, and the need for as much qualified input as you can obtain. This may not translate into a high degree of leverage, but it should ensure that the vendor does submit a competitive proposal. This approach applies to any new vendor, not just a marketing firm.

• Consistency of Behavior

Many companies operate in a totally predictable and consistent manner. Their policies and procedures are firm, if not carved in stone. They pride themselves on presenting one happy face to the customer. All sales teams are virtually interchangeable with each other. All employees are in agreement on what they propose, their pricing and their relationship strategy. These companies usually have a long history, mature product lines and intricate coordination mechanisms (because many employees have been with the firm for a long time). Don't expect much innovation or flexibility from them. Their solution is your solution, whether it fits or not. In many respects, marketing in these firms may be more concerned about satisfying internal management procedures than responding to customer requirements. You won't have much influence on improving their responsiveness to you, if that is the case.

> Before the PC revolution, the old Burroughs Corporation could be considered a representative of this type of firm. One didn't expect a lot of entrepreneurial accommodation from them in technical areas, though they did exhibit a lot of flexibility on price. You observed escape and evasion techniques every time you requested a special innovation. This behavior may be more characteristic of hardware vendors than software vendors.

A few vendor firms are loose confederations of design, development, implementation, sales and marketing. The firm is less a company and more like a group of fiefdoms. Each fiefdom has its own agenda, and concessions can sometimes be obtained by playing one fiefdom against another.

• Product Line Emphasis

This marketing driven company emphasizes a complete portfolio of solutions and a myriad of products. It wants to dazzle you with quantity, and the flexibility to solve any problem, even if the solution is vaporware today. The logic is: "We have a good solution to your problem, though you think it is not optimal. Well, we disagree. Even so, you know that our development people never stand still, and you can depend upon us, because we are committed to product improvements." In other words, buy their not-quite-right solution today, with the confidence it will be OK tomorrow.

Notice that the word "customization" is not in this vendor's vocabulary. This vendor is responsive only insofar that product evolution to respond to requirements is a true vendor goal. The product must be a general solution that can be sold many times, and not just for your requirements.

Despite this unwillingness to directly respond to this customer, this style of vendor marketing continues to have great success. Ultimately, the vendor does deliver, frequently with a product close to what was needed. What is the value of the time and productivity you lost while waiting for the vendor to improve the product?

How many firms waited years for LOTUS to deliver version 3.0 of 1-2-3? What was the productivity lost in not migrating to Excel, or Supercalc, or other spreadsheets? How many firms are waiting for Netview to answer their total network management prayers? They probably have a long wait.

If a naive customer listens carelessly to a product line vendor, vendor assurances about product innovation or modification can be misinterpreted to stand for "customization." This misinterpretation can be dangerous because the client is seduced into a level-of-expectation about the product that the vendor lacks intention of delivering. Beware of the semantic and real distinction in this instance.

In too many cases, customers hurt themselves by waiting for generic systems to be developed. People don't want to take risks. So they wait. Furthermore, since the opportunity costs of waiting for the vendor to produce are difficult to quantify, those who procrastinate are not brought to task by management. If the purpose of customization is to differentiate yourselves from the competition, it is never better to wait. Some investment in your own destiny is mandatory.

• Can You Leverage A Marketing Driven Firm?

To the extent we've already suggested above, yes. But your search for customized solutions to your requirements will probably not come from these sources.

A marketing company with a global image is already beyond your ability to leverage unless you are one of the top ten or twenty of their customers. There are even fewer firms that could possibly cause a major product line change by IBM. It didn't get where it is by responding to each customer's requirements. IBM became great because its products respond to the great majority of most firms' requirements. Some might call this the "least common denominator" solution.

In your pursuit of vendors, you can't ignore large firms or marketing driven firms. They might have the solution to your need, or may know so much about your industry that they could team with a smaller company to solve your special requirements. Therefore, you cannot ignore them, and should include them in your vendor list. On balance, your abilities to leverage these vendors are limited.

THE "ENGINEERING" OR TECHNOLOGY COMPANY

Technology firms originate in two ways: An inventor creates a product even before all the possible uses for the product can be understood (the transistor and the laser are two examples), or a visionary sees a void in current technology, a product line, or a service, and responds to that vacuum by creating a new enterprise with its new products.

The legendary Ken Olsen of Digital Equipment Corporation (DEC), and Steve Jobs of Apple, immediately come to mind in the latter category. Do you think Alexander Graham Bell visualized facsimile, voice mail, conference calling, videophones, or data communications as the inventor of the telephone? Recently, the cellular phone seems to have responded to a latent need for every driver to spend his freeway crawl hours on the telephone.

In contrast to marketing driven firms, companies that have their culture based upon technological roots may have less of a desire to get out and meet customers and respond to their needs. They may not even pay too much attention to maximizing their return on investment. To a technology company, the laboratory for innovation is much more comfortable than dealing with people and their insistent demands. Technology is implemented for its own sake, and the customer should perceive the "obvious solution to his needs" and respond accordingly by buying the product. It shouldn't have to be sold, for heaven's sake!

Until the arrival of the PC, DEC was perhaps the representative leader of this culture. DEC made highly reliable minicomputer systems primarily for scientists and engineers who had the technical qualifications to master the complexity of the products. It was a case of engineers being comfortable with other engineers. DEC's marketing focus was on lower prices and performance, and on writing up orders from a familiar clientele, not providing them with solutions.

Nevertheless, some white collar customer oriented packages did escape from the laboratories. One of the first in 1976 or 1977 was the DECMATE VT-52 based word processing system (WPS) with its Gold Key. This was followed in 1978 by the PDP-11 version of the software. The word processing software, at that time, exceeded in features and performance all other vendor systems, including WANG's and IBM's.

As one of the first purchasers of DEC stand-alone and minicomputer office systems, we had numerous system and hardware problems, and clamored for additional features and software. In conversations with Olsen we pleaded for increased investment in the product, and a global support policy. We could see the benefits in office productivity this new technology would bring, based upon the pilot program we had completed. Unfortunately, we received cursory attention, and shortly thereafter we adopted a global office automation strategy using other equipment. The rest is history. DEC missed out on being a leader in a $60 billion dollar industry. Its failure to have market share in PCs today can also be attributed to not listening to the customer. DEC had its own agenda at the time, bringing out the VAX architecture. In my view, DEC could have had both, success with the VAX, and success as a global power in office automation, if it had listened to the customer.

Despite the DEC example, there is considerable leverage that can be obtained in dealing with a technology based vendor. Because technology is important to a technology firm, your research and development or customization might get a favorable hearing. This would be particularly true if there was a high degree of congruence between what you required to be customized, and the vendor's own product development plans. The project becomes more of a partnership than a vendor-client relationship.

With these firms you obtain better leverage if you get past the sales personnel and form a liaison with the technical staff. You need to find an internal advocate of your requirements. That advocate must sponsor your project as a major benefit to the technology culture.

Since these vendors play to their vision rather than to the customers' visions, they can produce products that are totally out of the business mainstream. They also can produce brilliantly conceived and packaged products that find great acceptance.

The inability of Texas Instruments to establish a market for its PCs is an early example of the former, while the Macintosh Powerbook exemplifies the latter.

A good relationship with a technology vendor is valuable. They tend to be more willing to take risks in projects to customize products, as long as it advances the state of art. This could happen even if the customized product is marginally marketable at the time. This vendor substitutes research and development expenditures for marketing and sales promotion expenses.

Technology firms that do not also grow into marketing firms tend to have a more difficult time maintaining earnings' momentum. Since they market to end users, and not corporate executives, their credibility in the mind of the decision maker is likely to be lower. Your justification for selecting this vendor is correspondingly more difficult. In the long term, they must market like their competition, or fail. This begins the cycle anew for other technology companies.

THE SALES FIRM

A sales firm is one that competes on price or feature, not relationships or technology. Its sales personnel are "order takers" not account representatives, marketing representatives or customer engineers. They are not "solution" seekers.

Sears Roebuck is a sales firm. Your local real estate office is a sales firm. ComputerLand is a sales firm. All "black box" manufacturers are sales firms. The local telephone company is a sales firm. Those cited add little value.

These companies have solid products and services, backed by sound maintenance and customer services. In a highly competitive and rapidly changing industry, they may have a niche role, however, their cultures may reflect ambiguity in knowing what their roles are, or should be.

You will find that the sales personnel will likely be less technically qualified, and less aggressive in trying to help you solve problems. If you want any real leverage with this type of firm, you need to find the right button to push. You escalate your requirements directly to top management, to tell them of an opportunity they would otherwise not be told about by their sales staff, who would walk away from the sale if they did not have a directly conforming product. There may be an exception or two, but a winning proposal will not come from a firm with a sales culture.

In the early 1980s, international telex was a magnificent cash cow for telecommunications companies known as International Record Carriers. These included RCA, Western Union International (now part of MCI), ITT and a few other smaller companies.

When asked to respond to rapidly changing business needs as data communications and electronic mail started to replace telex, those firms that actively worked with customers prospered (MCI), while the others disappeared. The quality and mindset of management and sales personnel were the major difference. One group sold existing services. The other group helped solve customer needs.

FOUNDER'S FIRMS

A founder's company is characterized as one in which the original owner is still the chief executive officer, whether the firm is now public or not. In this example, we are referring to those firms that are successful, and have grown considerably since start-up. They now have the facade of a structured organization and administration, similar to public companies with hired chief executives.

In a founder's culture, control is centralized and real delegation of authority is non-existent. The company usually takes its personality from the founder. You cannot make an immediate assessment of what the behavioral norms really are, until you figure out the founder's personality. You make some delicate inquiries of customers, competitors and vendors about the firm to know how to proceed.

You can be sure that your ability to influence the firm to respond to your needs will be directly related to your ability to obtain a personal commitment from the founder. No one else can, or will, make the commitment you require. Even if that happened, turnover at these firms can be high enough that you have no guarantee that commitments would be honored after your sponsor departs. Therefore, when you recognize that you are dealing with a founder's culture, you must obtain your commitment from the boss.

When you do, you can have a fantastic, mutually satisfactory business relationship. This could even be the case whether there was no financial or competitive benefit perceived by the founder. He might just like you, or might be enchanted with your project enough to sign-up. These company heads like new toys to play with, and you should not deprive them of that opportunity by avoiding them because they can be difficult at times.

Founders can have totally unrealistic expectations or views on market opportunities. This is particularly true when they extrapolate from markets or industries they know about to other markets. Since they have been successful in one market, their egos won't let them admit to a lack of equivalent knowledge everywhere.

One founder's company built a very successful business providing customized software and hardware for the regulated telephone industry at premium prices. When the vendor attempted to market equivalent products to businesses operating private networks, potential customers regarded the pricing strategy as totally out of line with comparative offerings from other vendors that concentrated on end-users. The firm had to reassess its strategy.

THE SURVIVAL START-UP

Every large firm begins as a small company. They become large by growing. Sometimes doing things they really don't want to do is necessary to grow, but there is no growth if the firm can't meet its payroll.

An important characteristic of the software industry, and other industries that are at the leading edge of technological change, is that the great preponderance of these companies remain entrepreneurial and small. They usually are still founder's companies, but have not reached a size where the founder's vision is lost. Still at the forefront of product development, the founder is still a worker more than a manager.

It is likely that they got started by obtaining their first contract from a former employer or close business associate of the founder. Although they have elements of marketing and sales, they are more likely dependent upon referrals from their existing customers for new business. As a result, these firms have a great uncertainty in knowing where their next customer will come from. But, if you are a customer, they are very likely not to care if you are a small firm or a large one. These firms respond to potential clients with maniacal zeal. Their survival may be at stake.

They not only have to respond to any request for proposal that comes to them, they have to ensure that the proposal they provide is outstanding. Simultaneously, they must continue to provide high levels of satisfaction to existing customers for new referrals.

You will have the highest amount of leverage with these firms. They need you. They will respond to your needs. You can leverage their financial dependency to obtain concessions from them. It may be that their sunk costs in trying to win the contract are so great, winning becomes a "do or die" situation. At some point, they may capitulate and give you all that you want.

Beware of placing any vendor in such a situation. No one can function properly when they are under the stress of survival. Obtaining concessions and compromises is part of business. But with a barely surviving firm, you must be especially diligent in their commitment to you, not to force them to the financial and technical edge of the cliff.

> Whether dealing with a small vendor or an industry leader, the objective of a relationship has to be an equitable win-win result. Neither party is there to exploit the other.

After this is considered, the fact remains, you probably can obtain the best deal from such a firm. You don't, however, ignore the principles in this manual. You must take every precaution to ensure proper project management with survival firms because they may not practice such rigor, or may have priced their proposal on an assumption that their ad-hoc practices are sufficient. You can't afford to have that happen, no matter how much leverage you can exert.

There is much to gain and much risk in working with survival firms. Not enough businesses give these firms a fair and impartial assessment and opportunity. The smaller your firm, the more important it is to ally yourself with these entrepreneurial survivors. You are risk takers together. The benefits also may be proportionately higher than other relationships.

> Nothing stated in this chapter should be interpreted to mean that the process of qualifying vendors discussed in Chapter 5 is ignored in any way.

VENDOR MOTIVATORS, NEEDS AND CONSTRAINTS

Beyond the generic understanding of cultures, lies an even more pragmatic set of issues that you should recognize. What motivates vendors and what are their needs and constraints that permit further leverage opportunities for you?

THE VENDOR BRANCH OFFICE

Companies have needs that have nothing to do with their cultures. These needs can be strategic or they can trickle down to the local branch level. The vendor's needs at the branch is where you exercise leverage.

The vendor is represented by people. For all intents and purposes the vendor's sales agent is the vendor to you. If the sales agent can earn your confidence, you will have a tendency to have confidence in the vendor. If the sales agent is friendly, helpful and solicitous of your needs, you would prefer her or him to a sales agent who wasn't. You will therefore consider not only the vendor's goals, but how they translate to the salesperson's actions.

Examine your relationship with the branch. Can you figure out what percentage of that branch's total sales come from your company? Even better, does your company provide a significant percentage of the regional or corporate revenue? Even if your percentages are small, is your company growing at a rate, or establishing a major influence over an industry, which would promise significant future revenue to the local branch? The greater your impact upon local revenue, the greater the attention local and regional managers must pay to you. That is why you tolerate those periodic business lunches. So you can exercise leverage when you need it.

Few branches or regions have the wherewithal to support your project on their own. They have to direct your requirements through the chain of command, always competing internally for similar pleas from other branches. Your geographic location becomes important. If you are in a small town in the Northwest, and vendor headquarters is in Maryland, your local branch may have a difficult time getting attention at the head office, let alone getting a response to your needs for customization. If they are near headquarters, they may have more success.

Remember that the local branch is caught in the middle. It is the pincers applied by vendor bureaucracy on one side, and your insistent demands on the other, which causes the local salesperson to take up your cause, and make it theirs. That is the only way they eliminate the pressure, while serving their personal needs of making a living.

GROSS REVENUES

The vendor may not be making its target revenue goals for the quarter or year. Intense pressure builds on the sales force as each end of quarter looms. If they don't make their targets, they don't earn commissions. The twin elements of greed and fear begin to work in your favor. Sales agents hustle more, are more aggressive in marketing and in following up on your requests in the hope of booking the sale before the performance clock stops.

If you are aware of these factors, you can use the revenue shortfall to get additional concessions, discounts, or support from the vendor. This does not mean that you should buy from the vendor to satisfy the vendor's end of quarter. You just use time to squeeze harder.

Having got all you can out of this quarter, nothing prevents you from rolling over into the next quarter to begin the process over. We are not suggesting that you "jerk the vendor's chain" in this regard. We suggest that your timetable for decisions is not necessarily the same as the vendor's. Therefore, you proceed at your pace. However, the opportunity to get a better deal does present itself when you are aware of the vendor's sales targets and schedules.

PROFIT MARGINS

Some vendor sales goals could be based upon getting higher margins from sales, not just increasing gross revenues. Since you are procuring customized services that have lower margins than standard products, you won't find opportunities for leverage with this vendor.

MARKET PENETRATION

There are three situations that are typical of a vendor's pursuit of additional market share: geographic penetration or expansion into a new territory, industry segment penetration, and technical or product niche penetration. If you are eligible to be classified as a company that is in an expansion territory, or are a potential target company in a new industrial bracket, or are a possible buyer of a unique new product, your ability to leverage the relationship improves over those companies that don't qualify. Every time a vendor has uncertainty in his future, you can make that uncertainty an advantage. You obtain a better deal, while the vendor removes some risk in pursuit of market share.

PRESTIGE BUYER

The number of commercial pioneers in the adoption of technological innovation is limited. Risk taking is not a popular attribute of businesses when considering technology. They understand risk, particularly in software development. But few firms want the risk they take to be increased by technology that lacks market penetration. Therefore, the firms that do take these risks are highly desired by vendors.

In particular, if your company is a global or national firm with a solid image in business and technology, then the incentives to work with the vendor, to obtain a strategic edge over the industry, get price discounts and customization to meet your needs, are lucrative. The client needs to be influential, but the product does not necessarily need to be a massive procurement. Just the fact you've made a risk commitment to that vendor to adopt its product is sufficient. It helps the vendor tremendously if you also are willing to serve as a referral source for its product. The firms that are followers will note your procurement, and their perception of risk is reduced. The vendor will be further obligated to you for the additional sales your risk-taking has generated for him.

> As the highly competitive T1 multiplexer industry began to grow, vendors made enormous concessions to early potential clients. They left equipment in the client's care for live testing for six months or more without compensation. Discounts of sixty percent of list price were given to early referral prestige accounts. Market share needed to be obtained rapidly. Clients who were entrepreneurial enough to accept the risks of the technology had benefits in two ways: their equipment costs were low, and their telecommunications costs decreased dramatically. The recent shakeout on the vendor side testifies to the need for the vendor to ally with the "right" accounts.

This is why vendors seek out clients to serve as *Alpha* and *Beta* sites for the development of new products. Customers willing to go through the trauma of serving as the debugging agent for a vendor, deservedly obtain major concessions from the vendor. But not every company would qualify. Your firm should already be a major account of that vendor, be known as an industry innovator, and prestigious enough so that the effort is worthwhile to the vendor, since he will be taking a great deal of flack during the alpha or beta testing periods.

The United Services Automobile Association (USAA), a San Antonio, TX, insurance company serving military officers and their families, has been on the leading edge in adopting innovations in Automated Call Directories, Automated Number Identification and Image Technology. It is a prestige account for all vendors. Because of its dedication to the adoption of advanced technology, USAA is a highly successful, low-operating cost, insurance company.

The need for risk-taking clients doesn't always extend just to prestige relationships. Sometimes a vendor needs to demonstrate that it is competitive in order to maintain its credibility in its industry. This can happen when its product may have some limitations. The vendor may look for any customer to induce others to wait for the improvements. The leverage that this customer has in this circumstance is significant, only if it can live with the product as it is for the time being.

PERSONNEL RETENTION

This situation is somewhat less likely today in an era of corporate leanness, but you should note its possibilities for your benefit. Consider the example of a vendor that has highly trained and experienced technical staff who work on internal development projects. Perhaps a major effort was recently completed, and new assignments are not yet available. The vendor foresees the need to retain these temporarily surplus employees, yet does not want to displace them, even for a short time.

It is possible you could turn that need to retain those personnel to your advantage. They could be seconded to your project at a lower cost than would otherwise be the case. You win, because you obtain the services of a higher quality of technical expert than your project might deserve. The vendor wins because the costs of retaining these personnel are paid by you. Obviously, your requirements for customization must fit in somewhere with the vendor's plans for product evolution. Discovering circumstances when this opportunity might be available will take some investigation, but is worth doing. Not all leverage is financial. Having superior talent to help you is always a benefit.

## Chapter Seven

PROCUREMENT PROCESS OPTIONS

INTRODUCTION

The fundamental approach of this manual is that you choose a vendor through a competitive process by issuing a Request for Proposal (RFP) to qualified vendors. However, you have additional procurement process options to help you select the best vendor. In all cases, these options are used in addition to issuing an RFP. They cannot replace it.

Many of these options are used by large businesses, governments and institutions because the scope and complexity of the project requires more than review of the RFPs. It is worthwhile to know what these options are, and where they might be applicable to your situation.

NONCOMPETITIVE PROCUREMENTS

SOLE-SOURCE PROCUREMENTS

A *Sole-Source* procurement is a purchase of a product or service from a single vendor, without having a competitive process prove that the vendor's product or service meets requirements or is the lowest cost.

Competitive bidding is the standard by which governments, institutions and most commercial enterprises operate. Government agencies are required by law to conduct competitive procurements, though there are many exceptions, particularly in research and development contracts.

Companies also want to get the best deal (and prevent kickbacks to their employees, either offered or sought), so competitive procurements are usually part of internal corporate policy. Still, companies can, and often do, buy from a single vendor if they choose. Other than fiduciary responsibility to shareholders, there are no regulations prohibiting companies from buying from a single source.

Though competitive procurement policies may exist, a clever specification writer can write the requirements in such a way that only one, or a very few vendors may qualify. This is tantamount to a forced sole-source procurement. No vendor is going to waste effort on a proposal he has no chance of winning.

We think there are too many instances of sole-source procurements in business and government. Sometimes the procuring department or agency (for government) is too lazy to do the work required to hold a competitive process, or they are comfortable with an existing vendor. They write the specifications so that only that vendor can meet them.

Federal Government agencies time and again are forced to alter awards because they have "railroaded" an evaluation, or tried to purchase sole-source. The General Accounting Office has especially cited the Navy for using these practices in their procurement of data processing equipment and systems.

Sole-source procurements are not desirable because you almost never obtain the best financial deal. Your leverage decreases in direct proportion to the knowledge that the vendor has about your buying intentions, with solutions to your needs being limited to what that vendor presents. In addition your schedule will be effectively controlled by the vendor, which may cause peers or management to question the wisdom of your decision. Other vendors may hear of the purchase and try to have your management change the decision by appealing to its sense of commercial equity. In the long term, you will find that all vendors will be more responsive when you pursue competitive rather than single vendor procurements.

There are occasions when a sole-source procurement is indicated. The product you are buying may be such a standard product that price distinction between one vendor and competitors is negligible. Your firm may have standardized on a given vendor's product line for technical, operational or maintenance reasons, and the greater need for management control of the standard overweighs the competitive aspect. A vendor's service and support may be so superior that any benefits from lower prices or qualitative technical features are mitigated by the service quality. Finally, the vendor may have such a unique product that it may have a virtual monopoly on the technology. You have no where else to go.

It is interesting how quickly competitors fill the vacuum created by a product that lacks competition. You should assist that rush to fill a competitive vacuum by publicizing your interest in having more than one source for solutions to your needs.

The computer memory market has seen wild swings as American firms bowed to competitive pressures of price discounting from the Japanese and got out of memory chip manufacturing, only to find prices increased significantly once the Japanese became effectively the sole supplier. Reliance upon one source for anything is risky.

In the procurement of customized equipment and systems, the process of qualifying vendors may lead to a situation where you think only one vendor comes close to meeting the requirements. The inclination to contract directly with that vendor is very high. If you don't hold a competitive process, you may fail to discover other vendors that have product improvements or revisions already under way. Our guidance is as follows:

> Unless management two levels up agrees, or insists upon a sole-source procurement, a vendor selection based upon evaluation of competitive proposals is mandatory.

UNSOLICITED PROPOSALS

Vendor sales executives are always looking for a place for their products, and an edge in controlling existing accounts. They stay in touch. That's their job. Whether during business lunches, breakfasts or meetings, these vendor-client discussions often turn into brainstorming sessions on unsatisfied needs in the technology or service areas or the client's pie-in-the-sky requirements.

These discussions are useful for the customer because the vendor representatives sometimes know of solutions in other companies similar to the client's needs. Vendor representatives use the information they collect from these sessions to plan future marketing and to provide feedback for new technology to the vendor's product designers.

A more enterprising vendor may decide that they already have a solution to your requirements, and will prepare a proposal for you. By providing such an *"Unsolicited Proposal"* the vendor hopes to capture a contract without having to enter a competitive situation. The vendor hopes that you will be so pleased to receive this "added-value" solution, that you will overlook that other vendors may have a comparable answer. The vendor thus hopes to receive an award for a sole-source contract. This is a tempting situation for you, because you receive a proposal without doing any work.

Unsolicited proposals are offered more frequently in marketing to government, particularly in Defense Department programs where the vendor has a proprietary, but early life-cycle technology and wants federal research and development funding to develop weapon systems applications of the technology.

Sometimes vendors provide unsolicited proposals in the commercial market. After analyzing computer systems operating capacity and efficiency, it is common for a vendor to propose more memory, greater capacity disks, database management or even an upgraded CPU. Most of the time the proposal is in response to performance problems. Almost every such proposal is more hardware oriented than software. But occasionally a vendor prepares a proposal related to new software systems or systems or network integration projects.

What should your attitude be about unsolicited proposals?

Receiving an unsolicited proposal, particularly when you are about to issue an RFP, tends to compromise you in three ways.

1. By informally revealing enough information about your needs this vendor has gotten a competitive edge, by gaining time and knowledge. You have now compromised your relationship with other vendors.

2. The vendor's proposal may contain proprietary information. Even if you had the same idea, you are now beset with an ethical problem. If you accept the proposal, and include

the idea in an RFP, the vendor will feel that you have released confidential information to the entire marketplace. Your relationship with that vendor is jeopardized. If you don't include the idea in the RFP, the quality of the responses may suffer.

3. You may feel that the vendor is looking out for your best interests, and you may feel an implied obligation to him to evaluate his proposal more favorably than other vendors.

If you believe that competition is always in your best interest, then there is only one way to proceed. Send all unsolicited proposals back to the vendor unopened and unread. Inform the vendor that given the importance of your needs, you are pleased by the support, but professional ethics require that you return the proposal. Request the vendor to wait until you send an RFP, and they can respond with the other vendors.

No vendor will feel too badly about that. You demonstrated a high level of ethics. You protected the vendor's proprietary information. While you value his services, you consider it important that all vendors be given equal consideration.

OPTIONS BEFORE THE VENDOR EVALUATION

The vendor evaluation process begins when you receive proposals in response to your RFP. There are a number of procurement options that you can adopt before the beginning of the evaluation.

REQUEST FOR INFORMATION (RFI)

The *Request for Information (RFI)* is a formal way to request information from a vendor about the system or product you are about to procure. The formality alerts the vendor of your serious intent.

In qualifying the vendor, you may have not been able to learn enough about the vendor's specific capabilities to know whether the vendor is going to have a product responding to your need. The RFI can be used as a preliminary screening device to limit the recipients of the RFP to those who can provide a quality proposal based on their response to the RFI.

The RFI can be used as a second stage of the vendor validation process, in which you qualify the vendor in the first stage, and then qualify the product in the second stage. Some companies use the RFI itself as the first and only way to qualify the vendor company. For the reasons provided in Chapter 5, we don't recommend this approach. The RFI should be product, not company focused.

Sometimes, the RFI can also mean *Request for Interest*. This would be when you are trying to find whether the vendor has any interest at all in doing business with you along the lines of system customization you have laid out. This would usually occur when the vendor and you do not have a current business relationship.

The RFI usually states that any responses received are not binding upon the vendor or the requester. In this way you give the vendor flexibility to be creative in responding without incurring an obligation. Furthermore, the vendor won't have to spend too much money to respond to your request if it is non-bidding.

Exhibit 7-1 contains an example of an RFI transmittal letter.

EXHIBIT 7-1

EXAMPLE OF AN RFI TRANSMITTAL LETTER

BACCARAT BANK & TRUST CO.
1400 Gambler's Square
Middletown, NX 00417

Mr. Adolphus Gobaine
Director of Sales
Systems Support Systems
14 South Street
North City, NE 88222

REQUEST FOR INFORMATION

Dear Mr. Gobaine:

The Baccarat Bank & Trust is searching for software systems developers which have existing systems which can be modified to meet BB&T's new requirements to integrate their existing wholesale banking system with the retail system which will be called Branch Integrated Transaction System (BITS). The enclosed package describes the functional requirements of BB&T.

If your firm has the capabilities which meet or can be modified to meet BB&T's requirements, and you have an interest in being considered for inclusion as a vendor which will receive the BB&T Request for Proposal, please provide BB&T with the following information:

1. Complete corporate history, including financial history, banking relationship, officers and clients.

2. Documentation which describes your system.

3. Your indication of interest in supplying software to BB&T.

4. Your qualifications to become a vendor to BB&T.

BB&T assumes no liability or responsibility for any costs associated with your submission.

The due date for receiving all responses to this request is 4:00 p.m. June 1. You should deliver your response to Mr. Eternic at the above address, 5th Floor.

Should you have any questions and/or require additional information, please contact the undersigned at 222–7744.

Sincerely yours,

Monk Eternic
Systems Contract Administrator

Encl.:   Functional Requirements

REQUEST FOR QUOTATION (RFQ)

The *Request for Quotation (RFQ)* is a formal request for a firm fixed price from the vendor. It is applied to the procurement of standard off-the-shelf products that require no, or very little modification. The content of the RFQ is usually brief, and corresponds closely to the vendor's specifications for the product.

In other situations, an RFQ can be used when a combination of equipment and labor content are required. For example, a purchase of a local area network might require the equipment vendor to include a quotation for the installation costs of the equipment and the wiring and cabling to connect the terminals. The vendor should have a strong case history of installations, so that a fixed price can be quoted for the complete job.

RFQs are the principal domain of the company purchasing agent who buys supplies, furniture and other semi-commodity items. They are never used for technical products requiring high degrees of customization because the information about the requirements is too limited in an RFQ for the vendor to know what to propose.

The RFQ is contractually non-binding upon the requester, but it is binding according to the Common Commercial Code upon the vendor. The vendor's quotation however, usually has an expiration date from ten to ninety days from the date submitted.

Exhibit 7-2 contains an example of an RFQ transmittal letter.

PRE-PROPOSAL BRIEFING

A *Pre-Proposal Briefing* is a meeting hosted by the purchaser to determine whether vendors that attend wish to receive an RFP. During the meeting the host may inform the vendors of: the nature and needs of the organization requesting the proposals; the objectives of the project; members of the project team; the contents of the RFP; issues of critical importance to receive evaluation emphasis; and administrative details of procedure during the vendor evaluation process.

The pre-proposal briefing allows the purchaser to refamiliarize vendors (with whom there is no current relationship) about his organization, management, processes and the like, so they can be as fully competitive as possible.

The pre-proposal briefing has several benefits for purchaser and vendor. For the purchaser, it permits a less formal means of presenting the background story behind the project. Issues of a political or relationship nature, which cannot be documented, can be addressed. The briefing places the RFP in a business context. The vendor has a better idea of the ultimate user who might even participate in the briefing. The vendors may be able to design and implement the project in a more creative manner with this understanding.

Because the briefing is uniform for all vendors, any advantage a vendor might have because of an existing relationship with your firm, or some of your staff, will be neutralized, The presentation also identifies the individual who will control the vendor selection mechanism, so other avenues of influence the vendor might have are precluded. Control is clear and unambiguous.

The pre-proposal briefing provides a nearly instantaneous screening mechanism for eliminating those vendors that have no interest in the project, thereby saving the buyer reproduction costs, postage and future coordination time, and saving the vendor the expense of preparing a proposal. Usually, the vendor will inform the purchaser after the briefing whether or not there is interest. The vendor could save time by not attending the briefing

EXHIBIT 7-2

EXAMPLE OF AN RFQ TRANSMITTAL LETTER

BACCARAT BANK & TRUST CO.
1400 Gambler's Square
Middletown, NX 00417

Mr. Axle Sparkplug
Director of Sales
Sanded Ceramics Inc.
8484 Bayou Falls Street
New Lewis, LX 39679

REQUEST FOR QUOTATION

Dear Mr. Sparkplug:

Sanded Ceramics is requested to provide a firm fixed-price quotation to Baccarat Bank & Trust Co. for one standard ceramic hot tub for inclusion in the Corporate Executive Exercise Center.

The complete details, including floor plans, water piping, electrical circuits and pump location areas are included in the attached blue prints.

Your quotation must include the following details:

1.   Descriptive catalog showing photograph of proposed hot tub before and after installation.

2.   Cost of hot tub.

3.   Cost of all pumps, pipes, motors, and all other materials.

4.   Cost of all labor to install.

5.   Itemized cost of all permits, bonds.

6   Taxes on any materials or labor.

7.   All freight, handling or other service costs to deliver to BB&T premises and transport to the installation area.

Should you have any questions and/or require additional information, please contact the undersigned at 222–7744.

Sincerely yours,

Allen Wastervil
Purchasing Agent

Encl.: Blueprints.

and writing a no-bid response when the RFP is received. However, since pre-proposal briefings require considerable preparation by the purchaser, they usually represent a project of considerable scope and expense, and are not given on a whim. Therefore, most vendors will make an effort to attend.

Pre-proposal briefings are in common use by federal, state and city agencies. These entities have so many vendors on their vendor lists that screening out qualified vendors is both difficult and politically dangerous. Vendors eliminated by screening, except by their own choice, can always appeal to a politician who then gets involved in the process to everyone's regret.

Because governmental projects usually represent large to immense revenue sources for vendors, most vendors will attend pre-proposal briefings.

Pre-proposal briefings are less commonly used by business, ostensibly in the cause of time saving. We believe this is regrettable because the advantages outweigh the disadvantages.

The pre-proposal briefing enhances competitive psychology. Place a dozen candidate vendors in the same room and watch them squirm a bit. Since the vendor community has many rotating players on the sales and marketing teams, they frequently know one another. You increase competitive intensity by introducing each by name and company. The tension in the room increases. Your project suddenly takes on a new dimension for them, by subconsciously increasing the threat and the opportunity.

It's amazing how firms behave when they are in a position to be measured directly against their competition. They can't be casual and cavalier about a proposal in these circumstances. They all have a degree of *esprit de corps*. They want to win! This dynamic tension enhances the probability that their competitive juices will flow, and they will be stimulated to respond to your RFP. Because of these factors, the responses to the RFP should be better than if the briefing was not held.

REQUEST FOR PROPOSAL (RFP)

The *Request for Proposal* (RFP) is the standard for all procurements that require innovation or have significant costs, size, risk or complexity. The entire next two chapters cover the RFP package.

LETTERS OF CLARIFICATION (VENDORS)

After receiving an RFI, RFQ or RFP, the vendors may find some inconsistencies, omissions, or inaccuracies in the documentation. If serious, errors will impair the quality of the proposals, or confuse the vendors about how to respond. Therefore, most vendors will send a letter to the customer inquiring about the errors or discrepancies.

Since the nature of the questions may differ from vendor to vendor, and you want the best product, standard procedure in this instance is for you to list all questions received and your response, in one document, and mail the response to all vendors that have indicated that they will submit a proposal. The vendors adjust their proposals according to the new information.

The receipt of questions, follow-up research and preparation of the response takes time to complete. The net result of this question and answer process is a delay in the schedule for submission of the proposals. The best way to handle a situation of this nature is not to allow it to happen in the first place. Too many RFPs are issued by impatient and careless purchasers who then have to correct their mistakes.

> One to-remain-nameless government body issued a two inch thick RFP for a major systems procurement. The errors, inconsistencies and omissions were prodigious. The flurry of vendor letters was so extensive that after six months of interchange between the purchaser and the vendors, the entire RFP had to be withdrawn. Two years later it finally emerged in corrected form. Although in this case the system wasn't critical to life or safety, the productivity benefits would have been considerable. Instead, the taxpayer paid the price for a poor quality RFP, and the vendors committed a lot of resources with no payback.

BIDDERS CONFERENCE

Some persons familiar with the vendor selection process might consider that the terms pre-proposal briefing and bidders conference are synonymous. We make a clear distinction between the two. The pre-proposal briefing occurs before an RFP is issued. The *Bidders Conference* occurs after an RFP is issued, and includes only those vendors who will submit proposals.

Similar to the letter of clarification, a bidders conference might be called by the purchaser to clarify any questions received after the vendors have reviewed the RFP. The questions can be verbally addressed and written responses distributed to each vendor attending. Additional questions from the audience can be taken and clarification given by the host.

The bidders conference has the benefit that some time is saved and any additional or new questions can be dealt with. If the questions are of a highly technical nature, there may be some inconvenience and cost to a vendor who may have to send technical attendees from a distant location. The need to hold a bidders conference is a good indication that the RFP did not receive the attention to detail it should have.

OPTIONS DURING VENDOR EVALUATION

Once proposals are received, the formal evaluation begins. We define the next group of optional activities as taking place during that evaluation period. These activities could theoretically occur even before the RFP is issued. In cases where the purchaser is attempting to pre-qualify vendors, they should be. However, we prefer to have them occur during the evaluation for two reasons: economy in the deployment of buyer's resources; and concentration of focus on determining the winning vendor.

Sending an evaluation committee to various locations to visit distant vendors is an extremely expensive activity. If site visits to vendor installations, benchmark testing, or oral presentations are to occur, they should be done only with those vendors that have a serious chance of being selected. The emphasis should be on eliminating a list of vendors as quickly as possible, and focusing on those critical issues that differentiate among the best remaining vendors.

LETTERS OF CLARIFICATION (PURCHASER)

When proposals are read by the evaluators, it sometimes becomes obvious that all or most vendors missed a requirement or concept. In such a case, a reading of the requirements specification or the RFP may indicate that the purchaser wrote one thing and meant another. Because the vendors will therefore submit erroneous solutions, it is common practice for the purchaser to send a letter to the vendors identifying the issue, rephrasing the requirement, and inviting new responses. Unfortunately, this also means new pricing proposals as well, and a schedule delay, due to the time to respond and reevaluate.

Unless the issue is of such importance that the entire project is jeopardized without a letter of clarification, it is best to ignore the errors during the evaluation, and deal with the issue with the two or three highest evaluated vendors.

ORAL PRESENTATIONS

Sometimes the buyer will have the leading vendors supplement their proposals by making a presentation on it. The presentation could feature only the technological solution offered, or it could include management and cost issues. Often invaluable insights are obtained in presentations because the documented explanation may be obtuse or complex.

This approach can work well with smaller vendor companies that may not be adept at elaborate packaging of proposals, but possess superb technical talent that a presentation can exploit far better than a document. Oral presentations have the risk that better funded vendors will appear with an elaborate multi-media show that overwhelms the purchaser with gloss, glitter and smoke.

We think oral presentations should come before the RFP is issued, and be used to pre-qualify vendors' products, rather than be used to evaluate them. There is too much opportunity for a lack of equitable and uniform treatment of vendors under an oral presentation format. An undisciplined, agenda-less presentation without time constraints leaves too much opportunity for vendor appeals.

If an oral presentation is required to further differentiate among very closely competing vendors, then it should have a rigid agenda, strict schedule and identical content for all participants.

VENDOR CUSTOMER VISITS

No vendor demonstration at its own facility can duplicate an already installed and operating system. We would recommend that every evaluation (or vendor qualification) should take advantage of customer site visits if applicable to the project. The customer's candid comments (with or without the vendor present) are sought concerning the performance of the system, its reliability, the quality and timeliness of vendor support and other issues pertinent to the evaluation.

VENDOR SITE INSPECTIONS

We do not mean a visit to a vendor's demonstration room under this topic. One of the few reasons to visit a vendor location is when you are buying vendor manufactured equipment that accompanies the system. This is relevant only if the vendor is a low volume producer of the equipment, and you have personnel qualified to evaluate a manufacturing environment. If you don't, don't go. If the vendor manufactures thousands of items of equipment, don't waste anyone's time. If the vendor has that many buyers, its acceptable from an equipment point of view.

A better reason to visit a vendor's site is to witness a qualification, performance or acceptance test of equipment/systems for another customer of the vendor. A thorough test plan executed crisply is a good indication that when it comes time to test your system, the vendor will be equivalently thorough.

BENCHMARK TESTING

Benchmark Testing is the evaluation of competing systems against a standard or benchmark. Benchmark testing is common in evaluating competing computer hardware configurations. Several types of benchmarks representing differing application mixes have been devised.

Testing of prototype systems, analogous to the one that you are purchasing, may provide some indicators of performance, but the absolute value of a system that will only marginally resemble yours when development is completed is questionable.

The best benchmark for your purposes is the actual mix of programs you run every day. Organizing these for different manufacturer's environments may take more of your resources than you want to devote. Benchmark comparison is often of marginal value because of the pace of technological change. Nevertheless, comparing the performance of competing vendors' systems over standardized conditions provides additional indicators that can support the choice of one vendor over another.

PROTOTYPE RUN-OFFS

Prototype competitions are used primarily in Department of Defense weapons systems procurements. Prototypes are expensive, and only the high technological risk and the vast rewards of large production runs justify the expense. In the commercial world, a large customer can induce competing vendors to lend prototypes for evaluation in the purchaser's laboratory.

The competition for the Advanced Technology Fighter (ATF) between Lockheed and Northrop was an example of prototype competition.

The early years of T-1 Multiplexer development saw some large multi-location companies requiring vendors to submit their emerging T-1 multiplexers for evaluation. This usually occurred before an RFP issuance. The vendors didn't object because the potential purchaser helped to debug the equipment. Once the sale was made, the large customer became a valuable referral source for the vendor.

Software companies use *Beta* versions of operating systems to obtain other developers' recommendations and insights on new versions, particularly for the personal computer industry. There is a certain symbiosis among these groups that works for the everyone's benefit. The approach, however, does not translate well to customized systems. For unique proprietary software systems, there really is no adequate prototyping model available for comparison.

OPTIONS NEAR EVALUATION COMPLETION

Even after a thorough evaluation, several vendors might still be close, and any might be an acceptable vendor. There are several additional steps that can be taken to select the recommended vendor.

SHORT LISTS OF VENDORS

In some procurements, the number of vendors submitting proposals overwhelms the ability of the evaluation teams to review the documents. One approach to sort the wheat from the chaff is to evaluate all proposals at a high level, eliminating the obvious non-contenders. The remainder form a short list that is then evaluated in detail to select the final vendor.

Conversely, the evaluation can be done in two stages by issuing a general RFP to which all vendors respond, and then issuing a second highly specific RFP to those vendors culled into a short list remaining from the first evaluation.

Another use of the short list might be similar to the following example. A procurement for a telephone switch with unique requirements had an initial vendor response from eight vendors. The vendor evaluation results show that any of three vendors can adequately meet the requirements, yet all were not responding correctly to one specific major function. You might use the three vendors as a short list, to initiate a mini-RFP for the function, awarding the procurement to the vendor with the best response.

FACT-FINDING

Fact-finding is a term borrowed from government procurements where the technical detail in a proposal is so overwhelming (as are the cost and management proposals) that the evaluators cannot assimilate it all during the evaluation schedule. They reduce the number of vendors to a short list (could even be only one vendor remaining) intending to award the contract to the vendor providing the best response to the questions the evaluators select for further discussion.

Fact-finding is usually a meeting held at either purchaser's or vendor's premises to discuss all the remaining issues and questions that remain after all the proposals are evaluated.

Sometimes tragic flaws in a design, test plan or service agreement can only be discovered during fact-finding. This could be because the RFP did not address the issue, or new information was discovered during the evaluation.

On one procurement (in the early 1970's) for a command and control system, we engaged in fact-finding with a vendor to try to understand the costs associated with spare parts for the control center. One question led to another, until we finally understood that the vendor was converting a digital data stream into analog values so they could be displayed on dials on a control console. A simple question was asked: "Could the data simply be displayed on video display units that were recently installed in data centers?" The vendor responded responsibly, "Yes." The government was able to reduce the cost of the procurement by thirty million dollars because it could use plain metal desks and VDUs, instead of buying an elaborate console.

Fact-finding served a valuable purpose, without limiting the quality of the final system one iota.

Fact-finding can also be the first stage in contract negotiations with the selected vendor. The purchaser uses fact-finding to reduce the scope of the proposal, eliminate unnecessary features, or attempts to more clearly correlate technological capability with costs.

You get the best leverage by using fact-finding as the final step in obtaining clarification from the remaining contenders of items that remain technically ambiguous, or for which the costs seem too high. Vendors might reduce costs during fact-finding on their own volition if they perceive that they might lose the contract. The threat of alternate vendors is a powerful inducement for concessions before negotiation. Once told the vendor has one, reducing costs, or obtaining added capability at no cost is a difficult task. You lose valuable leverage by doing fact-finding with the one finalist.

We believe that fact-finding isn't used enough commercially. Perhaps it's because purchasers might not have experience in bargaining for concessions. Perhaps they think it unseemly, or believe that the vendor's proposal is immutable. Nothing could be farther from the truth. All proposals can be negotiated if the risk-reward threat stays in the vendor's mind.

MULTIPLE NEGOTIATIONS

Multiple negotiations are the practice of simultaneously negotiating with several leading vendors for the final price. Multiple negotiations are an extension of both the short list and fact-finding options. The technical and management issues have been resolved. Only three possible issues remain: the schedule to complete the project, the costs, or both schedule and cost.

In this situation the remaining contenders are considered equivalent, and you're now negotiating for the best price or an improved schedule. Price may become the primary differentiater under these circumstances, not technical merit. The leverage discussed above, under fact-finding, applies. You have the best of all worlds: requirements satisfied, and several vendors competing anxiously for the business. A good price is inevitable.

This approach unfortunately can't be used too often when customized solutions are needed, because the vendor proposals will have significant technical differences among them. This will create a greater spread among vendors in both the technical and the cost categories, and the technical merits will likely make the pricing negotiations moot. Multiple negotiations are covered in a little more detail in Chapter 11.

STAGED PROCUREMENT

"If you do the first one right, we'll buy others. If you design the prototype and its good, we'll purchase a production run. If you do a pilot project in one location and it's successful, we'll buy cookie cutter versions for other locations." Only the last of these examples really applies to the commercial world. The others apply to government, and for many procurements, only the Federal Government at that.

A staged procurement has real advantages for the purchaser because it reduces costs and risk when innovation or state-of-the-art solutions are required to meet needs. Pilot projects and staged procurements bring extended schedules as a trade-off. If you have the luxury of time to get successful results, then pilot projects or staged procurements can be very useful.

Staged Procurements come in two versions. In the governmental style, two or more vendors complete the prototype or pilot version, and the best one is selected for full funding. In the commercial version, one winning vendor is awarded the pilot. If successful, then that vendor also gets the production run. If unsuccessful, the purchaser goes back to the drawing board, or starts all over with a second RFP and procurement for another pilot.

Staged procurements are difficult to sell to management anxious for results, yet adverse to failure of any kind. It seems they would rather risk large sums on "guaranteed" quick solutions, than have a pilot project fail. A failure cannot be explained away in a pilot, and the costs seem like money thrown out the door. A massive failure can always be blamed on circumstances beyond control because by definition it was under control when the large project started. It would not have been approved otherwise.

If this convoluted management thinking surprises you, it shouldn't. Many of today's senior managers are still technologically illiterate. Technology executives, on the other hand, often lack the backbone to sell balanced risk proposals to management. And a pilot project is a defined possible loser. Funding for pilot projects appears to be anathema in these days of short term results. Therefore the technologists sell a big project at higher risk because it might be a winner after all. The pilot represents too much career risk for the technology executive. Therefore, a few big projects also become big losers. But, they needn't have.

RECOMMENDED OPTIONS

Which if any of these options should one use as a practical matter in business?

Exhibit 7-3 contains our choices for using procurement options. You will note that we position the timing of some of these options differently than presented in this chapter because we believe in qualifying vendors (Chapter 5) before-hand.

By the middle of June, the requirements collection process was completed. The requirements specifications was also done, and Ulrich's team was ready to begin preparing the RFP. Peyton's work of identifying vendors and receiving their information was complete. They were on schedule (Exhibit 4-8) according to Fred's plan. Fred reviewed the list Peyton provided him, and scheduled a pre-proposal briefing for all nine vendors on June 20th. All invited vendors attended the meeting.

There was considerable excitement, as they surveyed each other, and considered the lucrative contract to be awarded. Table 7-1 contains a list of the vendors and their principal contacts.

EXHIBIT 7-3

RECOMMENDED PROCUREMENT OPTIONS

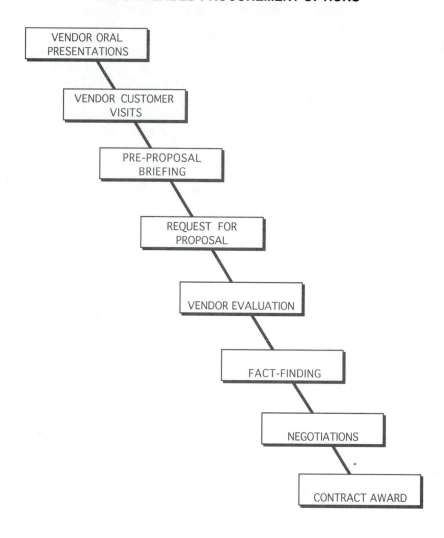

TABLE 7-1
CASE STUDY: LIST OF VENDORS

NAME	CONTACT
Advanced Systems International	Peter Aufrecht
Better Beta Systems	Robert Bender
Convulsive Transactions Inc.	Ed Cressop
Dogmatic Systems	Barry Dilgate
Ergonomic Transaction Systems	Susan Evansole
Fleece Banking Systems	Binge Fleesher
Grand Systems Designs	Orlando Gomez
Howitzer Retail Systems	Glendina Housin
Killian Data Systems	Julian Killian

## Chapter Eight

PREPARING THE REQUEST

FOR PROPOSAL

OBJECTIVE

By now, you should be anxious to get the *Request For Proposal* (RFP) out the door. You feel it is your final action item, and all the rest is left to the vendor. Not so. We need to visualize where the RFP will take us.

How will your management measure success? By RFPs? By proposals from vendors? Hardly. Management will measure success by the results achieved: a working system, meeting requirements, delivered on-time, and within the established budget. Intermediate milestones are of value for tracking progress, but they are not what management expects.

You've identified qualified vendors. Now you have to find the best vendor to complete the project. The request for proposal is the first step in preparing for the selection and management of the vendor through project completion. That is possible only if you can organize the RFP in a way that allows it to happen.

Considered in another light, the RFP is your opportunity to exercise nearly complete control and leverage over the vendor. If you structure the RFP and the proposal responses carefully, you will control your vendor throughout the implementation phase.

> The RFP is your best opportunity to exercise
> maximum control and leverage over a vendor.

It is also important to think of the RFP as a package of documents and not as a single document. A package is a grouping of documents linked to each other because of a unifying theme. The unifying theme for the RFP package is to organize the vendors so you will receive proposals that enable you to compare one vendor with another with the most convenience to yourself, not the maximum inconvenience. It seems to us that the time spent in realizing this objective is worthwhile.

THE RFP PROCESS

Many companies have some form of "standard" RFP format, which they've patched together by borrowing pieces from other RFPs they've seen. Unfortunately, no one can answer why the piecemeal collection is used and what purpose it serves.

We'll show you that creating the RFP is a deliberate, planned management process to reach your objective of successful conclusion of the project. But since the RFP package is only the first formal step in a process, we need to consider the remaining steps.

We use processes all the time in our personal lives, though we don't usually call them that. Let's say the family wants to take a vacation trip from Washington, DC to Los Angeles, which is about 2400 miles. You have 20 days of vacation and will return by air. You'll spend at least seven days in California, so that leaves thirteen days to travel coast to coast. Would you allocate your itinerary to travel an average of 200 miles per day? No, we'd think you would consider what sights you wished to visit on the way, and then see how your daily travel had to be adjusted.

For example, visiting the Smokies for a day might be fun. So would the "Grand Ol' Opry" in Nashville; Bourbon Street in New Orleans; water skiing on Lake Eufala in Oklahoma; Indian caves at Bandolier Park, north of Albuquerque; the Grand Canyon; Las Vegas; and camping in Zion National Park in Utah. You'll research the forward path to see what distance needs to be covered each day to have time for sightseeing. You'll analyze the route backward from LA to see if the schedule can still be met, and which locations might have to be eliminated.

You will finalize a schedule that has a daily milestone (lodging somewhere), a daily work effort (travel time spent in the car), and hopefully, some entertainment as well.

So too, the RFP process should take you on a journey that satisfies the objectives you've set for the project: successful requirements implemented, on-schedule, within cost, using a vendor to deliver a working system. What are the milestones that will mark interim completion points in the process? What are the efforts required to complete these milestones?

When considering milestones for completion, just like planning for the trip involved backward tracking, working backward from satisfied management at project completion can illustrate the milestones required to get there.

Exhibit 8-1 provides a flowchart of the next stage of milestones (phases) we are discussing.

EXHIBIT 8-1

PROJECT MILESTONES BEGINNING WITH THE RFP

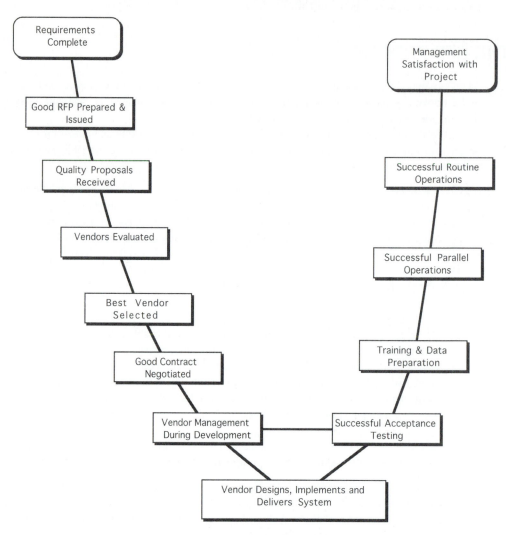

Requirements Complete

Good RFP Prepared & Issued

Quality Proposals Received

Vendors Evaluated

Best Vendor Selected

Good Contract Negotiated

Vendor Management During Development

Vendor Designs, Implements and Delivers System

Successful Acceptance Testing

Training & Data Preparation

Successful Parallel Operations

Successful Routine Operations

Management Satisfaction with Project

Starting from the far upper-right milestone in Exhibit 8-1, and working downward, you can see that these are also many of the phases identified in Exhibit 2-2, the Project Life Cycle Phases necessary for the success of a project. In this instance after being selected, the vendor will be doing most of the work. To make certain that you and the vendor are in harmony at each milestone, you must be certain that the vendor's efforts, not only during design and development, but during testing, training, systems parallel and operations are completed in a way that guarantees success.

Therefore a good contract has to be negotiated. You can only do that if you make provision to protect your firm before contract signing. Of course, you need to select the best vendor, using a proper and proficient selection process. This can only be accomplished if you're certain that you can unambiguously differentiate the vendors' proposals.

You achieve that differentiation by requiring the vendor to respond to your RFP in a manner and format that allows you to do that. You cannot depend upon the vendors to make it easy for you to compare them. You need good proposals, not only with respect to technical content, but for management, cost and controls as well. The way to do that is through a good RFP package that incorporates these elements.

The graphic shown as Exhibit 8-2 illustrates the desired objective. Recall the way the process works, by reviewing the discussion on Vendor Evaluation Policy in Chapter 4.

By keeping your eye on the final goal, you create a process to take you to that goal. That is why the RFP package is so critical to final success. It is your management tool, not just your technical request.

> ## The RFP Package is a management tool, not just a request!

RFP PACKAGE CONTENTS

The RFP package has two messages. You inform the vendors what you are doing, and you tell them what you want in return.

The RFP package can be one document, separate documents, or several documents referenced from a master document. The last method has the benefit of placing all relevant information in a specific sequence. The sequence acts as a check-list that all the required documents are included in the RFP. Furthermore, it enables voluminous documents such as the requirements specification to be prepared or formatted only once. The master document with referenced attachments is the preferred approach. The master document is called *The RFP Guidance Document*.

The RFP package contains:

• A Letter of Transmittal

• Technology Requirements and other technical documentation and references

EXHIBIT 8-2

A METHOD FOR ACHIEVING PROPOSAL STANDARDIZATION

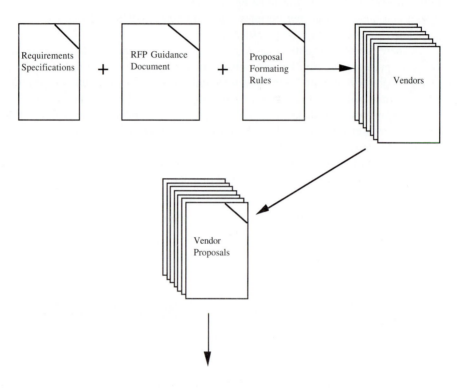

Vendor	Analysis of Requirements Fulfilled By Each Vendor								
	Technical Proposals			**Management Proposals**			**Cost Proposals**		
	1.1	1.2	1.n	1.1	1.2	1.n	1.1	1.2	1.n
A									
B									
C									
D									
E									
F									
G									
H									

Where 1.1, 1.2, 1.n represents sequencing through all requirements sections.

- The RFP Guidance Document

- Contract Terms and Conditions

The following sections discuss these documents.

LETTER OF TRANSMITTAL

The *Letter of Transmittal* is an individually addressed cover letter that tells the vendor that he is receiving an RFP, requests his proposal, identifies the principal contact at your company and may contain some last minute information that could not be included in other parts of the RFP package. You also need to specify some order of precedence of the documents that you are transmitting.

An *Order of Precedence* is a quasi-legal definition telling the vendor that if there is some anomaly or error in the documents you provide, and if the anomaly or error cannot be resolved, the document having the highest precedence will be the one that arbitrarily resolves the issue.

An example of a Letter of Transmittal using the BITS case study information is found in Exhibit 8-3.

TECHNOLOGY REQUIREMENTS

FUNCTIONAL REQUIREMENTS

As we discussed in Chapter 2, the functional requirements are the vision of how the buyer, or business unit of the customer, imagines the system will operate when completed. The functional requirements do not provide the vendor with sufficient technical information to develop or test the system. The requirements specifications do this.

Functional requirements give insight to the vendor on information, practices and person-systems interactions in business terms to help the design. We recommend that these user documents be included in the RFP package as background information.

THE REQUIREMENTS SPECIFICATION

The *Requirements Specification* is the technical document that describes what is to be designed, implemented and tested. It is the fundamental and only formal set of specifications produced by the customer. Any interface specifications that have been produced are included under this categorization. The requirements specification and all associated documentation mentioned in this section are incorporated into the RFP package by reference. Since these documents were discussed extensively in Chapter 2, they do not need to be discussed further here.

STANDARDS

Nearly every medium to large company that develops software recognizes the need to stan-

EXHIBIT 8-3

EXAMPLE OF A LETTER OF TRANSMITTAL

BACCARAT BANK & TRUST CO.
1400 Gambler's Square
Middletown, NX 00417

Mr. Ryewood Jester
Director of Marketing
Convulsive Transactions Inc.
11 South Promise St.
Anyburg, AK 44441

Dear Mr. Jester:

Enclosed herewith is one (1) copy of the Baccarat Bank & Trust's Request for Proposal (RFP) Package (A total of 7 documents) for the purchase of a computer system named the Branch Integrated Transaction System (BITS). The enclosed RFP package is the complete set of data that will be distributed by BB&T.

It is required that all bidders adhere to the entire set of RFP Instructions for submitting responses to this solicitation. A number of key instructions are:

1. All bidders shall furnish a conforming proposal in accordance with the specifications and guidance provided in the RFP package.

2. All bidders must submit a conforming proposal as specified in Section 6 of the RFP Guidance Document.

3. Bidders may furnish an alternative proposal(s), provided that the bidder has also furnished a conforming proposal.

4. The enclosed RFP package shall be maintained in strict confidence.

5. The bidder shall limit his contact with BB&T with regard to this RFP to: Mr. Monk Eternic.

6. BB&T assumes no liability or responsibility for any costs associated with the bidder's proposal(s) preparation efforts.

7. The due date for receiving all responses to this solicitation shall be no later than 4:00 p.m., August 31. This bidder shall deliver proposal(s) via certified carrier or by hand to Mr. Eternic at the above address, 5th floor.

8. The following documents are included within this RFP Package. In the event any document conflicts with any other, the conflict shall be resolved with the lower numbered document taking precedence.
    1. This Transmittal Letter
    2. BITS Requirements Specification and BITS Interface Specifications
    3. RFP Guidance Document
    4. BB&T Standard Contract Terms and Condition
    5. BB&T Systems Development Standards
    6. BITS Functional Requirements

Should you have any questions and/or require additional information, please contact the undersigned at 222-7744.

Sincerely yours,

Monk Eternic
Systems Contract Administrator

Encl.

---

dardize how it develops systems, and how it documents them. Similarly, standards have to be imposed on the vendors. All vendors, particularly software developers and computer manufacturers, have their own standards. The key issue for the buyer is to reconcile the compatibility, level of quality and comprehensiveness of two different standards.

Three approaches can be used to assure quality. The customer can mandate the vendor to use company standards. The customer provides copies of his standards with the RFP for the vendor to price the cost of conformity. Thus the vendor can understand the quality and content level of the equivalent documentation that the vendor must provide. This approach has the benefit of providing the systems and operations staff of the customer with familiar documentation. It has the deficiency of requiring the vendor to learn a new method or style of documenting its product, which leads to higher costs.

Alternatively, you can allow the vendor to use its standards and documentation. You will require examples of these standards to be delivered with the proposal. They will be evaluated and approved as part of the vendor selection.

The third option, lets the vendor choose either of the two or a combination, but requires the vendor to demonstrate where the standards are equivalent and where they are different. The choice is also evaluated and approved.

It is generally convenient to deliver your standards for comparison, but to accept the vendor's standards if they meet your criteria for quality. The vendor is more familiar with managing to his process, so the schedule is more predictable, and the costs have to be lower.

Since BB&T had always developed its own systems, it had a repository of standards that were acceptable by earlier fashions, but not pertinent today. Fred really didn't have an option, so he decided that he would deliver the BB&T standards to the vendors anyway, but expect that he would adopt the winning vendor's standards. The result may very well mean that the BB&T staff will learn some new techniques by using the vendor's standards.

THE RFP GUIDANCE DOCUMENT

The *Request for Proposal Guidance Document* is a document that provides direction to the vendors on what they need to know about your business requirements, how they should conduct themselves during the proposal and evaluation phases, what they should expect in terms of contractual requirements, and how they should prepare and format their proposal to you.

Exhibit 8-4 contains an outline for the RFP guidance document. In the sections that follow, only topics having a direct bearing on the evaluation will be discussed. Chapter 9, which contains an example RFP guidance document, has a presentation of specific terminology for each paragraph identified in Exhibit 8-4.

1.0 INTRODUCTION AND SCOPE

This section provides background discussion of the project, its business objective, and other orientation information. The knowledge obtained here allows the vendor to place its

EXHIBIT 8-4

OUTLINE FOR THE RFP GUIDANCE DOCUMENT

1.0 Introduction & Scope

2.0 RFP Administration

2.1 Precedence of Documentation
2.2 Bid/No-Bid Response
2.3 RFP Points of Contact
2.4 Costs of Preparation
2.5 Duration of Applicability
2.6 Alternate Proposals
2.7 Retention/Return of Proposals
2.8 Confidentiality
2.9 Contacts With Customer Personnel

3.0 Proposal Evaluation Administration

3.1 Basis for Selection
3.2 Non-Responsiveness
3.3 Site Visits
3.4 Fact-finding
3.5 Customer's Evaluation Schedule
3.6 Evaluation Methodology and Process
3.7 Notification

4.0 Administration of the Contracting Phase

4.1 Customer Standards
4.2 Customer Furnished Items
4.3 Contract Terms and Conditions
4.4 Regulatory Constraints and Requirements
4.5 Change Control and Amendments
4.6 Payments to Vendors
4.7 Ownership and Works for Hire
4.8 Post-Selection Process and Negotiations

5.0 Rules for Vendor's Response

5.1 Adherence to Rules and Formats
5.2 Page Limited Proposals
5.3 Delivery Conditions
5.4 Vendor Proprietary Information
5.5 Vendor Personnel
5.6 Subcontractors
5.7 Vendor Requirements Upon Customer
5.8 Project Management Process
5.9 Project Schedule

6.0 Format and Content of Vendor's Response

6.1 Statement of Work
6.2 Work Packages
6.3 Vendor Deliverables
6.4 Technical Proposal
6.5 Management Proposal
6.6 Cost Proposal
6.7 Requirements Traceability
6.8 Design Concept Document

response to the RFP in perspective. If a pre-proposal briefing has been held, this section can be very brief.

2.0 RFP ADMINISTRATION

This section contains rules for the vendors' behavior if they are going to respond to the RFP.

The primary purpose of this section is to communicate the systems contract administrator's intent to have an orderly and correct process for interaction between the customer and the vendors from the time they receive the RFP package until they are informed of a selection. This is to create a level playing field for all vendors responding.

A disclaimer related to the customer not bearing any of the costs of preparation of the proposals requirements for maintenance of confidentiality and intellectual property rights of the parties and other procedural details are also included.

There is a considerable amount of boilerplate in this section if your company frequently issues RFPs. Some of the clauses that belong here are found in Chapter 9. They are included so you can get a feel for the terminology, but they do not have a further influence on selecting the best vendor.

3.0 PROPOSAL EVALUATION ADMINISTRATION

This section provides the vendor with an understanding of how you will manage the process of selecting the best vendor.

• Customer's Evaluation Schedule

It is important for vendors to know the timetable of the evaluation from the time they submit their proposals to the time actual work begins. Their level of expectation can be managed and they can plan their resources better.

Nearly everyone underestimates the time it takes to conduct a thorough vendor evaluation process, and to obtain top management's approval to spend the funds.

Exhibit 8-5 contains a realistic timetable for preparation of proposals by vendors, the conduct of an evaluation, contract negotiations, management approval and contract award.

Inform vendors that following your selection of the winning vendor(s), you will hold fact-finding sessions. Assuming one or more vendors provided satisfactory responses, you might hold discussions with several prior to contract award. This takes time, and the vendors should know they may be called upon to participate.

We believe that sixty days from proposal submittal to start of work is a reasonable and manageable period for an evaluation process. If the customer is under severe schedule stress, or has management fully participating in the process, the timetable can be improved by a few weeks.

On the other hand, if the customer is the federal government or a public sector entity, the timetable can be a figment of the imagination. When a politician can influence a decision, you can be sure he will try. We've seen some evaluations suspended for years because of this interference. As a consequence many vendors will not bid on government contracts.

EXHIBIT 8-5

EXPECTED VENDOR EVALUATION AND NEGOTIATION TIMELINE

Calendar Days from RFP Issue	Activity
0	RFP Issued
25	Vendor Proposals Received
26-40	Evaluation Panels Review
41-42	Advisory Committee Review
43-45	Project Review Committee
46	Preliminary Approval Subject to Contract
46	Potential Winning Vendor(s) Notified
47-49	Fact-finding with Candidate Vendor(s)
50-51	Contract Negotiations
52	Recommendations to Management
57	Management Final Approval
58	Contract Award
60	Start of Work

We think the best way for government employees to protect themselves from interference is to ensure that their RFP preparation and evaluation processes are rigidly followed and codified as standards. Still, when it comes to political self interest, there are no guarantees.

• Evaluation Methodology

If the vendors are familiar with your vendor evaluation policy (Chapter 4), little more needs to be mentioned about how you will judge the best vendor. If the vendors are new, this section might mention that you use a standardized quantitative process. You evaluate not only the technical merit, but also the management and costs of the proposed solution. You have both peer and senior management reviews of the recommendations.

The objective of these statements is to provide assurance to the vendor that the investment made in responding to your RFP will not be wasted because of a frivolous or subjective method of evaluating proposals.

Some RFPs contain information about the evaluation review, including weighting algorithms, requirements priorities and the like. This is particularly true of public sector entities. We believe "sunshine laws" requiring this information to be published in advance of the evaluation are ill advised, and do not improve the quality of the project. We think this information tends to distract the vendor from the objective: a totally satisfactory working system.

If you provide many details of your evaluation process, the vendor might be tempted to play "proposal-itis," a guessing game to place extra emphasis on those work packages where he thinks he will be more competitive. Then the vendor reduces the quality of other sections of the proposal, hoping you won't notice.

However, if you have concern that the vendors may overlook a requirement because they will not understand its context (e.g., if audit controls are especially important), then you should specifically mention it as important, and requiring special vendor emphasis.

4.0 ADMINISTRATION OF THE CONTRACTING PHASE

This section provides an overview of some legal requirements that the customer will insist upon in the contract.

4.1 Customer Standards

This is where you inform the vendor which standards to use. If the vendor's are to be used, they must demonstrate that they meet the quality and content of your standards. You also state that you will be the judge of such conformity. You refer to your standards that you are including in the package.

4.2 Customer Furnished Items

You should identify those items or services that you are willing to provide to the vendor during the contractual phase of the project. These items are typically space, copiers, telephones, and reasonable access to customer personnel with adequate advance notification.

Exhibit 8-6 identifies typical items included in a customer furnished items list.

This commitment is often misunderstood or ignored by many buyers. The purpose is to recognize that there will be substantial interaction between the vendor and the customer during the project, and that the customer is prepared to provide these items.

Sometimes, such as access to key executives, there is reluctance to make an a-priori commitment for their availability to the vendor. But reasonable executives understand that need, and will respond positively at the appropriate time.

If customer furnished items are not disclosed in the RFP, some vendors will assume that the customer is providing these items anyway, while other vendors will assume they have to provide them and include them within their proposal. The result is a cost difference and level of expectation among vendor proposals.

Sometimes the vendor will not specify his requirements for customer supplied support until contract negotiations. Then he might surprise you with a request for more money or services. If you tell the vendors what they will receive, then if anything more is required, they must list them in their proposal and price it appropriately.

For example, if you are not providing a computer for the vendor's use, the cost of a rental machine may have to be included in the vendor's proposal. You could receive a large price shock in that event.

EXHIBIT 8-6

TYPICAL ITEMS FURNISHED BY THE CUSTOMER

- Clerical support
- Computer access and time for testing
- Computer time for programmming
- Customer Standards for systems development
- Customer Standards for testing
- Key executive interview scheduling & coordination
- Other customer documentation
- Software for Integration testing
- Software for Interface testing
- Supplies, copiers, telephones
- Systems Analysis staff support
- Work space at customer's facility

This section also may state what the customer will not provide: such as manufacturer's specifications for computer equipment, systems manuals and the like.

4.3 Contract Terms & Conditions

Nearly every company has its own standard contract for procurements. Contracts have evolved over the years of systems development. Many terms and conditions have become standard in the industry. Yet every year we read about lawsuits related to contract nonperformance. Between the efforts of the legal department and systems contract administration, a standard company contract for the procurement of systems should be developed.

Your protection is contained in that contract. Therefore, the vendor should be advised of what your contract terms and conditions are, as part of the RFP. The vendor should have an opportunity to refute, suggest alternate wording or additional terms to protect its rights, and object to terms considered onerous. Why allow the vendor the luxury of squeezing you on terms after you've told him he has the winning proposal? If the vendor doesn't object in his proposal, you have obligated him to sign your standard terms and conditions.

Appendix A contains an example of some standard terms and conditions used by BB&T. The paragraphs contained therein are not really material to the successful conclusion of a project, but address what to do when things go wrong. And this manual is about how to select vendors to deliver successful projects.

4.4 Regulatory Constraints and Requirements

This issue does not arise often in private contracts. However, if the RFP is issued by a public entity because of legislation by local, state and federal governments, there will be many terms and conditions related to EEOC, OSHA, and participation by minority firms and dozens of other affidavits that the vendor will be required to sign. The RFP package will mandate that the vendor must comply with these regulations. The number of forms and affidavits may require more work than the entire proposal.

4.5 Change Control and Amendments

We don't know of any systems contract that never had a change. If the probability that the customer or vendor will require contractual changes is high, then the contract itself ought to contain terminology that controls the process by which change is identified, negotiated and implemented.

The change management process is an integral component of project management and of the contract itself. This section in the RFP should tell the vendor what to plan for in terms of management overhead, to participate in changes during the term of the contract. You shouldn't have to wait for the problem to occur to invent a process to resolve the issue if it needs contract amendment.

4.6 Payments

It is customary, but not essential, to inform the vendor how you expect to pay for the work. Most contracts have progress payment clauses, either based upon monthly level of effort, or against customer approval of key deliverables or milestone accomplishments. We favor the latter.

The vendor has two recourses when you state your baseline approach to payments. He can negotiate with you for a more favorable payment schedule, such as 20% on contract signing followed by progress payments. Alternatively, a vendor can approach his banker for a loan against his receivables. When you state your position in the RFP, a vendor can use the time when you are evaluating his proposal to meet with his banker.

Another typical practice is for the purchaser to withhold final payment to the vendor until the installed system has operated through a critical accounting period, such as the month end processing cycle, or the end of a calendar quarter. Since the software vendor may not be highly capitalized, delays in payments on your part could impact his financial stability.

When the vendor is informed of your position, he can plan his cash flow, but, he can also price his project for the inconvenience the delays in payment will cause. These topics get resolved at the negotiating table. Having them above the table from the outset can only benefit both parties in the long term.

4.7 Ownership

One area you need to consider carefully is to decide what you want to do about ownership of the software developed for you. Under "works for hire" it should be the customer's property. Portions of code modified from an already existing shell are useless to the customer without the rights to the shell. Our recommendation is to cross license the software to both parties, with the purchaser obtaining some royalty from the vendor for future sales of the derivative system.

4.8 Post-Selection Negotiation

In Section 4.3 above, you informed the vendor about your expected schedule for the evaluation and selection of a winning vendor. In this section you provide any specific details that you expect to be addressed in depth when the actual contract terms and negotiations will be negotiated, agreed upon, and then signed into the contract.

5.0 RULES FOR THE VENDOR'S PROPOSAL

This section defines what the vendor must do, deliver or behave in order for his proposal to be accepted by you for evaluation.

5.1 Adherence to Rules and Formats

An initial statement should notify the vendor that to have a proposal that meets your requirements, the vendor must follow these rules, and the format and content requirements of the following sections.

5.2 Page Limited Proposals

In defining the packaging requirements for the proposal, there is some merit in requiring the vendor to limit the number of pages in his response. This is particularly true in this age of word processing where the vendor could inundate you with verbiage only peripherally targeted toward the design.

Page limitations to a vendor's proposal can force the vendor to concentrate on the meaningful parts of his proposal instead of providing such statements as: "We will have a quality control function for developed programs according to our standard practice." Unless you know the vendor's quality assurance function very well, this sentence lacks merit. Keep the writing terse, relevant and quantitative by limiting the verbiage.

> Even when the number of pages are limited by the customer, vendors get creative. Some will use the tiniest fonts they can find, and narrow the margins to get more words on the page. Others will deliver proposals on legal or larger sized paper, each folded over. If you require limited pages, you have to specifically define the page parameters as well.

5.3 Delivery Conditions

This section informs the vendor of the time, date and place for delivery of the proposal, the number of copies to be delivered, and the binding instructions for the separate volumes of materials.

If it is required that the vendor deliver the proposal in several separate volumes, (e.g., Design Concept Document, Technical Proposal, Management Proposal, Cost Proposal, Contractual Compliance Document, Standards example), the buyer should explicitly say so in the rules.

5.4 Vendor Proprietary Information

This section usually states that the vendor is required to explicitly label and mark every page containing proprietary information, otherwise the information will be considered in the public domain.

5.5 Vendor Personnel

This section requires all personnel that will be working on the project to be true employees of the vendor and not part-time help or consultants. Statements attesting to employee bonding, vendor performance bonds and liability insurance may also be required.

5.6 Subcontractors

The customer may, or may not, wish the vendor to use subcontractors to assist in the project. If the project is small enough, the customer usually prohibits the use of outside personnel. This is to assure that the vendor has all the personnel needed to do the project when the vendor writes the proposal. Otherwise, some vendors might try to get the job, then recruit the staff to do the work. Therefore, you must be explicit.

In very large projects, especially those involving both equipment and software, some provision for the vendor to subcontract may be practically necessary. In these situations, the buyer usually requires specific identification of all subcontractors that the vendor plans to use, and reserves the right to approve all such subcontractors prior to the vendor employing the subcontractor.

5.7 Vendor Requirements Upon Customer

This paragraph makes an explicit demand upon the vendor, that if the vendor requires any support or services from the customer (other than those already identified as customer furnished items) during the term of the contract, the vendor must document the requirements in the proposal. This is to preclude the possibility that the vendor will want a change in scope, or a schedule delay, because the customer couldn't provide required support.

5.8 Project Management Process

Although not something you strictly regulate, it's necessary to instruct the vendors that you require a project management process for the day-to-day management of the project. Vendors should be required to explain what their management process is, and what tools they expect to use. Tools include such project tracking methods as critical path scheduling, trigger events or milestone tracking, Gantt charts, review dates and task completion or resource tracking. During the negotiations you and the vendor will agree upon those methods to be used to report progress. This requirement is normally designated to be documented in the management proposal.

5.9 Proposed Project Schedule

This section specifies that the customer has a target schedule for the completion of the project. The schedule is included in the document. The vendor is required to propose that his schedule for completion of the project will meet the customer's schedule, or the vendor must propose another schedule that it can meet. The rationale for the vendor's alternate schedule must be included.

> Exhibit 8-7, Revised BITS Project Schedule, prepared by Fred Everet, would serve as a sufficient example for the vendor to critique.

Since customer's schedules can be optimistic at best, the vendor should be encouraged to propose a realistic schedule. The vendor should also be advised that it will not be adversely judged if an alternate schedule can be substantiated as reducing risk, improving performance, lowering costs or leveling personnel peaks.

6.0 FORMAT AND CONTENT OF THE VENDOR'S RESPONSE

The next section of the RFP package contains your direction to the vendors for the format and content of their proposals. Each of the proposal components discussed below is intend-

EXHIBIT 8-7

REVISED SCHEDULE FOR BITS PROJECT

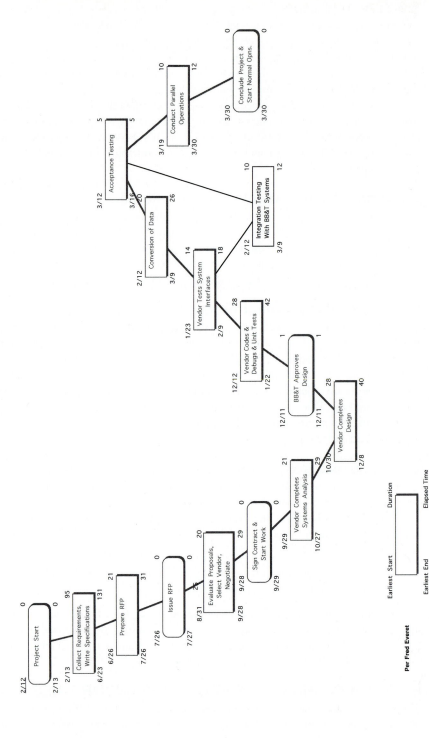

ed to fulfill the customer's objective: to receive proposals from every vendor that have the same format and content, and can be judged side-by-side.

The concept was depicted graphically in Exhibit 8-2. Refresh your memory of the structure required, by reviewing Exhibits 4-2, 4-3, 4-4 and Exhibit 8-2.

6.1 Statement of Work (SOW)

The *Statement of Work* (SOW) is historically the most important of all the documents to be provided by the vendor, because by custom, it has been the document of reference that supersedes all other vendor deliverables as a contractual statement. In that context, the SOW is the ultimate deliverable. Since the custom continues, we see no reason to eliminate the SOW, though it is more effectively superseded by Work Packages (discussed below).

In one instance a vendor provided elaborate discussion in the technical proposal concerning the wealth of capabilities the system would have, only to effectively eliminate those capabilities in his SOW, which took precedence over all other proposal documentation. If the discrepancy hadn't been caught, the customer may have been held for ransom in change orders to actually implement the system as stated in the technical proposal. Fortunately the difference was caught, and the vendor disqualified.

We believe the statement of work can be an umbrella statement in nontechnical language that accurately describes in general, what the vendor will provide, do, and deliver as contractually obligated. We believe it should be the reference point from which the vendor incorporates all the other items of the proposal, especially the work packages discussed below.

You could write your own statement of work in this section, and then have the vendor respond to it. However, it is difficult for the customer to anticipate the ways that vendor proposals might require different responses in the Statement of Work, so the details of the SOW are best left to the vendor to complete.

In conformity to the generic SOW mentioned above, a vendor response might be: "The vendor will do the work according to the requirements specified by the customer in his RFP package, by the vendor's work packages, the technical proposal and the management proposal for the price identified in the cost proposal. This is the best situation for the customer, because the vendor's proposal and the SOW are identical.

Exhibit 8-8 provides an example of how one vendor might phrase the Statement of Work in response to your guidance.

Customers frequently demand more from the vendor than the vendor originally specified. The contract that is negotiated from the statement of work (and the work packages) represents a governing control of what the vendor is obligated to do, and how much or little has been agreed upon when a customer's requirements change. Therefore, it is extremely important that you fine tune the SOW and the work packages before starting work.

6.2 Work Packages (WP)

In order for a project to be successful, the work must be defined so it is understandable, and can be integrated with other components of the effort.

EXHIBIT 8-8

AN EXAMPLE EXCERPT OF A STATEMENT OF WORK

- •
- •
- •

2.0   Systems Analysis

Convulsive Transactions Inc. (CTI) shall perform all the effort required to review the performance requirements specified in Requirements Specifications, Sections 2.1 through 2.6, and Sections 6.4.1, 6.4.2, 6.4.3, and Sections 11.02 through 11.11, and shall then analyze and document these performance requirements to determine and quantify the degree to which the CTI system will meet or exceed all the performance requirements so specified.

ALTERNATIVELY:

- •
- •
- •

2.0   Systems Analysis

Convulsive Transactions Inc. (CTI) shall perform all the work specified in Work Packages 2.0 (Systems Analysis), and 7.0 (Systems Testing), to validate and verify that the CTI system meets or exceeds all perfomance requirements.

The concept of a work package originated under another term, "Work Breakdown Structure" (WBS) in the 1960s in the procurement of space and weapon systems by the Department of Defense. Systems got to be too big to be understandable or manageable. Cost overruns were enormous. Many subcontractors were involved. The technical and management complexity were beyond anyone's previous experience. To piece it together "Systems Analysis" was invented. Decomposition into component parts and re-synthesis became necessary to integrate hardware, operations and software. The decomposition methodology became the WBS.

The underlying concept is simple: A *Work Package* is a separation and segregation of work into understandable independent functions or activities that can be integrated into the complete system, and which can be independently managed and priced.

The understandability is in two domains: the technology or product within a package is understandable, and the amount of effort or materials to produce that product or deliverable is also understandable. Therefore, a massive system that cannot be comprehended in total can be broken into components that are more easily managed and delivered. No better or more practical system seems to have evolved in the civilian marketplace. Therefore, we recommend its adoption as the best management tool yet devised.

Time and again this methodology has proved its value, though it is often obscured by the magnitude of the Department of Defense programs, (and because many are extending the state-of-the-art, and therefore are also research and development programs, which have higher elements of risk).

In practice this methodology is used (but not the name) in the construction industry where the general contractor hires many firms as subcontractors including electrical, mechanical, interior design, painting, landscaping and telecommunications companies in a schedule that he integrates.

The same approach also works with smaller systems developments. In such projects, the goal might be more control of costs than management of complexity, but it produces the same result, control of a process.

The subdivision of a project into *Work Packages* has the following results:

1. They effectively define the schedule for the project.

2. They allocate the vendor's resources by task (and by inference, the customer's resources too).

3. They highlight interfaces among tasks where integration or coordination is required. The transition from one work package to another work package identifies the need for new or joint responsibilities, activities and actions.

4. They define milestones and deliverables within the project where review and control can be exercised. A built-in tracking mechanism is established.

5. They inherently establish a cost basis for every deliverable, and a comparative assessment of cost differences among vendors for similar work.

6. They allow a one-for-one technical comparison between one vendor's tasks within a work package with other vendors' proposals for the same tasks.

7. As a result of the above, they permit better insight into each vendor's creativity in design tasks.

8. They permit quantitative comparisons among vendors in performance areas.

9. They allow comparisons among management style, process and talent for each task within the project.

10. They allow you to remove those tasks that you do not want the vendor to provide (descope), while establishing a ceiling price for the task if it is added later.

11. They allow you to draw a blueprint for the entire program from the beginning. You will understand everything the chosen vendor will do.

There are several ways to break down a project and its work packages into component parts. These can be by dollar value of the work (e.g., $10,000 tasks); by the schedule (e.g., one week's or one month's worth of work); by the level of effort (e.g., 600 labor hours); by the function, task or phase level (e.g., administration, systems analysis, testing); or by the deliverable for that part (e.g., module test plan). We suggest that a combination be used where applicable, overlaid upon a baseline of the project life cycle phases (Exhibit 2-2).

The degree of subdivision of any package into sub-packages, or tasks, will depend upon the total scope of a project, its schedule and its complexity. For example, a small project might be divided into a single work package for each phase of the project.

Exhibit 8-9 shows how such a work package for a small system might be defined.

A large project will have many subdivisions to provide insight into all the work and deliverables. There can be a matrix of organizations, engineering talent and labor grades that participate in a task. It's important to know where responsibility is assigned.

Exhibit 8-10 provides an example of an outline for work packages in which several subdivisions are needed to provide adequate understanding about what is being delivered.

These work packages must have a corresponding set of definitions that state what is, and is not, included within each Work Package. A set of definitions that can be used in a systems procurement is found in Appendix B. We urge you to read these definitions in detail to understand the distinctions that are made in work packages.

Exhibit 8-11 provides an example of how a vendor might respond to a portion of the requirements for Work Package 2.4.1 related to Systems Analysis specified in Exhibit 8-10.

> The underlying concept of the *Work Package* is simple: Segregate independent functions or activities into understandable packages that can be built and integrated.

EXHIBIT 8-9

AN EXAMPLE OF GENERIC WORK PACKAGES FOR
A SMALL SYSTEMS PROCUREMENT

WORK PACKAGES	DESCRIPTION
1.0 Project Management & Administration	All vendor activity related to the administration of each aspect of the vendor's activities: technical, management and cost administration and liaison and reporting to the customer.
2.0 Systems Analysis	The effort related to perform technical trade-off analyses and calculations required to validate that the design will meet performance requirements.
3.0 Systems Design	The effort related to design of the vendor's solution and the modifications to the existing systems. This design effort could be formats, databases, programs or screens.
4.0 Coding, Debug and Unit Testing	The effort required to reduce the design of the vendor's solution to computer instructions, and their testing as units of delivered code.
5.0 Vendor Interface Testing	The effort related to the vendor's testing of the modules and software built with models or real interfaces from the client's other interfacing software systems.
6.0 Integration Testing	The effort related to test all of the functioning parts of the vendor's system and the interfaces among all other systems to validate correct processing by all.
7.0 Conversion of Data	The effort required by the vendor to support the conversion of information from the formats of the old system into the required formats used by the new system.
8.0 Acceptance Testing	The effort related to proving that the vendor's system performs according to the requirements, within the performance specifications, according to the approved design without error.
9.0 Cutover and Parallel	The effort related to support of the customer while the new system becomes operational, and to verify the accuracy of its processing as compared with the old systems.
10.0 Operations Support	The effort related to providing support to the customer after the system has been accepted and is operational.

EXHIBIT 8-10

AN EXAMPLE OUTLINE OF WORK PACKAGES FOR A MAJOR SYSTEMS PROCUREMENT

1.0 Project Management & Administration
1.1 Organization, Manpower & Controls
1.2 Scheduling
1.3 Contracts Administration & Change Management
1.4 Client Reporting
1.5 Deliverables Production

2.0 Systems Analysis
2.1 Hardware Capacity Analysis
2.2 Hardware Performance Analysis
2.3 System Module Performance Analysis
2.3.1 System Module **1** Performance Analysis
2.3.2 System Module **2** Performance Analysis
2.3.3 System Module **3** Performance Analysis
2.4 Interface Performance Analysis
2.4.1 Interface System **A** Performance Analysis
2.4.2 Interface System **B** Performance Analysis
2.4.3 Interface System **C** Performance Analysis
2.4.4 Interface System **D** Performance Analysis
2.5 Total System Performance Analysis
2.6 System Reliability Analysis
2.7 System Security and Audit Analysis
2.8 System Analysis Deliverables

3.0 Systems Design
3.1 System Module **1** Design
3.2 System Module **2** Design
3.3 System Module **3** Design
3.4 System Module **4** Design
3.5 System Module 5 Design
3.5.1 System Module **5** Program **1** Design
3.5.2 System Module **5** Program **2** Design
3.5.3 System Module **5** Program **3** Design
3.5.4 System Module **5** Program **4** Design
3.6 System Design Documentation Deliverables

4.0 Coding, Debug & Unit Testing
4.1 System Module **1** Code, Debug & Unit Test
4.2 System Module **2** Code, Debug & Unit Test
4.3 System Module **3** Code, Debug & Unit Test
4.4 System Module **4** Code, Debug & Unit Test
4.5 System Module **5** Code, Debug & Unit Test
4.6 Code & Documentation Deliverables

5.0 Interface Testing
5.1 Module **1 & 2** Interface Testing
5.2 Module **1 & 3 & 4** Interface Testing
5.3 Module **1 & 5** Interface Testing
5.4 Module **3 & 4 & 5** Interface Testing
5.5 Interface Testing Deliverables

6.0 Integration Testing
6.1 System Timeline Testing
6.2 Interface Integration Testing **A, B, C, D** With Modules **1, 2, 3**
6.3 Interface Integration Testing **A, B, C, D** With Modules **4, 5**
6.4 Input-Output Controls Testing
6.5 Integration Testing Deliverable

7.0 Data Conversion
7.1 Operations Process **J** Data Conversion
7.2 Operations Process **K** Data Conversion
7.3 Operations Process **L** Data Conversion
7.4 System Interface **A, B, C, D** Data Conversion
7.5 Data Conversion Verification
7.6 Data Conversion and Database Deliverables

8.0 Acceptance Testing
8.1 Systems Test Plan
8.2 Systems Test Procedures & Script
8.3 Data Base Verification Testing
8.4 Acceptance Test Criteria & Data
8.5 Systems Acceptance Test, Results & Reports

9.0 Cutover & Parallel
9.1 Operational Process **J** Cutover & Parallel
9.2 Operational Process **K** Cutover & Parallel
9.3 Operational Process **L** Cutover & Parallel
9.4 Operations Acceptance

10.0 Operations Support
10.1 Software Maintenance Support
10.2 Database Support
10.3 Operational Procedures Support

EXHIBIT 8-11

AN EXAMPLE OF VENDOR TERMINOLOGY IN A WORK PACKAGE

-
-
-

2.4   Interface Performance Analysis

2.4.1 System A Interface Performance Analysis

Using the existing Convulsive Transactions Inc. Retail Banking System (CTI-RBS) before BB&T modifications, CTI will prepare dummy input and output subroutines and model data based upon the System A interface specifications, to:

1. Feed input data to CTI-RBS to test compatibility of the existing CTI-RBS for System A data. This test will be run on the BB&T KRV computers to test CTI-RBS operating performance prior to the BB&T modifications and to test the accuracy of the interface. Operating times of the CTI-RBS system will be tracked for the impact of two hundred dummy confirmations from System A.

2. Output data from CTI-RBS will be electronically sent via dummy subroutine call to a copy of the System A software to determine its ability to receive and process the data. Operating times will be tracked for the data transfer rates, and the production processing time by System A for a two hundred transaction batch from CTI-RBS.

Although this processing will not be exactly equivalent when the BB&T modifications have been made, it will provide assurance that CTI has correctly interpreted the interface specifications, and correctly designed the input-output subroutines. A two hundred dummy transaction batch should have negligible increases in either systems' stand-alone run times as a result of this interface.

6.3 Vendor Deliverables

Vendor deliverables are those items that the customer expects the vendor to deliver during and at the conclusion of a project.

> Since buying a car is a process most people experience, one might believe there is an analogy between systems projects and delivery of a car. When you buy a car, the dealer or the factory specifies what it contains and you consent to the list of options you are given. Then you take possession and pay for it with a high degree of confidence that you will receive what you ordered.

> With systems projects there is no common baseline of understanding of what constitutes the complete deliverables for the project. Unlike cars, there is no consistent set of specifications that makes one system comparable to another. Therefore, it is up to the purchaser to define what is wanted.

You have to tell the vendor what you expect. The alternative is that each vendor picks and chooses among the many possibilities of deliverables that will make his proposal look best and cost the least. The vendor will thus understate the real costs if you want more than the vendor's minimum deliverables. A worse consequence is that you will have no means of comparing one vendor's quality and costs related to the deliverables with any other vendor's deliverables.

Since vendor deliverables are no different from the normal deliverables of your standard system development methodology for internal projects, you should adopt them to fit the vendor relationship. It is usual practice to enumerate the deliverables in a list, and by reference, attach a set of definitions of what each deliverable contains. This set of definitions can be highly stylized, formatted and structured, or they can be a single paragraph. The definitions can include requirements as when the deliverables are due to be delivered, the media they are to take, and the number of copies. These *Vendor Deliverable Definitions* should be included as a section in your systems development standards document included in the RFP package and referenced from this section.

> Exhibit 8-12 contains the list of minimum deliverables that we would expect from a software systems vendor.

Vendor deliverables include all the tools and documents needed to manage the project and report to the customer on it. The RFP format forces the vendors to expose how they cost out this management overhead. If you want to be more informal, you can delete what you don't need during negotiations. In this way you can measure and price the overhead you need to impose.

If every vendor is required to respond to your deliverable requirements, lean operating companies will have lean overhead costs and a competitive advantage, with your money put to better use on the product. Firms that carry an abundance of overhead costs embedded throughout the proposal will be exposed. Where once you may have given them the benefit of a doubt on a task's costs, now you can truly measure the cost of each deliverable of every vendor's proposal.

Why should vendor's accept this situation? Because they want the contract!

EXHIBIT 8-12

TYPICAL VENDOR SYSTEMS DELIVERABLES

(Alphabetically)

Acceptance Test Plan

Acceptance Test Report

Acceptance Test Script

Conversion Plan

Development Test Plan

Discrepancy Report

Financial Summary Reports

Interface Specification

Operational Manuals

Operational Procedures

Preliminary Design Specification

Program Design (as Built)

Program Object Code

Program Source Code

Requirements Traceability Matrix

Status Reports

System Design Specification

System Installation Procedures

System Requirements Allocation Specification

Systems Analysis Document

Training Plan

User Manuals

EXHIBIT 8-13

AN EXAMPLE EXCERPT OF A VENDOR'S TECHNICAL PROPOSAL

- •
- •
- •

Work Package: 3.5 System Module 5 Design

3.5.1 System Module 5 Program 1 Design

Program 1 provides input and output processing controls for Module 5's programs. All data provided to other programs in this module will enter Program 1 and, depending upon the characteristics of field 4 in the first record, will be filtered and checked for accuracy according to the data integrity requirements specified in requirements specification section 5.4.1-5.4.6.

Data meeting the filter and integrity checking will be passed directly through a subroutine call, identified in field 7 of the first record, to the corresponding program in Module 5.

Data failing to meet the filter and integrity checking will be held in an error bin numbered according to the characteristic nature of field 4 in the first record of the batch, until the entire batch has been processed, at which time a summary statistical alarm denoting the batch, number of records and the number of errors contained therein will be sent to the console, while a detailed listing of the errors found for each record will sent to the repair and restore printer/workstation #5.

The batch will be dumped to an error queue corresponding to the error bin from which it can be re-started after repair and restore, and after audit verification of repair and restore has been authorized.

The system will automatically re-synchronize for missing batch numbers, batch totals and completed processing provided that the repair is completed prior to the total completion of Module 5 processing (assumed 25 minutes).

6.4 Technical Proposal

The *Technical Proposal* contains the detailed description in technical language of the technical work and products that the vendor will deliver. The proposal will provide item by item traceability to the requirements specification that you have provided to the vendor, and will be organized according to the flow of the work packages. The vendor's technical proposal is naturally the most voluminous document submitted, and can be several hundred pages for a major system.

Exhibit 8-13 provides an example of how a vendor might describe what might be done to design a control program that funnels data to other processing programs.

6.5 Management Proposal

The *Management Proposal* specifies how the vendor will manage resources during the project. Different management approaches will be required during the phases of the project. For example, the vendor's role will be very direct and hands-on during systems coding, but will be more supportive during conversion and parallel, when the customer's personnel are heavily tasked.

The management proposal includes the vendor's discussion of the personnel resources that will be deployed, including roles, responsibilities and contributions by work package. The development team's identification is part of the management of the project. The staffing profile proposed for the project will also reveal the management skills of the vendor. A rapid rise in staffing might indicate that the vendor will be recruiting new personnel during the project. An unexplained change in personnel in the middle of the project might suggest that the vendor is rotating personnel out of your project, replacing them with perhaps less skilled individuals. The customer should have confidence in the labor plan, in the same way he has confidence in the technology proposed.

Besides the management tasks of each work package, the vendor has an overhead management responsibility of managing resources and work as a total entity. This role is usually covered in the first work package that addresses all the administrative tasks of the project. Project management techniques, status reporting and customer relations are included in this package.

Exhibit 8-14 contains an outline of the kind of information that the vendor would cover in the management work package complementary to the technical effort described in Exhibit 8-13.

The management proposal also serves as the document of convenience for the vendor's response, and includes several other deliverables as separate chapters, in addition to the work packages corresponding to the management effort. Table 8-1 provides an outline of the contents of the complete management proposal document.

EXHIBIT 8-14

AN EXAMPLE EXCERPT OF A VENDOR'S MANAGEMENT PROPOSAL

> - •
>
> - •
>
> - •
>
> **Work Package: 3.5   System Module 5 Design**
>
> **3.5.1   System Module 5 Program 1 Design**
>
> Program 1 requires design from the most experienced input-output controls designer at CTI. Mr. Randy Ruchard will be assigned to the effort. Controls and filter design will be reviewed by the designer of each receiving or sending program to/from Program 1 as the design progresses, but not less than weekly. The review by each designer will be by direct analysis of output, error reports and code inspection if required.
>
> It is expected that this effort will require three weeks of effort, including the reviews.

TABLE 8-1

FORMAT OF THE MANAGEMENT PROPOSAL

CHAPTER	TITLE	DISCUSSION OF CONTENTS
1.0	Statement of Work	Contains the vendor's SOW that incorporates all work packages.
2.0	Management Proposal Work Packages	Contains the work packages describing the management effort by the vendor to deliver the project.
3.0	Deliverables	Describes the vendor's deliverables and incorporates examples by reference that may be appended separately.
4.0	Schedule	Gives the vendor's detailed proposed schedule.

TABLE 8-1 (continued)

5.0	Standards	Describes the vendor's standards and processes for developing documents/code. Discusses choice of standard, and by reference, includes copies of documents completed according to the standards.
6.0	Issues and Objections	Contains any items the vendor has flagged as a result of considering problem requirements (technical or contractual) and which the vendor requires to be resolved before the start of work.
7.0	Resumes	Contains the resumes and job function and responsibility to be taken by the vendor's key personnel assigned to the project.
8.0	Requirements Traceability Matrix	Contains the Requirements Traceability Matrices required to track conformity of the vendor's proposal to the requirements.
9.0	Vendor's Chapter	Contains any other information, discussion or documentation that the vendor wishes to address.

The management proposal gives the customer insight into how the vendor works and manages. With this insight a judgment can be made whether this vendor has the capability and the people to deliver what has been described in the technical proposal.

6.6 Cost Proposal

You want to understand the price you will pay for the system, as well as for the price you pay for the various components of the system. You want to make a judgment that the price you are paying for a component is consistent with the degree of technical complexity for the same component.

Comparing various vendors' prices across the same work package will reveal significant differences for what is purportedly similar work. When you see these differences, you'll ask yourself and (rhetorically) the vendor, "Why is the work you propose so expensive (so reasonable) given the complexity of the task as we currently understand it?" When you see a cost that exceeds your expectation, you can examine the technical effort to see if too much capability is being delivered. Perhaps you can descope that capability and obtain a satisfactory solution at lower cost.

In addition to the pricing of the work packages, you need to know whether there are any other costs, such as licensing fees, that are not included in the work packages. Because you may need to change specifications, or add new functionality at some time during the project, it is essential to also understand the hourly labor rate per engineering grade or title that the vendor quotes. Then you can also estimate the costs of new functionality, by comparing your estimate of the labor effort with the quoted labor effort per task in labor-hours or labor-months for comparable tasks quoted in the proposal.

The insights on cost versus technology discussed above reveal the benefits of matching technical, management and costs across the work packages. The information contained in one of the proposals can lead to enlightened questions concerning the other proposals. This is why we believe reviewers of vendor's proposals should know what is contained in the others. The reviewers can determine if they are obtaining their "bang for the buck." In the absence of financial data, technology personnel will usually choose the most advanced sophisticated design and opt for the highest performance possible. But you don't need a Ferrari to drive to the store.

Exhibit 8-15 contains an example of the way one vendor might submit the costs for work package 3.5.1 in a cost proposal.

6.7 Requirements Traceability

Now that you've told the vendor to provide technical, management and cost proposals, and that each proposal must be organized according to work packages, one last issue needs to be resolved. We must know in each case, which of the technical requirements are being satisfied by which of the work packages.

Conversely, we have a detailed requirements specification. If the vendor has proposed a solution to requirement 3.4.5.2, then we need to find that solution in the vendor's proposal.

Therefore, a *Requirements Traceability Matrix* is required from every vendor that maps, or cross-correlates each proposal (work packages) with the requirements specifications and vise-versa.

Exhibit 8-16 provides an example of a requirements traceability matrix starting from the work package listing.

Exhibit 8-17 provides an example of the cross-correlation of the requirements specification with the contents of a hypothetical vendor's proposals.

With the use of these traceability matrices, the vendor and you can be assured that all requirements have been addressed. The traceability matrices are an essential tool during testing.

6.8 Design Concept Document

Although not considered essential and not a document that will be included in the evaluation process, a design concept document is often requested by the customer. A *Design Concept Document* is an explanation, in easily understandable, nontechnical, business language of what the vendor has developed or will develop. The purpose of the design concept document is to respond to the functional requirements. The document might include overview charts, man-machine operating examples and functionality. If the vendor has developed and is marketing the system, the marketing materials, suitably adjusted for the peculiarities of this project would serve effectively as the design concept document.

The nontechnical user will be able to conceptually understand what the system will do, without having to muddle through the technical jargon in the specifications.

The project manager can use the material as supporting information when the presentations are made to the project review committee on the recommended vendor.

EXHIBIT 8-15

AN EXAMPLE EXCERPT OF A VENDOR'S COST PROPOSAL

-
-
-
-

Work Package: 3.5   System Module 5 Design

3.5.1   System Module 5 Program 1 Design

Program 1 requires three weeks of labor effort. The estimated cost is $6,700.00. Labor Grade: "Designer" will perform this effort. Project manager's directly billed time is 3 hours.

3.5.2   System Module 5 Program 2 Design

Program 2 requires........

CONTRACT TERMS AND CONDITIONS

The contract terms and conditions, referenced from Section 4 of the RFP guidance document are the packaged set of legalese that your legal department and the systems contract administrator have pieced together to form the basis of your contract.

These are a separate document to allow the vendor's legal department to review them, while the vendor is writing the proposal. The vendor can object to any clauses that are unacceptable when submitting a proposal based on this legal input.

Appendix A contains some example clauses for BB&T's Standard Contract Terms and Conditions.

REGULATORY CLAUSES AND AFFIDAVITS

If you are a public entity or governmental body, you will require your vendors to submit documents, certifications and affidavits testifying to all sorts of nondiscriminatory practices, procedures and the like.

Sometimes, the amount of paper and legal effort that goes into filling out these requirements exceeds the value of the contract. If you are a vendor and want to play in the government's playpen, you don't have much of an option but to comply. In commercial procurements you won't be bothered with this stuff.

EXHIBIT 8-16

EXAMPLE: "CONVULSIVE TRANSACTIONS, INC." REQUIREMENTS TRACEABILITY MATRIX

WORK PACKAGE #	WORK PACKAGE NAME	TECHNICAL PROPOSAL PAGE REFERENCE	MANAGEMENT PROPOSAL PAGE REFERENCE	COST PROPOSAL PAGE REFERENCE	REQUIREMENTS SPECIFICATION (R); INTERFACE SPECIFICATION (I) SATISFACTION REFERENCE SECTION NUMBERS
1.0	Project Management & Administration		1-2	1-2	RFP Guidance Section 5.4
2.0	Systems Analysis	7-11; 14; 33 - 38	3; 7; 13	1; 3; 5	R: 1.4-17; 2.4-2.6; 5.2; 7.1-7.4; I: 1.5-1.9; 2.1-2.3; 3.1-3.3; 4.1-4.4
3.0	Systems Design	12; 39-75	14-25	6	
3.1	Retail Subsystem	39-58	15-19	7-8	R: 2.7-3.0; 4.1-4.6; 5.1-5.9
3.2	Interface Modules	59-66	19-22	8-9	I: 2.4-2.7; 3.1-3.6; 4.1-4.6; 5.1-5.6
3.3	Audit Controls	67-75	23-25	10-11	R: 6.1-6.5
4.0	Coding, Debug & Unit Testing	76-80	26-30	12-15	R: 7.1-7.3
5.0	Interface Testing	82-87	31-33	16	R: 3.8; 4.8; 5.8 I: 2.6; 3.6; 4.6;5.6
6.0	Integration Testing	88-93	34-35	17	R: 7.4-7.7 I: 6.1-6.5
7.0	Data Conversion	94-97	36	18-20	R: 7.8
8.0	Acceptance Testing	98-104	37-40	21	R: 7.9 I: 6.6
9.0	Cutover & Parallel	105-107	41	22	R: 7.10 I: 6.7-6.9
10.0	Operations Support	108-110	42-44	22	R: 8.1-8.3

EXHIBIT 8-17

EXCERPT FROM A REQUIREMENTS TRACEABILITY
CROSS-CORRELATION MATRIX

WP#	NAME	DOCUMENT / PAGE / SECTION REFERENCES (Note 1)		TECHNICAL PROPOSAL REFERENCES	MANAGEMENT PROPOSAL REFERENCES	COST PROPOSAL REFERENCES
1.0	Project Management & Administration	RFP 4.0,	p 45-50		2	1
		RFP 5.0,	p 51-53		3-7	2
		RFP 6.3,	p 67		2, 4, 8-10	3
2.0	Systems Analysis	SRS 2.0				
		2.1	4	7	11	3
		2.2	4	8-11	11	3
		2.3	5	12	11	3
		2.4	5	13-15	12-14	3
		2.5	6	16	14	4
		2.6	6	17-20	14	4
		2.7	7	21	15-16	4
		2.8	8	22-24	17	5
		IS 2.0	2-4	12, 23-30	11, 13, 18	6
3.0	Systems Design	SRS 3.0				
		3.1	3	31-35	19	7
		3.2	9-11	36-39	20	7
		3.3	12-14	40-42	20	7
		3.4	15-19	43-47	20	8
		3.5	20-24	48-50	21	8
4.0	Code, Debug & Unit Testing	etc.		etc.	etc.	etc.
5.0	Interface Testing	etc.		etc.	etc.	etc.
6.0	Integration Testing	etc.		etc.	etc.	etc.
7.0	Data Conversion	etc.		etc.	etc.	etc.
8.0	Acceptance Testing	etc.		etc.	etc.	etc.
9.0	Cutover & Parallel	etc.		etc.	etc.	etc.
10.0	Operations Support	etc.		etc.	etc.	etc.

Note 1: RFP = Request For Proposal Guidance Document Reference Requirement
SRS = Systems Requirements Specification Document
IS = Interface Specifications Document

CASE STUDY

Fred Everet, Ulrich Schmidt and their team worked long hours from the end of February through the end of June to assure themselves that the requirements specifications were completed and signed off by the respective business managers. Lisa supported their effort by reengineering some wholesale system operating processes, so that the man-machine interfaces with the new BITS system would be simpler, more controllable and easier to fix if something went wrong. She developed manual operational contingency plans for various processes should the completed BITS system not work totally as planned.

Monk Eternic searched his contact lists of former military associates and government contractors and was able to obtain some public domain boilerplate related to RFPs that helped him better understand the unique procurement requirements of a software system.

These efforts resulted in an improvement on the original schedule that Fred had outlined. Instead of having an RFP ready to be sent to vendors by August 15 (Exhibit 4-8), they were able to send out the RFP package by July 26th (Exhibit 8-7), an improvement of 20 days, which could be added to the development cycle.

The final work packages were completed and the RFP package was sent. Chapter 9 contains the exact wording of the BB&T RFP Guidance document.

Exhibit 8-18 contains the BB&T work packages as sent in their RFP package.

EXHIBIT 8-18

WORK PACKAGES CHOSEN BY BB&T FOR THE BITS SYSTEM

1.0 Project Management & Administration
1.1 Organization, Personnel & Controls
1.2 Scheduling of Work
1.3 Contracts Administration & Change Management
1.4 Client Reporting
1.5 Deliverables Production

2.0 Systems Analysis
2.1 KRV Computer Capacity Analysis
2.2 KRV Computer Performance Analysis
2.3 System Performance Analysis
    2.3.1 Personal Loans Perf. Analysis
    2.3.2 Student Loans Perf. Analysis
    2.3.3 Home Loans Perf. Analysis
    2.3.4 Checking Accounts Perf. Analysis
    2.3.5 Term Deposits Perf. Analysis
    2.3.6 Savings Deposits Perf. Analysis
    2.3.7 Credit Card Processing
2.4 Interface Performance Analysis
    2.4.1 General Ledger Interface Perf. Analysis
    2.4.2 Income & Expense Accounting Interface Performance Analysis
    2.4.3 Central Liability Interface Perf. Analysis
    2.4.4 Customer Profitability Interface Performance Analysis
2.5 Total System Performance Analysis
2.6 System Reliability Analysis
2.7 System Security and Audit Analysis
2.8 System Analysis Deliverables

3.0 Systems Design
3.1 Personal Loans Module Design
3.2 Student Loans Module Design
3.3 Home Loans Module Design
3.4 Checking Accounts Module Design
3.5 Term Deposits Module Design
3.6 Savings Deposits Module Design
3.7 Credit Card Processing Module Design
3.8 Audit Tracking and Reporting Module Design

4.0 Coding, Debug & Unit Testing
4.1 Personal Loans Module Design
4.2 Student Loans Module Design
4.3 Home Loans Module Design
4.4 Checking Accounts Module Design
4.5 Term Deposits Module Design
4.6 Savings Deposits Module Design
4.7 Credit Card Processing Module Design
4.8 Audit Tracking and Reporting Module Design

5.0 Interface Testing
5.1 General Ledger Interface Testing
5.2 Income & Expense Accounting Interface Testing
5.3 Central Liability Interface Testing
5.4 Customer Profitability Interface Testing

6.0 Integration Testing
6.1 System Timeline Testing
6.2 Integration of General Ledger with all Modules
6.3 Integration of Accounting System / all Modules
6.4 Integration of Central Liability / Loan Modules
6.5 Integration of Customer Profitability / all Modules
6.6 Input-Output Controls & Audit Tracking Testing
6.7 Integration Testing Deliverable

7.0 Data Conversion
7.1 Loan Operations Data Conversion
7.2 Deposit Operations Data Conversion
7.3 Credit Card Operations Data Conversion
7.4 Checking Accounts Data Conversion
7.5 Data Conversion Verification
7.6 Data Conversion and Database Deliverables

8.0 Acceptance Testing
8.1 Systems Test Plan
8.2 Systems Test Procedures & Script
8.3 Database Verification Testing
8.4 Acceptance Test Criteria & Data
8.5 Systems Acceptance Test, Results & Reports

9.0 Cutover & Parallel
9.1 Loan Operations Cutover & Parallel
9.2 Credit Card Operations Cutover & Parallel
9.3 Checking Account Operations Cutover & Parallel
9.4 Deposit Operations Cutover & Parallel
9.4 Operations Acceptance

10.0 Operations Support
10.1 Software Maintenance Support
10.2 Database Support
10.3 Operational Procedures Support

## Chapter Nine

A REQUEST FOR PROPOSAL "SCRIPT"

This chapter contains a completed request for proposal guidance document as it was prepared by Fred and his staff at Baccarat Bank & Trust. The text corresponds to the terminology you might actually use in your RFP, and corresponds directly to the perspective presented in Chapter 8. When you prepare your own RFP, you will of course make whatever changes your own requirements necessitate, but the verbiage here will point you in the direction to take.

Baccarat Bank & Trust
Request for Proposal Guidance Document

1.0 INTRODUCTION & SCOPE

The purpose of this RFP Guidance document is to:

• Solicit vendor proposals to design, code and deliver the system described in this RFP package.

• Receive vendor proposals that conform to the requirements and format as specified in this document.

• Guide the response of all vendors submitting proposals to assure the most uniform basis for evaluation.

• Instruct all vendors on BB&T's Standard Contract Terms and Conditions.

The specifications for this effort are contained in the following documents, which are attached hereto, and incorporated herein:

1. Baccarat Bank & Trust System Requirements Specification (SRS) for the Branch Integrated Transaction System (BITS).

2. Baccarat Bank & Trust Interface Specifications (IS) for interface of the vendor's system with existing BB&T systems.

3. This document, *RFP Guidance Document*, which includes requirements for deliverables, proposal rules and formats for the vendor's submission.

4. BB&T Standard Contract Terms and Conditions.

5. A BITS Functional Requirements document that describes the business issues and operational requirements in nontechnical terminology.

6. BB&T System Development Standards.

This Request For Proposal Package constitutes the sole and total BB&T requirements and deliverables for the BITS Project.

It is possible that the vendor may require additional information from other vendors, computer manufacturers, or other distributors in order to complete the proposal. BB&T assumes no obligation whatsoever to provide you with such information, or to assist you in obtaining such information on your own.

These proposal instructions, unless specifically exempted in the Request for Proposal (RFP) transmittal letter, must be followed for all proposals. Failure to comply with these instructions will result in your proposal being considered as non-responsive and rejected for cause.

2.0 RFP ADMINISTRATION

2.1 Precedence of Documentation

Should there be any inconsistency between this RFP Guidance Document and any additional documentation furnished with the RFP or the transmittal letter, the order of precedence shall be:

1. Letter of Transmittal.

2. This document, *RFP Guidance Document*, which includes all proposal rules, requirements for deliverables, and formats for the vendor's submission.

3. BB&T Standard Contract Terms and Conditions.

4. BB&T System Requirements Specification (SRS) for the Branch Integrated Transaction System (BITS).

5. Baccarat Bank & Trust Interface Specifications (IS) for interface of the vendor's system with existing BB&T systems.

6. BB&T's System Development Standards.

7. BITS Functional Requirements document that describes the business issues and operational requirements in nontechnical terminology.

Vendors are requested to indicate areas of inconsistency among these documents, if any, to the BB&T Systems Contract Administrator (SCA).

2.2 Bid / No-Bid Response

Vendors are requested to advise the BB&T contact of the vendor's intention to bid or not to bid on the RFP. This intention should be communicated via telephone within four business days of receipt of the RFP.

2.3 RFP Points of Contact

The points of contact with BB&T personnel in order of preference are the BB&T Systems Contract Administrator, Mr. Monk Eternic; the Project Manager, Ulrich Schmidt, V. P.; then any other individual identified in the transmittal letter. Contact with any other personnel at BB&T on this RFP is prohibited. Such contact is sufficient reason to reject a vendor's proposal for cause without further explanation or obligation.

2.4 Costs of Preparation

BB&T assumes no liability for any costs whatsoever associated with a vendor's response to this RFP.

2.5 Duration of Applicability

The vendor (you) agree that the proposals (including pricing) shall remain valid for 90 days from receipt of the proposal by BB&T and shall be the basis for negotiation of a firm contract with BB&T. Should BB&T select you as the vendor and enter into negotiations with you, the proposal shall remain valid during the duration of the negotiation until a contract is signed or negotiations terminated, even if the ninety day applicability period is exceeded, unless modified by written agreement of both parties.

2.6 Alternate Proposals

Vendors are required to submit a proposal that conforms with the requirements of the RFP. If a vendor takes objection to the RFP or to other BB&T requirements, these objections should be clearly indicated in the transmittal letter and in Chapter 6 of the management proposal. It is possible that such exceptions may result in a reduction in score of the vendor's proposal. On the other hand, added-value suggestions as alternatives to the specifications are welcomed.

Vendors may submit one or more alternate proposals to the RFP provided that at least one conforming proposal is received. Multiple versions of alternate proposals, although not prohibited, are discouraged.

2.7 Retention / Return of Proposals

If a vendor is unsuccessful in obtaining a contract award from BB&T, they are requested to destroy all copies of BB&T's documentation and inform the SCA by registered mail.

BB&T will retain one archive copy of a vendor's proposals in the systems contract administrator's files in secured cabinets as reference for future potential contracts. This archive copy will also permit internal audit of BB&T's standards and policies in contract awards. If the vendor is unsuccessful in obtaining a contract award, BB&T will destroy all other copies.

2.8 Confidentiality

BB&T considers all proposal activity to be confidential in nature. BB&T does not wish its activity with regard to this Request for Proposal to be available to other than the vendor's own personnel. Therefore, the vendor shall not disclose to anyone other than BB&T personnel directly involved with this request for proposal and the vendor's personnel directly associated with response to this request for proposal and who have a need to know, any information concerning this RFP.

No news release or announcement on the existence of, or subject matter of this request for proposal or any phase of any project entered into hereunder may be announced, without prior written approval of the BB&T systems contract administrator.

3.0 PROPOSAL EVALUATION ADMINISTRATION

This section contains information for the vendor to understand the manner in which BB&T will make its judgment on the best proposal.

3.1 Basis for Selection

The vendor will be selected on the basis of the data submitted and contained within the vendor's proposals. All vendors who have been requested to respond to this RFP are considered fully qualified. As a consequence, performance history, financial status and any information from previous relationships with BB&T have already been factored into the proposal invitation.

Therefore, it is incumbent upon the vendor that the proposal submitted contain that information, and only that information, absolutely essential for BB&T to obtain a full and complete understanding of the vendor's capability to deliver the BITS system and perform the work contained within the proposal. Any other information is unnecessary, unless there has been a material change in the technical, management, personnel or financial status of the vendor, in which case, the vendor must include relevant information within Chapter 9.0 of the management proposal.

3.2 Non-Responsiveness

Non-responsiveness includes failure to add value to the specifications and requirements provided in the Request for Proposal. This would include parroting back of content already within the Request for Proposal documentation.

Non-responsiveness also includes failure to submit to the packaging requirements contained within this Request for Proposal Guidance Document.

3.3 Site Visits

BB&T does not expect to have a requirement to visit the vendor's site or any installed customer sites as part of the evaluation process.

3.4 Fact-finding

Should BB&T determine that a vendor is their choice for the procurement, prior to negotiation, BB&T may request the vendor to attend a review session of fact-finding. The purpose of the fact-finding would be to establish a further understanding of the detailed technical design that has been proposed. The primary intention is to amplify items which have been identified as requiring further definition or clarification.

The BB&T evaluation team will also conduct a detailed analysis of the management plan and the cost profile with particular emphasis on the correlation of management activity with the associated cost per task. The evaluation team may also have a goal of determining which items in the vendor's proposal it wishes to delete and no longer consider for procurement. It will use the information provided by the fact-finding process during the forthcoming negotiations. The fact-finding process is considered an essential element of your response to the request for proposal.

3.5 BB&T's Evaluation Schedule

The vendor responding to the request for proposal should assume that BB&T wishes to give the vendor's response the maximum opportunity for review and discussion with BB&T senior management. Therefore, in planning resources, the vendor should assume that BB&T will operate according to the following internal timeline:

Days from:	Activity
0	Vendor Proposals Received
1-14	Evaluation Panels Review of Proposals
15-17	Advisory Committee Review
18-20	Sr. Project Review Committee
21	Preliminary Approval Subject to Contract
21	Potential Winning Vendor(s) Notified
22-24	Fact-finding with Candidate Vendor(s)
25-26	Contract Negotiations
27	Recommendations to Management
32	Management Final Approval
33	Contract Award
35	Start of Work

For purposes of planning the start of work date, you should assume that the Start of Work Date will be September 29.

3.6 Evaluation Methodology and Process

BB&T will evaluate the proposals on the basis of the content of the work packages containing technical information, management capabilities to do the work described, and costs and the statement of work. The methodology by which the relative merits for technical, management and cost factors are considered in the evaluation process is considered proprietary to BB&T.

Although by the nature of the technology considerations contained in this request for proposal, technical merit will have a higher degree of importance, the vendor must be certain that the management capability described to implement the technical features of the proposal and the costs for implementing it, must be fully acceptable and within the range which BB&T will consider to be competitive.

The qualifying vendor must be fully satisfactory in all categories of technical, managerial and cost elements of the proposal. These three factors are all required to insure high probability of successful project completion.

3.7 Notification

Although it is BB&T's intention to complete all evaluation work according to the above schedule, there are no guarantees that this can be achieved. Furthermore, until a contract has been signed with the successful vendor, any vendor, unless rejected for cause, may have a continuing probability of obtaining the contract award. Therefore, BB&T will not advise any vendor of the disposition of the award until the contract with the successful vendor has been signed.

4.0 ADMINISTRATION OF THE CONTRACTING PHASE

This section describes what BB&T expects of the winning vendor during the performance under the contract, and defines the groundrules for the conduct of both parties during the project.

4.1 BB&T Standards

BB&T has provided the vendor with a copy of BB&T's System Development Standards to permit the vendor to establish whether the vendor's own system development standards meet or exceed the rigor, quality and comprehensiveness of BB&T's standards. The vendor will be required to demonstrate that the vendor deliverables will meet such standards should the vendor prefer to use his own methodology. The justification for the use of the vendor's choice of standards will be presented in Chapter 5 of the management proposal.

BB&T will rigorously review all submissions for the requisite quality, and should the deliverables not meet such quality standards, the vendor will be required to rectify the submission at his own cost.

4.2 BB&T Furnished Items

BB&T shall provide certain documentation, equipment, facilities and personnel to the successful vendor as contained in the following list:

• Office Space

Four hundred square feet including one conference room seating six, one office for the vendor project manager (100 sq. ft.), desks, chairs as required, a convenience document copier (shared), and one telephone instrument per desk.

• Review of Vendor Deliverables

BB&T shall review, comment and return to the vendor its comments concerning the deliverables, according to the schedule agreed to between the vendor and BB&T, or in five business days from receipt if not so specified.

- **BB&T Key Personnel Access**

The vendor must identify key BB&T personnel who are required for interviews, briefings, etc., within the proposal. BB&T will make every reasonable effort to have these personnel available for reasonable periods of time with 6 business days advance request.

- **Computer Time on BB&T KRV Computers**

BB&T will make computer programming time available to the vendor during normal business hours in a segmented partition at a priority below all BB&T production processing, and at a priority equal to all other BB&T requests for computer processing, limited to six concurrent sessions or jobs.

BB&T will make off-hours computer time for programming and debugging available on an as-available basis. BB&T will allocate test time on the computer in accordance with the BB&T approved test plan submission by the vendor.

Should the vendor require additional services or support, other than that indicated above, these requirements must be identified in Chapter 6 (Issues and Objections) of the management proposal.

4.3 Contract Terms and Conditions

If a contract is to be negotiated with the vendor, the terms and conditions contained in the appended document, BB&T Standard Contract Terms and Conditions will be the basis for the contract.

In the time between vendor notification and contract signing, BB&T and the vendor will enter into negotiations as to the scope and cost of the contract.

BB&T may, at its own initiative, determine to proceed with the work by issuing a *Start of Work Order* contingent upon satisfactory contract negotiation. This start of work order would be to expedite the schedule, will be of limited scope, and will be a limited dollar investment by BB&T.

Should the vendor not wish to engage in such an activity without the execution of a formal contract, this should be specified within Chapter 6.0 of the management proposal. This action will not be prejudicial to the award of a contract to a vendor who options for such a procedure.

The vendor shall be required to post a performance and completion bond for this contract.

4.4 Change Control and Amendments

BB&T does not expect that it will change any requirements that would need contract amendment during this project. Should the vendor identify the need for a change in scope, or BB&T require a change in scope, all changes will be submitted on a Systems Change Request Form (format to be agreed to during contract negotiations) that will be given to the SCA for action.

Only after both parties agree to the change in writing, and the price and schedule associated with the change are agreed, will the SCA issue a Contract Change Order. Until a Contract Change Order has been issued, no vendor work can be started, and if started, will not be compensated by BB&T.

4.5 Payments to Vendors

BB&T will provide progress payments to the vendor only on completion of critical milestones that will be identified in the mutually agreed schedule. BB&T will withhold a final payment of 10% of the contract price for 60 days following completion of parallel operations to ensure all identified bugs and performance tuning have been completed by the vendor, and that all as-built documentation has been delivered and approved.

4.6 Ownership and Works for Hire

BB&T regards the work performed and the deliverables provided to BB&T, to be the sole, exclusive property of BB&T and to be a Work For Hire under existing law. Should the vendor wish to pursue licensing of the BB&T property, the vendor should indicate this in Chapter 9.0 of the management proposal.

5.0 RULES FOR VENDOR'S RESPONSE

This section contains guidance for the vendor in preparing proposals.

5.1 Adherence to Rules and Formats

It is mandatory that the rules established in the RFP Guidance Document and the formats required in Section 6 and its Exhibits be strictly followed. BB&T has established an elaborate, consistent and fair evaluation methodology that ensures each vendor will receive a thorough review of his submission when the rules and formats are followed. Any vendor not following the formats in structure and intent will be rejected for cause.

5.2 Page Limited Proposals

It is not BB&T's intent to limit the amount of material that the vendor provides within each submitted document. Nevertheless, voluminous materials not pertinent to the exact work package deliverable can only impair the value of the vendor's proposal. BB&T recommends judicious prudence by the vendor in restraining his proposal to excel in quality, rather than quantity of presentation material.

5.3 Delivery Conditions

All proposal documentation must be physically delivered to the BB&T systems contract administrator no later than 4:00 P.M. on the date specified in the transmittal letter.

A total of five (5) bound or loose-leaf copies of each of the vendor's proposals and other documents are to be submitted, not combined into sets.

5.4 Vendor Proprietary Information

The vendor will clearly mark on each and every page of the proposal those contents considered proprietary. However, BB&T need not protect information labeled as proprietary should it be available in the public domain or obtained from other legitimate sources.

BB&T will treat all vendor submissions to this request for proposal with the same degree of confidentiality and secrecy that it uses in its internal controls of confidential information. This includes: physical security in a secure container, limitation of access to this information by the personnel of BB&T with a need to know, and maintenance of traceable records of personnel with access to the information contained within the proposal.

BB&T expects that the vendors will maintain the same degree of confidentiality with respect to its request for proposal.

5.5 Vendor Personnel

The vendor agrees that all personnel assigned to work on this contract will be full-time, permanent employees of the vendor. Furthermore, the vendor shall ensure that each employee is bonded, and that the vendor shall provide a performance bond for his work equal to two times the value of the contract.

5.6 Subcontractors

BB&T will not authorize the use of subcontractors or consultants by the vendor at any time during this contract.

5.7 Vendor Requirements Upon BB&T

From time to time in order to execute the terms of the contract, the vendor is required to obtain documentation from other vendors (namely, computer manufacturers or other distributors of equipment). In addition, US Government publications or references may be useful or necessary in completing work. BB&T assumes no responsibility in providing the vendor with any documentation of this nature and all needs of this kind must have been considered within the vendor's proposals.

Should the vendor have the need for any other services or customer furnished items, they should be specified in Chapter 6.0 of the management proposal.

5.8 Project Management Process

At a minimum the vendor will use appropriate project management and scheduling tools necessary to control the development and coordinate the activities of the parties. BB&T will evaluate these tools as part of the evaluation of management capabilities and processes in Work Package 1 of the management proposal.

The project will be scheduled in phases according to the schedule to be negotiated. The phases for this project will correspond to the sequence specified in the work packages, Exhibit 9-1 included herein. There shall be no deviation from Exhibit 9-1.

5.9 Project Schedule

To assure uniformity in the comparative analysis of schedules, the vendor shall use a project start date of September 29th for his schedule proposal.

BB&T will conduct major reviews of project status and milestone completion during the project to confirm the appropriate progress. These milestones will be identified in the vendor's management proposal. Milestone completion, deliverables approvals and progress payments will be directly linked.

In addition to the above, the BB&T project manager will conduct weekly status review meetings with vendor project management. These status reviews will normally require an hour and will include at a minimum the following:

- Cost review (to whatever detail necessary)

- Personnel Tasking, Issues

EXHIBIT 9-1

BB&T WORK PACKAGES FOR THE BITS SYSTEM

1.0 Project Management & Administration
1.1 Organization, Personnel & Controls
1.2 Scheduling of Work
1.3 Contracts Administration & Change Management
1.4 Client Reporting
1.5 Deliverables Production

2.0 Systems Analysis
2.1 KRV Computer Capacity Analysis
2.2 KRV Computer Performance Analysis
2.3 System Performance Analysis
    2.3.1 Personal Loans Perf. Analysis
    2.3.2 Student Loans Perf. Analysis
    2.3.3 Home Loans Perf. Analysis
    2.3.4 Checking Accounts Perf. Analysis
    2.3.5 Term Deposits Perf. Analysis
    2.3.6 Savings Deposits Perf. Analysis
    2.3.7 Credit Card Processing
2.4 Interface Performance Analysis
    2.4.1 General Ledger Interface Perf. Analysis
    2.4.2 Income & Expense Accounting Interface Performance Analysis
    2.4.3 Central Liability Interface Perf. Analysis
    2.4.4 Customer Profitability Interface Performance Analysis
2.5 Total System Performance Analysis
2.6 System Reliability Analysis
2.7 System Security and Audit Analysis
2.8 System Analysis Deliverables

3.0 Systems Design
3.1 Personal Loans Module Design
3.2 Student Loans Module Design
3.3 Home Loans Module Design
3.4 Checking Accounts Module Design
3.5 Term Deposits Module Design
3.6 Savings Deposits Module Design
3.7 Credit Card Processing Module Design
3.8 Audit Tracking and Reporting Module Design

4.0 Coding, Debug & Unit Testing
4.1 Personal Loans Module Design
4.2 Student Loans Module Design
4.3 Home Loans Module Design
4.4 Checking Accounts Module Design
4.5 Term Deposits Module Design
4.6 Savings Deposits Module Design
4.7 Credit Card Processing Module Design
4.8 Audit Tracking and Reporting Module Design

5.0 Interface Testing
5.1 General Ledger Interface Testing
5.2 Income & Expense Accounting Interface Testing
5.3 Central Liability Interface Testing
5.4 Customer Profitability Interface Testing

6.0 Integration Testing
6.1 System Timeline Testing
6.2 Integration of General Ledger with all Modules
6.3 Integration of Accounting System / all Modules
6.4 Integration of Central Liability / Loan Modules
6.5 Integration of Customer Profitability / all Modules
6.6 Input-Output Controls & Audit Tracking Testing
6.7 Integration Testing Deliverables

7.0 Data Conversion
7.1 Loan Operations Data Conversion
7.2 Deposit Operations Data Conversion
7.3 Credit Card Operations Data Conversion
7.4 Checking Accounts Data Conversion
7.5 Data Conversion Verification
7.6 Data Conversion and Database Deliverables

8.0 Acceptance Testing
8.1 Systems Test Plan
8.2 Systems Test Procedures & Script
8.3 Database Verification Testing
8.4 Acceptance Test Criteria & Data
8.5 Systems Acceptance Test, Results & Reports

9.0 Cutover & Parallel
9.1 Loan Operations Cutover & Parallel
9.2 Credit Card Operations Cutover & Parallel
9.3 Checking Account Operations Cutover & Parallel
9.4 Deposit Operations Cutover & Parallel
9.5 Operations Acceptance

10.0 Operations Support
10.1 Software Maintenance Support
10.2 Database Support
10.3 Operational Procedures Support

- Coordination Issues and Plans

- Interfaces and Operational Plans

- Schedule Adherence and Plans

- Technical Progress

The vendor will provide other written reports as necessary to assist in monthly updates for BB&T's senior management.

6.0 FORMAT AND CONTENT OF VENDOR RESPONSE

The primary objective of BB&T is to evaluate all proposals from a single reference point. This requires that competing submissions be structured according to a standard format, the Work Package.

There shall be three physical proposals submitted: a Technical Proposal, a Management Proposal and a Cost Proposal. A fourth document called the Design Concept Document, described below, is optional.

In addition a Company Supplementary Document may be included, which may contain reference materials, corporate information and other such materials which may be of a clarifying nature concerning the company, only if a material change has occurred to the vendor's technical, management, personnel or financial status in the last 90 days. A statement describing the essence of the changes must be added to Chapter 9.0 of the management proposal. If included, this supplementary document <u>will not be used to evaluate the vendor's proposal</u>.

6.1 Statement of Work

The Statement of Work is the generic statement from which a contract will be executed. The Statement of Work (SOW) will be organized by work packages. The SOW will be included as the first chapter in the management proposal.

The vendor will, by reference, incorporate the work effort and specifications contained in the technical, management and cost proposals into the SOW. Where there are limitations on level of effort or constraints on bounds of the vendor's performance, these must be clearly specified in the proposal.

6.2 Work Packages

The standard management and evaluation tool used by BB&T is the Work Package (WP). The work packages applicable to this project are contained as Exhibit 9-1 of this RFP guidance document. All technical, management and cost proposals must be organized according to the work packages specified in Exhibit 9-1. Definitions of the contents of each work package are contained in Appendix B of this RFP.

6.3 Vendor Deliverables

A listing and description of the Deliverables that the vendor will be providing during the contract will be included in Chapter 3.0 following the SOW and the management work packages in the management proposal. The deliverables identified in Exhibit 8-12 shall constitute the minimum deliverables.

6.4 Technical Proposal

The technical proposal will provide a detailed description of the vendor's solution to the technical, performance and operational specifications. The solution to be implemented must respond to the requirements as specified the Systems Requirements Specification, the Interface Specifications or in this RFP guidance document as applicable. The technical proposal will be subdivided and organized by work packages as shown in Exhibit 9-1.

6.5 Management Proposal

The management proposal will describe the methodology that the vendor will use to implement the technical effort. Since each kind of effort requires somewhat different management techniques, the management proposal effort supportive of the technical solution will be organized by work packages corresponding to Exhibit 9-1.

The management proposal shall include all descriptive information to deliver the completed project to BB&T, and will be organized according to the format and contents of Table 9-1.

6.6 Cost Proposal

The Cost Proposal will contain three chapters. Chapter 1 will contain a single page summary cost table by major work package, and any additional costs not included within a work package. The total cost of all work packages and the grand total will be provided.

Chapter 2 will contain the detailed costs for each work package. The work packages for which detailed cost data is required are listed in Exhibit 9-1. Each work package task, sub-task and sub-sub-task will contain a separately priced level of activity that includes one column for vendor technical effort and one for management effort.

Chapter 3 will list all vendor personnel to be assigned to the project, their labor grades and titles (e.g., systems analyst; librarian) and their billing rate per hour. Alternately, the vendor may list actual salaries plus benefits actually paid per individual, plus the vendor's profit. Overhead is included in work package #1 and therefore, cannot be included in compensation information. Chapter 3 will also include a section describing in detail any supplemental costs not included within the work packages and the rationale why BB&T should pay for them.

TABLE 9-1
FORMAT OF THE MANAGEMENT PROPOSAL

CHAPTER	TITLE	DISCUSSION OF CONTENTS
1.0	Statement of Work	Contains the vendor's SOW which incorporates all work packages (WP).
2.0	Management Proposal Work Packages	Contains the work packages describing the management effort of the vendor to deliver the project, according to the WP format provided by BB&T.
3.0	Deliverables	Describes the vendor's deliverables and incorporates examples by reference which shall be appended separately.
4.0	Schedule	Provides the vendor's detailed proposed schedule, and discusses differences between BB&T's proposed schedule and the vendor's.
5.0	Standards	Describes the vendor's standards and processes for developing documents/ codes, and compares the vendor's standards with BB&T's and makes the recommendation as to which to use. Incorporates by reference, vendor documents that have been prepared to the vendor's standards if they are selected.
6.0	Issues and Objections	Contains any items the vendor has flagged as a result of considering BB&T's requirements (technical or contractual) and which the vendor requires to be resolved prior to the start of work.
7.0	Resumes	Contains the resumes and job function and responsibility to be taken by each of the vendor's key personnel assigned to the project by Work Package.
8.0	Requirements Traceability Matrices	Contains the Requirements Traceability Matrices required by BB&T to track conformity of the vendor's proposal to BB&T's requirements.
9.0	Vendor's Chapter	Contains any other information, discussion or documentation that the vendor is required to, or wishes to address.

6.7 Requirements Traceability

The vendor will submit two Requirements Traceability Matrices (RTMs) which will be included in Chapter 8 of the management proposal. One RTM will match each section and page of the Technical, Management, and Cost Proposals with each requirement specified in this RFP Guidance Document, the Systems Requirements Specification or the Interface Specifications as applicable. Every Requirement must be matched by a corresponding proposal section.

The second RTM named a Cross-Correlation Requirements Traceability Matrix will list each Section of the above Specifications and then the corresponding pages of the Technical, Management and Cost Proposals. The formats for the RTMs will be as depicted in Exhibits 8-16 and 8-17.

6.8 Design Concept Document

A Design Concept Document is an optional submittal, and is a part of the proposal in which the vendor may present his ideas and technological solutions in a manner and format in which he is most comfortable. The purpose of the design concept document is to provide BB&T nontechnical personnel with a clear understanding of the technological solution proposed by the vendor in the vendor's own terms, if the vendor feels that including a design concept may improve BB&T's understanding of their design. The design concept document is not a specification, and will not be evaluated or included in the contract. It will be used only as a descriptive addendum tool to the specifications.

## Chapter Ten

EVALUATE THE VENDOR PROPOSALS

CREATE THE EVALUATION METHODOLOGY

You've delivered the RFPs, and while the proposals are being prepared, there is still much to do. In Chapter 4 we deferred presenting a specific vendor evaluation methodology, so we'll need to develop one here. This chapter is the most important one in the book, because it validates all the good work you've done up to here, by ensuring that you do indeed select the best vendor. The many exhibits will require study to get the most out of this chapter.

EVALUATION WORK FLOW

We know that the result of the evaluation process will be the writing of a vendor evaluation report and a recommendation to management on the best vendor. Therefore, the evaluation should follow a process that ensures this is where the evaluation will lead. This would be a good time to revisit Chapter 4 and review the Evaluation Hierarchy, Evaluation Panel composition, the Review Panels and the Vendor Evaluation Report.

Exhibit 10-1 provides a flow chart that will serve as a frame of reference for the following discussion.

The vendors' proposals are evaluated with three distinct evaluation paths, technical, management and cost, as shown in the three top sets of boxes in row 1 in Exhibit 10-1. The evaluators of each proposal may be the same persons or different persons. For convenience, we've shown these as different persons (#1 through #18) in row 2. Each evaluator evaluates each vendor in turn (rows 2 and 3), and then prepares a summary for each vendor (row 4). The individual vendor evaluations are then combined into a composite summary for each category of evaluation (row 5). Finally, the three categories are combined to give a composite comparison among all vendors (row 6). This chapter describes in detail how this work flow leads to the effective selection of the best vendor.

EXHIBIT 10-1

EVALUATION WORK FLOW

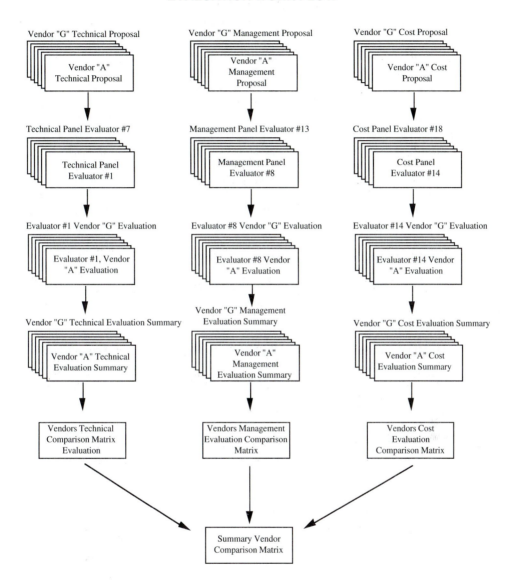

SELECTING THE EVALUATION PANELS

In Chapter 4 we discussed some aspects of panel composition and responsibilities, without analyzing too deeply what the professional capabilities and talents of the members of the panels should be.

Technical Panel

What kind of distribution of talent would contribute to the best evaluation? Some expertise you may find valuable to include on your technical panel are the following:

- Application specialists are required with expertise in the software to be developed. These are the experts who will be the primary judge of whether the vendor's system will meet the requirements. It is understandable that the technical panel should have several application specialists to ensure the most thorough evaluation.

- A specialist (systems engineer) in the operating system of the computer, including memory management, input/output processing, paging, queues, and system overhead affecting the application systems design; and application systems design which may impact operating system overhead.

  There are many instances in software systems development where application systems are completed, only to find that when the full transaction load is processed, the computer can't meet performance (timeliness) requirements. A major insurance company developed a complex applications system, only to discover they would need to spend $15 million more for computer equipment to process the load. They canceled the project and returned to older systems.

  The systems engineer evaluates the proposals from the perspective of his or her experience, challenging every processing function to determine if the computer will process the vendor's system.

- Since systems now serve geographically remote users, a telecommunications specialist with knowledge of transmission bandwidth options, equipment timing delays and teleprocessing throughput analysis, should analyze the proposals to ensure that terminal users at remote locations will have the response times they require.

- Accounting/audit experts evaluate proposals looking for threat models for security breaches, accounting errors, and adequacy of problem and error reports and batch totals, to ensure that the application meets with audit requirements.

- An industrial engineer work flow specialist can review the proposals to see if the man-machine interface proposed by the vendor results in efficient work flow and paper flow if non-computer-processable input or output requires further processing.

- A database expert can analyze proposals for the efficient use of files, their data integrity, structure and compatibility with other files in the system.

- A test engineer can evaluate proposals with testing requirements in mind.

     Depending upon the system to be implemented, other experts should be included on the panel to provide their input.

Management Panel

The principal requirement for membership on the management panel should be managerial experience. The membership should have a broad background in project management, since different experiences can offer excellent examples on whether a vendor's project can be delivered with the management controls, personnel and tools proposed.

- Project control specialists often help the management panel to review schedules and management control systems for reasonableness and effectiveness.

- Industrial engineers focus on the project's process of management to visualize work force loading effectiveness, expense management, and quality controls over the technical effort.

- The systems contract administrator must be a member of this panel because of his role in contract performance.

Cost Panel

Just as for the management panel, the principal criterion for membership on the cost panel should be managerial experience. Only persons who have budgeted and paid bills can understand the value of labor effort connected to deliverables. Many, if not all the cost panel members, will also serve on the management panel.

- The systems contract administrator; must be a member of this panel because of his role in project control and progress payments.

- Financial analysts can often provide various calculations on cost effectiveness in support of the cost proposal evaluation effort.

Fred and Ulrich's early request for additional technical and business analysts was prudent. It allowed the managers of the persons requested to participate in the evaluation, to plan for their absence from normal duties during the evaluation period. The evaluators are identified at the bottom of Table 4-1.

TRAINING THE EVALUATION PANELS

With all this expertise assembled, why should these panels require any training? If the work of the evaluation panels is to be completed in the scheduled fourteen calendar days, there must be an efficiency about the evaluation process. Otherwise, managing the opinions of a herd of evaluators will be chaotic. The training of evaluation panels involves nothing more than perhaps a week of collective meetings and individual readings.

The objective of the training activity is to have all evaluators do their evaluation from the same perspective. This is the same as "singing from the same page of the hymnal." While a diversity of experience is necessary to do a good vendor evaluation, a "loose cannon" or "prima donna" with their own views of the process cannot be tolerated.

- A reading of the Vendor Evaluation Policy should be the first task assigned to the panel members. They will then understand the end of the process they are trying to support, so they can focus their efforts on reaching that stage.

- Each panel member should be familiar with the functional requirements, so that the business issues can form the background perspective on why detailed technical requirements exist to begin with. When you understand the business issues, you can identify excessive technical designs when not required. The business component may not need the elegant solution nor wish to pay for it.

- Since the vendor will deliver a solution in response to the requirements, a full comprehension of the Requirements Specification and the Interface Specifications is mandatory for each panel member. We recommend that the systems analysts who had the responsibility for writing the requirements documents take the lead in explaining various requirements to the panel members.

- Finally each panel member should read the RFP Guidance Document to understand the ground rules under which the vendors are delivering their proposals. If you evaluate proposals frequently, you'll probably know the RFP Guidance Document from memory.

- The concept of the "Fully Acceptable Response" should then be established by the accountable executive or panel committee chairman.

The concept of the Fully Acceptable Response has its basis in an understanding that every person brings his own experience, biases, frame of reference, and level of expectation to what he observes or reads. Without some common frame of reference, two persons reading the same material can have vastly different opinions about the merit of the material. There will be differences among the panel members in any event. It is desirable to have these differences channeled and narrowed.

A *Fully Acceptable Response* is defined to be that response, by any vendor, that minimally meets the requirements for that function or deliverable. A Fully Acceptable Response, a *Fully Satisfactory Solution*, or a *Minimally Acceptable Response* are identical. Everyone will have a slightly different idea of what constitutes fully acceptable, but everyone can agree, that there is some minimal solution that does meet the requirement. If a minimally acceptable solution can be assigned the midpoint in a range of possible values (say a score of five), then better or worse proposals can be graded on the deviation from what is fully acceptable.

This fully satisfactory approach is in contrast to many evaluations that start from a floor of a zero score, thus allowing infinite gradation from the totally unacceptable.

The panel chairman should hold a session in which the panel should try to speculate about what will constitute a minimally satisfactory solution to each requirement. Although the participants will not have a clear idea of the exact solution proposed (If they did, they would develop the system themselves.), they will converge on a common level of expectation of what is minimally satisfactory. Having established mutual agreement on what constitutes a minimally satisfactory solution, the panel members will get a higher degree of consensus on the truly good proposals and the truly poor ones.

> A minimally satisfactory solution is, by definition, a fully satisfactory solution.

> A fully satisfactory solution is the standard upon which other more, or less elegant, solutions are compared.

The beauty of comparing the solutions of other vendors against a vendor proposal considered to be fully satisfactory in whole or in part, is that the cost effectiveness of the solutions, or the cost versus elegance can be quantitatively measured. In other words, not only does the technical solution sort itself out by the fully satisfactory definition, but the cost of the solution can also be measured from a norm.

PREPARATION OF THE EVALUATOR'S "TOOL KIT"

Since the vendor evaluation report will be assembled from input from the panel members, make it easy on yourself. Anticipate the need for data to prepare the report by preparing an Evaluator's "Tool Kit."

The *Evaluator's Tool Kit* are those documents, working papers and forms that enable the evaluator to perform his role in the vendor evaluation, and document his results.

Exhibit 10-2 graphically shows the documents that each evaluator requires.

The Requirements Specifications will need to be reproduced so that each evaluator has a copy. The preliminary Requirements Traceability Matrices, and each vendor's version should be handy for quick cross-reference among documents.

Five proposals from each vendor are sufficient, since the reading of each proposal will be rotated among the evaluators (next section).

An evaluation questionnaire should be prepared. The *Evaluation Questionnaire* is a list of questions corresponding to the work packages. The questions relate to the intelligibility, credibility, rationale, and feasibility of the vendor's effort in that work package. The questions will vary by work package and by the kind of system being evaluated.

Exhibit 10-3 contains an example of the type of questions that might be relevant to the Systems Analysis Work Package featured earlier in Exhibit 8-10.

The principal benefit of the questionnaire is that it creates a concentrated focus of skepticism about each vendor's proposal. This skepticism helps to ensure that only those vendors who can clearly define and explain their solution will receive fully satisfactory evaluations.

EXHIBIT 10-2

THE EVALUATOR'S "TOOL KIT"

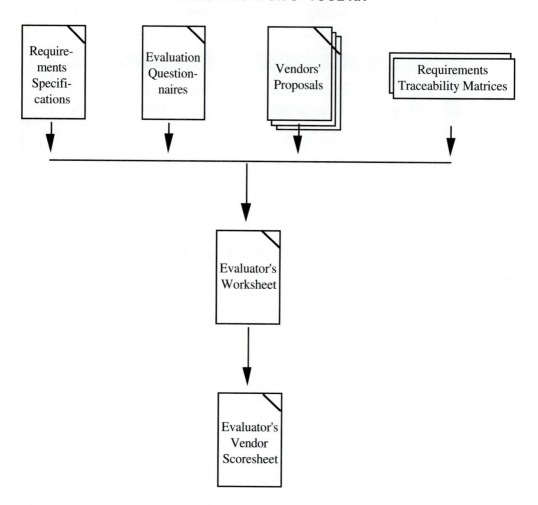

To enable each evaluator to document his rationale for assigning values to the vendor proposals, a standardized *Evaluator's Worksheet* form is prepared, and filled in and scored as the evaluation progresses. As each work package is completed, the evaluator adds the score for that work package to a summary scoresheet for that vendor. When a vendor's proposal has been completed, the evaluator turns in the worksheets and summary to the panel chairman.

Exhibit 10-4 provides a suggested format for the Evaluator's Worksheet. Note that the worksheet can be used for any Category, any vendor or any evaluator.

We'll discuss the filled-in worksheet and the summary scoresheet under Individual Evaluation.

EXHIBIT 10-3

EXCERPT OF A TECHNICAL EVALUATION QUESTIONNAIRE

Work Package: 2.0 Systems Analysis

For this vendor's proposed effort in performing studies, trade-off analyses and systems analysis to predict successful operation of the completed system, has the vendor:

2.1 Hardware Capacity Analysis

- Defined the methodology by which capacity will be determined? Is the method credible?
- Made allowances for changes to the system? Considered the system's interfaces to existing BB&T systems?
- Sized memory, disk storage, tape capacity, or defined a method to validate adequacy of existing equipment?

2.2 Hardware Performance Analysis

- Defined how the performance will be estimated?
- Specified a job mix to measure estimated performance? Is the benchmark reasonable? Credible? Does it correspond to anticipated transaction volume?
- Modeled the performance on the basis of existing customer transaction workloads? On Mimosa Street Banks' service bureau transaction workload?
- Defined or estimated queues? Determined interrupt priorities, or a method to allocate them and adjust when necessary?
- Made reasonable estimates on I/O times, contention? Planned for adequate contingency?
- Made adequate provision for human interaction?
- Done trade studies of requirements against design options to assure best design and performance?
- Done any trade studies which are trite, obvious or superficial?
- Included all system level performance requirements into the hardware performance analysis?
- Included a module-by-module build-up in estimating performance to potentially find a non-conforming module to module performance, or a module to BB&T system interface which is non-conforming?

2.3 System Module Performance Analysis

- Taken each performance requirement for each module and defined how the performance will be estimated? Measured?
- Taken all the requirements and considered them as a whole in establishing a module level estimate of performance?
- Defined I/O options for analysis based on feeder modules or interfacing systems?
- Determined how transaction calculation accuracy will be measured?
- Determined how each transaction batch will have traps for audit? Assessed the performance impact of audit and control logic? Done trade studies to minimize performance impact?

·

·

·

(etc.)

EXHIBIT 10-4

EVALUATOR'S WORKSHEET

Vendor ID: [_____] Category: [____] Technical: [____] Management: [____] Cost: [____]

Evaluator ID: [____] Work Package: [_____]

Work Package Sub-element	Vendor Proposal Page Number	Requirements Reference	Comments (Use Questionnaire)

Work Package: [_____] Work Package Raw Score: [_____]

FINAL PLANS

A few days before the proposals are due, the panel chairman should check that the rooms reserved for the evaluation are equipped with the appropriate amenities and essentials.

Each panel member should know where to go when the evaluation is to start. Each should have an assigned desk or table. Since by this time, the vendors that will not provide a proposal have identified themselves, the panel chairman can now assign the schedule for reading the proposals.

Ulrich Schmidt knows the panel membership. If he takes the names in the order listed in Table 4-1, and assigns a number to each, he will have a corresponding Evaluator # ID for each person (refer to row two, Exhibit 10-1). Table 10-1 shows the results of Ulrich's assignment.

TABLE 10-1
EVALUATOR'S ASSIGNMENTS AND ID

TECHNICAL PANEL	ID#	MANAGEMENT PANEL	ID#	COST PANEL	ID#
Ulrich Schmidt	1	Ulrich Schmidt	1	Ulrich Schmidt	1
Peyton Somers	2	Peyton Somers	2	Peyton Somers	2
Rip Scali	3	Rip Scali	3	Rip Scali	3
Tony Scerbo	4	Tony Scerbo	4	Tony Scerbo	4
Walt Smerski	5	Walt Smerski	5	Walt Smerski	5
Alvin Eberhardt	6	Monk Eternic	9	Monk Eternic	9
Dwayne Eber	7	Toshio Sumizaki	10	Toshio Sumizaki	10
Dmitri Sorjak	8	Roger Eilinger	11	Peijun Shun	12

There are twelve evaluators in total. As is evident, some evaluators (the more senior personnel) evaluate all proposals, while the other panel members evaluate only those categories pertinent to their expertise.

Seven vendors informed Monk that they would submit proposals to BB&T. Dogmatic Systems (Table 7-1) declined because they were being acquired by Big Systems Corp. and couldn't spare the management time. Killian Data Systems declined because of the founder's illness. Ulrich then assigned the vendors codes as follows:

Advanced Systems International	*VA*
Better Beta Systems	*VB*
Convulsive Transactions Inc.	*VC*
Ergonomic Transaction Systems	*VE*

Fleece Banking Systems   VF

Grand Systems Designs   VG

Howitzer Retail Systems   VH

Ulrich then completed a more detailed schedule for the evaluation to make certain that each panel member would work with the utmost urgency. Table 10-2 shows his timetable for the first fifteen days of the evaluation period. .

The schedule in Table 10-2 is ambitious. If you assume a technical proposal will average 100 pages, a management proposal about 40, and a cost proposal 15 pages, then a total of 155 pages times seven vendors is plenty of material to read, review and comment upon.

TABLE 10-2
EVALUATION PANEL SCHEDULE

Days from:	Activity
0	Vendor proposals received.
1-5	Review 1-2 technical proposals per day.
6	Technical panel consensus review.
7	Technical commentary and scoring revisions completed.
8	Chairman summarizes technical scoring & results.
8-9	Management panel reviews four proposals per day.
10	Management panel consensus review.
11	Management commentary and scoring revisions.
10-11	Cost panel reviews four proposals per day.
12	Cost panel consensus review.
12	Cost commentary and scoring revisions.
13	Comparison review of all vendors and all categories.
14	Sensitivity and risk analysis.
14	Chairman and panels select best vendor.
15	Chairman provides overview to advisory committee.

There is a shortcut that can relieve the burden: quickly identify any proposal that is clearly non-responsive, nonconforming or just extremely poor. Part of the first day could be used for such scanning. If you can eliminate one or two proposals (but provide substantiating documented justification) you have more time to review the quality proposals. The other alternative is to work 12 hour days. This seems to be the norm in vendor evaluations.

Note that Ulrich allocated five days to reading the technical proposals. In such a period of time, even with documented worksheets, the evaluator can be dazed by the sheer volume of information. One vendor seems like the one just reviewed. When the evaluator gets to the last proposal, he has learned a lot from the previous ones. He will subconsciously favor the latter proposals, for that early skepticism will be dissipated. (This is similar to the judging process in Olympic Ice-Skating or Gymnastics where there is a built-in bias in favor of the last competitor.) If every evaluator followed the same sequence of reading, the entire evaluation could be subconsciously skewed. Therefore, the sequence of reading of the vendor proposals should be randomized among the evaluators to eliminate sequential bias.

Exhibit 10-5 provides an example of how Ulrich Schmidt might structure a reviewing sequence for the evaluators reading the technical proposals. Similar sequencing would be done for the management and cost proposals.

EXHIBIT 10-5

READING SEQUENCE OF VENDOR TECHNICAL PROPOSALS

Vendor ID

Evaluator ID	VA	VB	VC	VE	VF	VG	VH
#1	1	2	3	4	5	6	7
#2	2	3	4	5	6	7	1
#3	3	4	5	6	7	1	2
#4	6	2	7	1	4	3	5
#5	4	6	1	7	2	5	3
#6	5	4	3	2	1	7	6
#7	6	5	4	3	2	1	7
#8	7	6	5	4	3	2	1

Evaluators are to read the proposals in the sequence indicated in their row.

CREATE A METHOD TO COMPARE VENDORS QUANTITATIVELY

Although the evaluators' comments are the definitive assessment of the vendors' proposals, a mathematical computation has traditionally been used to provide a numeric (or graphic) comparison among vendors. This section presents a rigorous and consistent mathematical framework for finding the best vendor. The methodology should be used as described, without option or deviation.

CATEGORY PERCENTILE CONTRIBUTION (CPC)

We previously defined an intrinsic requirement for a customized system. This requirement expressed that the technical, management and cost contributions to the system all had to be acceptable. Technical, Management, and Cost are named evaluation "Categories."

To obtain a definitive comparative final score among vendors, we assign each Category a percentage contribution, equivalent to the importance of that Category relative to the other Categories. The sum of the contributions from the Categories will add to 100% of a vendor's score.

Then we can show that if:

VG = Vendor "G" (for example).

T_{VG} = Total Technical Score for Vendor G.

M_{VG} = Total Management Score for Vendor G.

C_{VG} = Total Cost Score for Vendor G.

T_{PC} = Percentage Contribution for the Technical Proposal expressed as a decimal fraction.

M_{PC} = Percentage Contribution for the Management Proposal expressed as a decimal fraction.

C_{PC} = Percentage Contribution for the Cost Proposal expressed as a decimal fraction.

$100\% = T_{PC} + M_{PC} + C_{PC}$ (definition).

Then Vendor G's (VG) total score is:

$$VG = (T_{PC} \times T_{VG}) + (M_{PC} \times M_{VG}) + (C_{PC} \times C_{VG})$$

If we decide that the technical proposal should be worth 65% of the total percentage contribution while the management proposal is 20%, and the cost proposal is 15%, the above equations would be:

$$100\% = 65\% + 20\% + 15\%$$

$$VG = (0.65 \times T_{VG}) + (0.20 \times M_{VG}) + (0.15 \times C_{VG})$$

Identical expressions would apply for vendors VA, VB, VC, etc.

Although it seems intuitively right that a purchase of customized technology would allocate the highest percentage for the technical solution, different percentile allocations would apply for different types of procurements.

Exhibit 10-6 provides some examples where different percentile allocations for the Technical, Management or Cost Categories might apply. We do not have space to develop these percentile contribution allocations any further here, but common sense should rule your allocation approach. There are built-in safeguards against unreasonable allocations. These are discussed in the section on sensitivity analysis.

WEIGHT ASSIGNMENT

The score the vendor obtains for any Category before the application of the Category Percentile Contribution needs to be examined next.

Since we've spent so much effort preaching the merits of the work packages, it is obvious that the score the vendor will get is the sum of the scores for each work package.

How do we determine what the work package scores should be? Two concepts apply. First there is the score assigned by the evaluator as he reviews the vendor's work packages. This is defined to be the *"raw score."* We'll discuss this a little later.

Then there is the relative value or *"Weight"* that is applied to each work package relative to the other work packages in that Category. The sum of the weights of the work packages for each Category is equal to 100% of the weights for that Category. The sum of the weights can actually equal any absolute number, as long as all Categories add to the same absolute total for the sum of the weights. Multiplication of all terms in an equation by the same constant (e.g., *100, or *1000) does not change the value of the expression.

Although we've asked the vendors to respond to ten work packages in the case study, nothing forces us to place a value or weight on any work package.

For example, Work Package #10, Operations Support (Exhibit 9-1) comes after the project is essentially over. This package is useful for estimating the cost of future vendor support, but is not critical toward choosing the best system. Therefore, we could assign a zero weight to it.

There are two methods for assigning weights to the work packages. We call these the *"Assigned Weight Method"* and the *"Equal Weight Method."*

Exhibit 10-7 provides an example of how these two methods would be applied. We'll use the highest levels of the work packages from Exhibit 9-1 to illustrate the example.

The *Assigned Weight* method is intuitively the more obvious and comfortable for evaluators. For a systems procurement it is natural that the more important differentiating aspects of a vendor's system design (e.g., WP 3.0) receive more emphasis than other work packages. This is the approach we'll follow here.

However, there are times, particularly when there are a fewer number of work packages, or there are only little differences among the intrinsic importance of the work packages, when an equal weight assignment is as good as any. The benefit of the equal weight assignment method is that there are fewer calculations to make, and sensitivity analyses do not need to be made to the degree found in the assigned weight method. Furthermore, the evaluator's focus is distributed over the entire proposal, not just the "most important" sections. One deficiency is that you may need to plan more carefully on creating equal value (weight) work packages.

EXHIBIT 10-6

CATEGORY PERCENTILE CONTRIBUTIONS FOR A VARIETY OF PROCUREMENT SITUATIONS

Procurement Situation	Technical %	Manage-ment %	Cost %	Comment
Four door sedan	Low	None	High	Cars are technically almost alike.
High-Fi System	High	None	Medium	Quality depends on your budget.
Software for your PC	Medium	None	Medium	Sort of a balance between features and cost.
Recruitment of a new Chief Executive Officer	None	Very high	Low	If the CEO is the best, any salary and bonus price is OK.
Outsourcing your Data Center	Medium	Medium	Medium	Delicate balance required among all categories.
Paper clips	None	None	High	The ultimate commodity.
Electricity	Low	Very high	Low	Service quality is everything. Technical and cost are the same for everyone.

EXHIBIT 10-7

AN EXAMPLE OF WEIGHT ASSIGNMENT METHODS

FOR THE TECHNICAL CATEGORY

WORK PACKAGES		Assigned Weight Method (%)	Equal Weight Method (%)
1.0	Project Management & Administration	5	10
2.0	Systems Analysis	15	10
3.0	Systems Design	40	10
4.0	Coding, Debug and Unit Testing	15	10
5.0	Vendor Interface Testing	5	10
6.0	Integration Testing	5	10
7.0	Conversion of Data	2	10
8.0	Acceptance Testing	8	10
9.0	Cutover and Parallel	5	10
10.0	Operations Support	0	10
Total:		100	100

When we consider the *Assigned Weight* method, the weight assigned to a Work Package within a Category does not have to have the same weight in another Category. Exhibit 10-8 shows how the weight assignment might be distributed within each Category.

Since Work Package 1.0, Project Management and Administration (Exhibit 10-8), has most of the management effort, it is proper that it has a higher weight in the management category than the technical category. But that doesn't mean that it should cost more than a nominal overhead cost of 10-12% of the total project cost.

From here on we'll follow the example of the Technical Category. The Management and Cost Categories follow identical steps, using their assigned symbols and sub-scripts.

The evaluation chairman and accountable executive should prepare the initial weight assignments. In fact, if there were sufficient time earlier, this weighting effort might more properly be done concurrent with completion of the requirements specifications or by the complete panel prior to issuance of the RFP. In practice, there is seldom enough time to do it then.

They will then hold a forum of the evaluation panel, to obtain their input, so that a consensus on the weight to be assigned to each work package can be achieved before the proposals arrive. The participants will allocate weights to the major work package subdivisions first (Exhibit 10-8). Then weights will be further distributed to the next lower level, and if required, to whatever sub-level is necessary to ensure comprehensive review.

For example, in Exhibit 9-1 for the BB&T work packages, the allocation of weights may include individual weights for Work Packages 2.3.1, 2.3.2, 2.3.3, etc. Work Package 3.0, Systems Design, might have weights assigned only to the 3.1, 3.2, 3.3, etc., levels. In any event, the sum of the sub-level weights will be equal to the next higher level assigned weight.

Although the sum of the weights will always equal to 100% of the weight assigned, the actual sum of the weights could be 100, 1000 or even 10,000, if you want to avoid decimal differences. If the sum of the weights for the Technical Category is 1000, then the sums of the Management and Cost Categories must equal 1000 as well. (You've already differentiated among the Categories when you applied the Category Percentile Contribution percentage. Weight assignment is used only within the Category.)

An example of Weight Assignment, where the sum of the weights of the Work Packages for each Category is 1000, is shown in the bottom example of Exhibit 10-8. We will use this alternative.

The mathematical way of expressing the weight assignment for the Technical Category is:

$$W_T = W_{T,WP_1} + W_{T,WP_2} + W_{T,WP_3} + W_{T,WP_4} + \dots \text{ (or)}$$

$$W_T = \sum_1^z W_{T,WP_i}$$

$$100\% = W_T = \sum_1^z W_{T,WP_i}$$

where W_T is the Total Assigned Weight for the Technical Category, W is the weight value for the Work Package, WP_i is the weight assigned to Work Package 1, WP_2, etc., and where the work packages are summed from 1 to z, however many there are.

$W_T = W_M = W_C$ by definition is mandated by the methodology.

EXHIBIT 10-8

EXAMPLE OF ASSIGNED WEIGHTS FOR ALL CATEGORIES

	WORK PACKAGES	Technical (%)	Management (%)	Cost (%)
1.0	Project Management & Admin.	5	30	12
2.0	Systems Analysis	15	5	20
3.0	Systems Design	40	20	25
4.0	Coding, Debug and Unit Testing	15	15	23
5.0	Vendor Interface Testing	5	5	5
6.0	Integration Testing	5	5	5
7.0	Conversion of Data	2	0	0
8.0	Acceptance Testing	8	15	5
9.0	Cutover and Parallel	5	5	5
10.0	Operations Support	0	0	0
	Total:	100	100	100

EXAMPLE OF ALTERNATIVE ASSIGNED WEIGHTS

	WORK PACKAGES	Technical (10*%)	Management (10*%)	Cost (10*%)
1.0	Project Management & Admin.	50	300	120
2.0	Systems Analysis	150	50	200
3.0	Systems Design	400	200	250
4.0	Coding, Debug and Unit Testing	150	150	230
5.0	Vendor Interface Testing	50	50	50
6.0	Integration Testing	50	50	50
7.0	Conversion of Data	20	0	0
8.0	Acceptance Testing	80	150	50
9.0	Cutover and Parallel	50	50	50
10.0	Operations Support	0	0	0
	Total:	1000	1000	1000

Ulrich and the panel have agreed upon the weight assignment shown in the alternative in Exhibit 10-8 where the sum of the weights in each Category equals 1000.

THE SCORING RANGE

If you recall, we discussed the importance of the concept of the *Fully Satisfactory* score in establishing a common understanding among the evaluators. Now let's see what kind of scoring range can be used to evaluate the proposals.

When we speak of "*Score*," we mean the numerical value that corresponds to a judgment of quality placed upon a portion of the vendor's proposal by an evaluator.

Some vendors will provide a design that exceeds the minimum acceptable, while other vendors will fall short of that minimum. It is desirable in evaluating proposals that the scoring system allow for a wide range in the score a vendor might deserve for a work package. On the other hand, a scoring range with tremendous span (e.g., 1 to 100) significantly increases the nuances of a score, without necessarily increasing the accuracy of the score.

> Behavioral psychologists describe a phenomenon called "*The Just Noticeable Difference*." It seems that the human mind has a limited capacity to notice differences, and does so, as much by patterns as by quantification. This differential capacity has been measured to be about 15% before most people will notice and be able to quantify a difference between two items.

On the above basis, a score of 94 versus 96 lacks real meaning, since in terms of our recognition capabilities, it is a difference without a distinction. Yet, we readily comprehend the distinction between a school grade of 95 versus an 80, or an A versus a B. What we need are ways to indicate distinctive differences between vendor's proposals. With this in mind, we can take advantage of our behavioral pattern to create a scoring range that maximizes distinctions. We've identified two options for scoring ranges. One is the "Ternary Range" and the other is the "Gradation Range."

The Ternary Range

With the *Ternary Range*, each work package (or subdivision of a work package) is evaluated as less than satisfactory, fully satisfactory, or better than fully satisfactory.

> Exhibit 10-9 illustrates the definitions that are used in establishing a score using the Ternary Range.

Since ternary means three levels, any range of values could be used for the three numbers. A range of -1, 0, +1 will work, though many people are bothered by negative values, and probably by the realization that a fully satisfactory proposal would receive a net score of zero! A range of 0, +1, +2 rectifies this problem. A range of +1, +5, +9 apparently denotes even greater distinction, but it is psychologically difficult to make a jump in value to +9 for a vendor whose proposal may be only somewhat superior to one who is given a +5. In any event, whatever the number range selected, the difference between score levels is about 50%. This is certainly a "noticeable difference."

We prefer the 0, +1, +2 approach shown in Exhibit 10-9. Using this range, a vendor with a near satisfactory work package will receive a score of +1. Those that are noticeably

EXHIBIT 10-9

THE TERNARY RANGE FOR PROPOSAL SCORING

Evaluator's Judgment:	Definition	Mandated Score
Noticeably Exceeds Satisfactory	The vendor's response to the requirement and work package provides a capability that exceeds satisfactory in an outstanding manner.	**+2**
Fully Satisfactory	The vendor's response fully meets, almost meets or just barely exceeds the minimum acceptable response.	**+1**
Noticeably Less Than Fully Satisfactory	The vendor's response is deficient in a sufficient number of characteristics that it is noticeably below the minimum acceptable.	**0**

Notes to Evaluators:
1. No scores other than the mandated scores are permitted.
2. For each score in a work package, a set of comments justifying your score, and a reference to the vendor's proposal section are required on your worksheet.

better receive a +2, and the noticeably inferior a zero.

The ternary range has the salient value that it is simple. Once the concept of fully satisfactory or equivalently, minimally satisfactory is grasped, the evaluation process can be accelerated. Outstanding proposals are quickly recognized, as are the poor ones. The ternary range eliminates the need to distinguish quantitatively among small differences. It has the deficiency that if the proposals are very competitive, making a decision of the best vendor based on a small difference in numerical rating is intuitively unsatisfactory and not obvious. (Which is why we use commentaries as the primary differentiating factor in evaluations.)

We've used the ternary range satisfactorily in evaluating fourteen vendors offering to supply satellite transmission facilities. Since the Cost Category was the most important, it was easy to bracket the cost proposal with this simple method. We recommend you try this approach with a simple procurement and see how useful it can be.

The Gradation Range
Using the principle of Just-Noticeable-Difference, a scoring range having approximately 15% difference between scoring levels can be created. This is called the *Gradation Range*.

Exhibit 10-10 illustrates the definitions and the scores to be assigned using the gradation range.

You'll notice that the scoring ranges are not equally spaced, but scatter on either side of a score of 5 that is defined to be fully satisfactory. A favorable score of 6 and a slightly deficient score of 4 are a little closer to fully satisfactory than better or worse scores. Making an exact 15% difference (e.g., 3.5 and 6.5) doesn't seem worth the effort or preci-

EXHIBIT 10-10

THE GRADATION RANGE FOR PROPOSAL SCORING

Evaluator's Judgment:	Definition	Mandated Score
Outstanding	The vendor's response to the requirement and work package provides a capability that exceeds satisfactory in an outstanding manner.	**10**
Superior	The vendor's response significantly exceeds a fully satisfactory response.	**8**
Good	The vendor's response is somewhat better than what would be fully satisfactory.	**6**
Fully Satisfactory	The vendor's response fully meets, but does not exceed the minimum acceptable response. Included in this score would be alternative solutions proposed which may have been unanticipated, but which nevertheless solve the requirement.	**5**
Adequate/Fair	The vendor's response does not meet the minimum satisfactory solution, but can be rectified, or a work-around can be devised.	**4**
Inadequate	The vendor's response is not satisfactory, and significant difficulty would be encountered in employing a work-around, or in negotiating a suitable alternative solution.	**2**
Unacceptable	The vendor did not respond to the requirement or the solution proposed was totally unacceptable.	**0**

Notes to Evaluators:
1. No scores other than the mandated scores are permitted.
2. For each score in a work package, a set of comments justifying your score, and a reference to the vendor's proposal section are required on your worksheet.

sion. Besides, it is intuitively sensible that a design that can be remedied shouldn't be penalized too much, while one only slightly better than the minimum acceptable shouldn't be rewarded too much either.

It is anticipated that most proposals will be scattered in the 4 to 6 range, with some 2s and some 8s and very few outstanding or unacceptable scores. The distribution might resemble a Gaussian distribution curve centered somewhere near 5. An outstanding vendor will have his distribution of scores centered at a much higher value.

Limiting the number of possible scoring levels to seven (rather than 10 or more), forces the evaluators to validate distinctions between vendors.

If you use the gradation range, and a total weight of 1000 for each Category, then the theoretical maximum score a vendor could obtain would be 10 * 1000 or 10,000 for each Category. If you use the ternary range with a maximum score of +2, then the maximum vendor score with a weight of 1000 per Category would be 2000.

It is possible that using either method of scoring, the differences between vendors may be too close to designate a winner. Then the use of sensitivity analysis (readjusting weights or scores) might indicate a winner. We'll discuss sensitivity analysis later. If sensitivity analysis doesn't work, then you escalate the problem to management. After all, that is why you have an advisory committee and a project review committee. They may need to earn their salaries rather than rubber stamping your recommendation.

DO THE VENDOR EVALUATION

INDIVIDUAL EVALUATION

The big day finally arrives and each member of the evaluation team assembles his tool kit, and begins to read the assigned vendor's proposal. As evaluator #5 (Walt Smerski) reads, he makes notes on his evaluation worksheet. He adds page and section references along with his comments, to be certain that he can substantiate his comments against what the vendor has documented. The traceability matrix furnished by the vendor allows him to correlate the vendor's proposal against the relevant sections of the requirements specifications. Finally, he assigns a score to that work package section.

Exhibit 10-11 contains an example of a completed evaluator's worksheet. We will use the gradation range for the examples that follow.

The evaluator will assign a score based on the credibility of the vendor's response, as stimulated by the questions in the evaluation questionnaire pertinent to that work package. The evaluator doesn't have to comment on everything because an evaluator's "rule" states that the absence of commentary explicitly implies that the vendor's content for that portion of the proposal is fully satisfactory. The evaluator comments only on differences from the satisfactory.

Sometimes comments about why a work package is fully satisfactory will need to be included if the vendor has an unusual feature or design. You can see from the comments in Exhibit 10-11 that questioning of the vendor's analysis is quickly established. The com-

EXHIBIT 10-11

EVALUATOR'S WORKSHEET

Vendor ID: [VF] Category: [ ] Technical: [XXXX] Management: [ ] Cost: [ ]

Evaluator ID: [#5] Work Package: [2.0 Systems Analysis/ 2.1 Hardware]

Work Package Sub-element	Vendor Proposal Page Number	Requirements Reference	Comments (Use Questionnaire)
2.1.01	2.02	2.1.1	Capacity estimates by dynamic memory usage is insufficient. CPU loading does not include monitoring overhead.
2.1.03	2.03	2.1.14	Chose wrong disk drives to model. Didn't read spec?
2.1.05	2.06	2.1.16	Sample size of 400 transactions per batch is too large, but # of batches at 20 per hour is too low by 40. Will they even out? Depends on interfaces output from transaction processing.
2.1.06	2.11	2.1.18	Different style to modeling I/O here, but satisfactory.
2.1.08	2.13	2.1.23	Interface to Accounting system doesn't show how performance can be measured, or even estimated. Where are acct. controls in the transaction performance estimate?

Work Package: [2.1] Work Package Raw Score: [4]

EXHIBIT 10-12

PARTIALLY COMPLETED EVALUATOR'S VENDOR SCORESHEET

Evaluator ID: #5   Vendor ID: VG

Work Package	Description	Assigned Weight	Raw Score
1.0	**Project Management & Administration**	50	N/A
1.1	Organization, Personnel & Controls	20	*6*
1.2	Scheduling of Work	5	*6*
1.3	Contracts Administration & Change Management	5	*4*
1.4	Client Reporting	10	*8*
1.5	Deliverables Production	10	*5*
2.0	**Systems Analysis**	150	N/A
2.1	KRV Computer Capacity Analysis	10	*4*
2.2	KRV Computer Performance Analysis	20	*5*
2.3	System Performance Analysis	10	*6*
2.4	Interface Performance Analysis	30	*6*
2.5	Total System Performance Analysis	30	*6*
2.6	System Reliability Analysis	10	*2*
2.7	System Security and Audit Analysis	20	*2*
2.8	System Analysis Deliverables	20	*5*
3.0	**Systems Design**	400	N/A
3.1	Personal Loans Module Design	50	*8*
3.2	Student Loans Module Design	50	*10*
3.3	Home Loans Module Design	50	*4*
3.4	Checking Accounts Module Design	70	*8*
3.5	Term Deposits Module Design	50	
3.6	Savings Deposits Module Design	50	
3.7	Credit Card Processing Module Design	50	
3.8	Audit Tracking and Reporting Module Design	30	
⋮	⋮	⋮	⋮
8.0	**Acceptance Testing**	80	N/A
8.1	Systems Test Plan	20	
8.2	Systems Test Procedures & Script	10	
8.3	Database Verification Testing	30	
8.4	Acceptance Test Criteria & Data	10	
8.5	Systems Acceptance Test, Results & Reports	10	
9.0	**Cutover & Parallel**	50	N/A
9.1	Loan Operations Cutover & Parallel	10	
9.2	Credit Card Operations Cutover & Parallel	15	
9.3	Checking Account Operations Cutover & Parallel	10	
9.4	Deposit Operations Cutover & Parallel	5	
9.5	Operations Acceptance	10	
10.0	**Operations Support**	0	N/A
10.1	Software Maintenance Support	0	
10.2	Database Support	0	
10.3	Operational Procedures Support	0	
	TOTAL	1000	

ments will be helpful in assisting the evaluator defend his score during the evaluation panel reviews. They will continue to be useful in any requirements revisions, during negotiations to require corrective remedy and in writing the vendor evaluation report.

As the evaluator completes the worksheets for each work package, he fills in the score assigned on an evaluator's vendor scoresheet that he maintains for each vendor.

Exhibit 10-12 contains an example of one page of a completed evaluator's vendor scoresheet.

This Scoresheet corresponds to the work packages for the BITS project, and contains the weight that was assigned for each work package and each sub-work package for the Technical Category by Fred, Ulrich and the panel. Notice that evaluator #5 (Walt Smerski) is finding some significant unevenness in Vendor G's (Grand Systems Designs) proposal. The 2s in WP 2.6-2.7 versus the high marks for 3.1-3.2 are often characteristic of vendors who do not have experience in RFPs that require extensive modeling and analysis, but who have a strong design.

CALCULATING THE VENDOR'S SCORE

The panel chairman posts each evaluator's vendor scoresheet on a Panel Vendor Scoresheet, which is a worksheet on which each evaluator's raw score for each work package is tallied. The Panel Vendor Scoresheet can be one large tally sheet, or several sheets each containing one work package for calculations.

Exhibit 10-13 contains a completed Panel Vendor Scoresheet for Vendor VG for just Work Package 3.0 for the Technical Category. Use the Exhibit to track the mathematical derivation below.

The Panel Vendor Scoresheet is the primary document for calculating the Score T_{VG}. This document is the source document for comparing the differences in how each evaluator considers this vendor. After all of the scores have been posted, they are added across for each work package component. Then the sum is divided by the number of evaluators who scored that work package. This computes the *Average Raw Score*. Then, the average raw score is multiplied by the weight assigned for that work package component to give the score for that work package component. The work package component scores are added to give the work package score for the major work package (in this example WP 3.0).

Mathematically, this would be designated as:

$$\overline{ARS}_{WP_{3.x}} = (RS_1 + RS_2 + RS_3 + \ldots RS_y)_{WP_{3.x}} \div n \text{ (where)}$$

$\overline{ARS}$ = Average Raw Score

$WP_{3.x}$ = Symbolizes that Work Package 3.x, where x (1,2,3, . . . etc.), is the Work Package

being considered, and

RS_1, RS_2, RS_3, etc. = the Raw Scores of Evaluators #1, #2, #3, . . . etc.), and

EXHIBIT 10-13

PANEL VENDOR SCORESHEET

Version # ___1___

Category: [Technical]   Work Package: [3.0]

Vendor ID: [VG]

Evaluator ID:

Work Package	Weight	#1	#2	#3	#4	#5	#6	#7	#8	Total	Average	Vendor's Score
3 Systems Design	**400**											
3.1 Personal Loans Module Design	50	8	6	10	6	8	N/A	6	4	48	6.9	342.9
3.2 Student Loans Module Design	50	8	6	10	6	10	N/A	8	4	52	7.4	371.4
3.3 Home Loans Module Design	50	5	5	8	5	4	N/A	10	4	41	5.9	292.9
3.4 Checking Accounts Module Design	70	8	6	8	8	8	6	8	2	54	6.8	472.5
3.5 Term Deposits Module Design	50	8	6	8	6	6	6	6	5	51	6.4	318.8
3.6 Savings Deposits Module Design	50	6	5	8	6	8	6	6	4	49	6.1	306.3
3.7 Credit Card Processing Module Design	50	4	5	6	5	6	5	5	5	41	5.1	256.3
3.8 Audit Tracking and Report Module Design	30	10	6	10	8	8	8	8	5	63	7.9	236.3

Individual's Average | 7.1 | 5.6 | 8.5 | 6.3 | 7.3 | 6.2 | 7.1 | 4.1 | | | 6.5 |

Vendor's WP Score: ___2597___

n=the total number of evaluators of that work package.

Then to calculate the work package sub-component score for vendor VG for the technical category (T and VG subscripts assumed throughout):

$$T_{WP_{3.x}} = \overline{ARS}_{WP_{3.x}} \times W_{WP_{3.x}}$$

And the sum of all the component Work Packages of Work Package 3.0 for example, would be:

$$T_{WP_3} = \Sigma \, (\overline{ARS}_{WP_{3.i}} \times W_{WP_{3.i}})$$ where 3.i is summed from 1 through however many sub-components the work package may have.

When all work packages have been completely scored, the vendor's score for the technical category T will be:

$$T_{WP} = \Sigma \, (T_{WP_i})$$ where **i** is summed from 1 to z (or as many as there are) work packages.

The use of the averaged raw score has a significant benefit to the evaluation process. In the event that there was some very specialized technical area that needed to be reviewed (e.g., computer operating system issues), an expert could be brought in to evaluate only those sections pertinent to his expertise. He or she would not be burdened with evaluating every work package. Averaging the scores avoids skewing the evaluation due to differences in the number of evaluators.

> In Exhibit 10-13 Evaluator #6 (Alvin Eberhardt) had a plumbing leak in his house on the day he was to evaluate Work Packages 3.1-3.3. Rather than delay the evaluation, he just skipped them. The results were not materially affected by his absence.
>
> You can see that when you average, it's important to have enough evaluators evaluating each work package so that you can obtain a reasonable sample of opinion. We think that number should be at least five. Therefore, the original panel staffing level of 7-8 will provide adequate representation should some evaluators need to be excused temporarily.

PANEL REVIEW MEETINGS

The panel chairman collects the Evaluator's Vendor Scoresheets, copies the data onto the Panel Vendor Scoresheet and does the calculations indicated in Exhibit 10-13 to calculate the vendor's score for each work package. On the sixth day, according to the schedule in Table 10-2, all of the technical evaluations should have been completed, and the Technical Evaluation Panel meets to review the results.

Each work package is reviewed in turn for consensus among the panel. Using the commentaries they wrote, each vendor is discussed in turn for strengths, weaknesses, areas for improvement and closeness to the ideal solution. The combined panel essentially creates a composite profile for each work package for each vendor. While the discussion is going on, the panel chairman uses the Panel Vendor Scoresheet to check for significant differences of opinion among panel members.

For example in Exhibit 10-13, Evaluator #3, Rip Scali, has given vendor VG scores that are a significant difference above the panel average: 8.5 vs. an average of 6.5. Similarly, Evaluator #8, Dmitri Sorjak, has given the same vendor an average score of 4.1, far below the panel average.

When significant differences do occur between either average scores or individual scores for a particular work package component, the persons differing from the majority of the panel members are asked to reveal the information they found in the proposal that caused them to assign the score they gave. Sometimes the entire panel might have overlooked an issue, which is brought to light because of the experience of that evaluator. On other occasions, the person scoring the proposal was the one who overlooked an issue. Using the information from their commentaries, the questionnaire, the requirements, and the vendor's proposal, the panel re-visits the issue in question.

Often a panel member is a pessimist and grades low. Other panel members might be more optimistic and give high grades. Neither of these approaches is erroneous as long as that panel member scores consistently across all vendors reviewed.

However, when it can be demonstrated that the panel member was in error in an evaluation, or the panel itself was, then the panel or the individual(s) should take the opportunity to update their original score to make it accurate. That is why Exhibit 10-13 has a place for a Version # to be entered, so that full traceability of the evolution of the scoring can be preserved.

The panel chairman has a burden to try to ensure that erroneous impressions are corrected. However, strong feelings about a score by an evaluator should also be acceptable, as long as not obviously in error. There should be no requirement that any panel member must change his score, even when significant differences do exist.

In the case of BB&T, let's assume that Rip Scali was generally more optimistic than the rest, and in the discussions made his case strongly for his opinion, though he did yield that he was too generous in scoring WP 3.1. On the other hand, Dmitri did not quite comprehend the driver program for the modules, and thus gave every module a low score. After Dmitri learned what the driver design really was doing, he adjusted his scores upward so that even in his opinion, vendor VG was more than satisfactory.

Exhibit 10-14 shows what the revised Panel Vendor Scoresheet might look like after the panel meeting. The average moves up a little and the range in panel scores are a little tighter.

The panel discussion process can have the effect that strong personalities exercise pressure on junior members to alter their score. On the other hand, some members of the panel can have their horizons expanded and benefit from learning from their peers. Therefore, the panel chairman must exercise a great deal of patience, and firm but fair control over the sessions to ensure each panel member can express his or her opinion unconstrained by others.

EXHIBIT 10-14

BITS PANEL VENDOR SCORESHEET

Version # ___2___

Vendor ID: VG

Category: Technical   Work Package: 3.0

Evaluator ID:

Work Package	Weight	#1	#2	#3	#4	#5	#6	#7	#8	Total	Average	Vendor's Score
3 Systems Design	**400**											
3.1 Personal Loans Module Design	50	8	6	8	6	8	N/S	6	6	48	6.9	342.9
3.2 Student Loans Module Design	50	8	6	10	6	10	N/S	8	6	54	7.7	385.7
3.3 Home Loans Module Design	50	5	5	8	5	4	N/S	10	6	43	6.1	307.1
3.4 Checking Accounts Module Design	70	8	6	8	8	8	6	8	5	57	7.1	498.8
3.5 Term Deposits Module Design	50	8	6	8	6	8	6	6	6	52	6.5	325.0
3.6 Savings Deposits Module Design	50	6	5	8	6	8	6	6	6	51	6.4	318.8
3.7 Credit Card Processing Module Design	50	4	5	6	5	6	5	5	5	41	5.1	256.3
3.8 Audit Tracking and Report Module Design	30	10	6	10	8	8	8	8	6	64	8.0	240.0

Individual's Average | 7.1 | 5.6 | 8.3 | 6.3 | 7.3 | 6.2 | 7.1 | 5.8 | 6.7

Vendor's WP Score: ___2674___

When the technical proposal review process is completed, the panel chairman retains the scoresheets while awaiting the results of the management and cost panel evaluations, and for further compilation to compare all vendors' scores.

MANAGEMENT PROPOSALS EVALUATION

Beginning on the eighth day of the evaluation, the management panel members begin their evaluation of the management proposals. The process is identical to that described above, except that the vendor's presentation has to be considered in the light of what was described in his technical proposal.

The major factor in the management evaluation is whether the vendor can deliver his technology with the human resources he will assign, and the management process he will use. The evaluator must be assured not only that the vendor can accomplish the development task, but also how the vendor will accomplish the task. The presentation by the vendor can be generic in some work packages, and quite specific in other work packages. The evaluator will need to use his management experience to make a business judgment about the vendor's management capability. The results are likely to be a little more subjective than the technical evaluations.

Exhibit 10-15 contains an excerpt of a Management Proposal Evaluation Questionnaire that would be used by the panel members to assist them in the management evaluation.

Besides the review of the work packages, each panel member must also make an assessment of the other related parts of the Management Proposal as identified in Table 9-1. In particular the deliverables, the schedule, the standards and the résumés of the contributing resources must be examined on their own merits for consistency, and double checked against the work packages for credibility and applicability. This task can be time consuming, but since most development teams will have a limited number of resources, once the quality of the contributors has been assessed by review of résumés, the correlation with the work packages is straightforward.

The management proposals are then scored and summarized. Significant deviations among evaluators are discussed in the panel meeting, and scores adjusted if required.

COST PROPOSALS EVALUATION

The cost panel evaluators assemble to match the technical solution and the management resources and processes proposed against the suggested cost. This is why the cost proposal is evaluated last. If you don't have a complete picture of how the vendor is doing the project, you have no way of knowing whether a proposed cost is too high or not enough to do the job.

The evaluators rely on their historic experience in managing projects to figure out whether the price for a work package is appropriate. Since the detailed technical analysis and commentary has already been accomplished by the other panels, they can treat the technology as a "black box," relying on their counterparts for the proper evaluation. The technical validity does not need to be questioned again.

The cost panel's scores will reflect the determination of whether the cost proposed matches the technical quality proposed. Is the cost fair? Is it consistent with the amount of work to be done? If the cost is lower than what the technical complexity suggests, how will

EXHIBIT 10-15

EXCERPT OF A MANAGEMENT EVALUATION QUESTIONNAIRE

Work Package: 1.0 Project Management & Administration

- Are senior management in the vendor's organization committed to the success of this project? Are they involved through their **active** participation? Is there appropriate and adequate customer liaison established at this level?

- Have contingency plans been developed to support this project with additional quality and /or quantity of human resources should problems occur?

- Does the vendor demonstrate that he has sufficient resources to complete the project if turnover occurs on the project team?

- Does the vendor have a clearly defined and appropriate process for problem identification and resolution?

- Have critical skills been identified for contributions to the project? Are they found within the vendor's organization and are they deployed at the appropriate time and task?

- Has the vendor allocated appropriate general and administrative resources to assist the project manager to perform his function?

Work Packages: 2-10 As Applicable

- Is there senior level experience allocated to this task?

- Have the resources allocated performed an identical or similar task before?

- Is there adequate experience with the system's operating system and hardware?

- Is there sufficient functional and application knowledge of this task? With previous experience in identical or similar tasks in the past?

- Is the applications knowledge consistent with the objectives of this project and related to it in terms of past experience?

- Has the vendor recognized any weaknesses in his capability? Has he proposed ways in which those weaknesses will be overcome?

- Does the vendor have a consistent transition plan to complete one phase (work package) and move on to the next?

- Are adequate quality controls established over the coding and debug cycle?

- Has the vendor provided the necessary tools to the implementation staff such as: programming languages, test bed, turn-around time for large batches, debugging aids, librarian and standard code modules?

- Are sufficient resources and time allocated to all aspects of the vendors debug and testing?

- Has the vendor provided adequate assurances and processes to deliver all documentation as required at each stage of the project?

the vendor do it? Will quality suffer? If the vendor's technical proposal is deficient, are the proposed costs consistent with that deficiency? Can a remedy be arranged within the costs proposed, or must the cost also be increased to pay for the remedy? A cost evaluation worksheet is completed for each of the work packages based upon the answers to the cost questionnaire.

Exhibit 10-16 contains an excerpt of a questionnaire that can be used to evaluate the vendor's cost proposal.

It is evident from Exhibit 10-16 that considerable judgment is required by the evaluators. They will judge, based on their experience in developing or paying for systems, whether the "bang for the buck" proposed by the vendor is fully satisfactory, a bargain (therefore a high score), or too pricy for the technology delivered. It is likely that there will be significant differences across work packages because of infrastructure differences among the vendors. These all have to be considered in this relative assessment of cost effectiveness.

However, in contrast to the technical and management panels, the cost judgments may not necessarily be reconciled during the panel sessions. This is because while the evaluation process achieves extremely good correlation across all categories, (and therefore ensures that each vendor's proposal is totally consistent), it has not yet considered the absolute cost of the proposals themselves. It is only in the vendor summaries and comparison reviews that final judgments about the absolute costs can be made.

Let's assume that you are doing a simple technical and cost evaluation to buy a car. The cars you've chosen to evaluate against your list of technical criteria are a Saturn and a Lexus. The Lexus gets a technical score of 80 and the Saturn receives a technical score of 50 (fully satisfactory). When you evaluate relative costs, the cost score for Lexus is 60, on the basis of value for the high degree of technical expertise. You score Saturn at 80, based on the value for the performance it delivers. Both are satisfactory. Which is the winner? It will depend upon the Category Percentile Contribution you gave to the cost category versus the technical category.

However the Lexus costs $45,000, and the Saturn costs $13,000. Which is the better choice for you? If your budget is only $25,000, a higher final score for the Lexus is irrelevant. You can't afford it. The absolute cost of the Lexus is too high.

The same applies, only more so, to the software system you want to buy. The "great solution" may not be the affordable one. Therefore, when evaluating costs, additional evaluation procedures are required. The distinction made in evaluating the cost category needs reemphasis. The weight assignments and scores for the cost category reflect relative cost-effectiveness of the technical and management proposals for that work package, and do not reflect the absolute dollar cost. The absolute cost comparison among vendors is discussed in the section on Real Costs. The Cost Category evaluation reflects judgments about relative cost effectiveness of the technical and management proposals, not absolute dollars.

The requirements imposed by governmental bodies that force purchasing departments to buy from the lowest absolute cost vendor ignore the very significant distinction between relative costs or "value" as described here and the real costs. The prevalence of low-ball bids, shoddy work, and cost and schedule overruns are the inevitable result.

EXHIBIT 10-16

EXCERPT OF A COST EVALUATION QUESTIONNAIRE

- Does the cost of this work package correlate with your understanding of the management effort to manage the task, and with the technical resources required to perform this task over the schedule identified?

- If the technical merit of this work package is outstanding or superior, is the cost reasonable? Should a lesser capability be sought at a reduced cost?

- If the management merit of this work package is outstanding or superior, are we paying an unnecessary premium for management overhead?

- Is this vendor delivering high quality at reasonable prices because he has demonstrated how to be highly cost effective in his development and management process?

- Is this vendor providing a product at a price which on average might be the standard price upon which others should be compared?

- If the technical proposal or the management proposal for this work package requires improvement to make it satisfactory, are there minimal or substantial higher costs likely to meet the satisfactory score?

- Are there any areas where the cost proposal is dependent upon work to be performed by the Purchaser? Which are they? Do they increase the probability of a higher cost change of scope later?

- If we were to do this work package internally at fully loaded costs and benefits, and then added 20% general administrative expense and 10% profit, would the cost we derive for the identical work proposed be reasonably close to what the vendor is proposing?

- Are there any areas where the vendor has proposed deliverables of a minimal nature at minimal cost, where we know a more substantial effort is required? Should we boost the cost and deliverable during negotiation, or wait until the issue surfaces during the project?

- Are there any areas where the vendor has low-balled his costs? What do you consider the reasons? What should we do about it?

- Is there anything in this work package which will cause much more time to be spent than is reasonable?

- Is there anything in this work package which will cause me to increase my costs, in lieu of paying the vendor?

- Is the quality of resources proposed in the management plan consistent with the labor rate or cost per man-month indicated in the cost proposal? Is this a likely "bait and swap" gambit by the vendor?

- Is the vendor making maximum use of whatever he has previously developed, and is not burdening us for the full costs a second time?

THE VENDOR SELECTION

TABULATION OF RESULTS

As the evaluation of each category nears completion, the panel chairman compiles the material used in the evaluations and calculates summary tabulations of the scores.

The compilation volume is extensive. In the examples used in this manual, there are 7 vendors with 3 categories to be evaluated by 8 evaluators. If each of the 10 work packages (Exhibit 9-1) were evaluated, and each person used only one page of worksheet (Exhibit 10-11) per work package, then a total of 7 x 3 x 8 x 10 x 1 or 1680 pages of worksheets would have to be collected. There would be 7 x 3 x 8 or 168 Individual Evaluator's Vendor Scoresheets (Exhibit 10-12). There would be 7 x 3 x 10 or 210 Panel Vendor Scoresheets (Exhibit 10-13), and double that, if a second version of each were required for scoring reconciliation. This information is summarized onto one sheet for each vendor (7 sheets). This calculates to a minimum of 1680 + 168 + 210 + 7 or 2065 pages of paper, not including archival copies of each vendor's proposals, evaluation questionnaires, correlation matrices, RFP documentation, specifications and whatever else has been prepared. This roughly corresponds to the contents of a five drawer filing cabinet.

Is all this paper necessary? If you want to avoid controversy, challenges (legal and other) to your recommendation and unwanted second guessing, not to mention bad publicity (particularly if you are a public or governmental function), you must insist on full traceability for every aspect of the evaluation process. The traceability will ensure that any independent audit will verify the integrity, consistency and fairness of your process, of your recommendation, and of the contract award.

> Careful record keeping of all aspects of the evaluation process is your only guarantee that your evaluation will not be overturned.

Up to this point we haven't examined any vendor's score in comparison with other vendors' scores. This is the next step in the process. All the material above can now be held for reference, while the panel chairman uses the Vendor Summary Scoresheets (row 4 in Exhibit 10-1 and Exhibit 10-17) to begin the comparison process.

Exhibit 10-17 contains a completed Vendor Summary Score for Vendor VG (one of seven vendors), which would reflect the final scores in each category for VG.

The score for each major work package for each vendor is transcribed onto a Vendor Comparison Summary Sheet. At this point in the process it is sufficient to consider only the summary work packages, and not the work package components, for you are beginning to analyze the vendors from a "big picture" view of buying the system, not just the components.

Exhibit 10-18 contains a blank Technical Proposal Vendor Comparison Summary form into which the scores will be entered. Similar forms are used for the Management and Cost Proposals. Exhibit 10-18 corresponds to row 5 in Exhibit 10-1.

TECHNICAL PROPOSAL VENDOR COMPARISON

The panel chairman enters the technical scores onto the summary sheet.

Exhibit 10-19 contains a completed Technical Proposal Vendor Comparison Summary. The following discussion will examine the scores in Exhibit 10-19 in detail. Since the BB&T team decided not to evaluate Work Package 10.0 in any proposal, only nine work packages have scores. BB&T has the suggested level of effort for Work Package 10.0 and can negotiate this task nearer to the cutover date.

Because percentage differences can vary considerably, depending upon what term is used in the denominator to measure the relationship, throughout this chapter we will measure the percentage difference between two vendors' scores with the <u>mean</u> score (all vendors) as the denominator.
From Exhibit 10-19, we find that:

1. The average or mean score of all vendors is 5595 or almost six hundred points over 5000, which would be a fully satisfactory response. This is reasonably high, and indicates a competitive situation. If you subtract the lowest score from the sum and then re-average those remaining, the mean score is 6094, a "good" score on the gradation scale.

2. One vendor, VF, had a score of 2749 which falls at the inadequate level. The score is so out of line with the others, it would appear the vendor didn't give it much of an effort, or perhaps didn't understand the requirements. Debriefing should determine this. Barring unforeseen circumstances, and because of many better proposals, this vendor would be rejected at this point. However, we'll continue to include vendor VF in the analysis just for completeness.

3. Vendor VB had a score of 4557, just below satisfactory. Presumably the proposal could be made satisfactory with further negotiations.

4. Two vendors had fully satisfactory scores, vendors VE and VH.

5. Three vendors had scores between good and superior. Vendors VA, VC and VG had strong proposals, a situation the evaluators should cheer. Vendor VA had the highest score of 7501, followed by vendor VG with 6956 and vendor VC with 6755. The percentage difference between VA and VG is (7501-6956)/5595, or 9.7%. The percentage difference between VA and VC is 13.3%.

Examining the summary scores that reflect the weighting function sometimes masks patterns because of the wide discrepancy between one work package score and another. It is useful to look at two other ways of comparing the vendors.

EXHIBIT 10-17

VENDOR SUMMARY SCORE

Vendor ID: VG

Category: Technical

	Work Package	Weight	Score
1	Project Management & Administration	50	340
2	Systems Analysis	150	1065
3	Systems Design	400	2674
4	Coding, Debug & Unit Testing	150	1110
5	Interface Testing	50	380
6	Integration Testing	50	340
7	Data Conversion	20	132
8	Acceptance Testing	80	640
9	Cutover & Parallel	50	275
10	Operations Support	0	0
	Vendor's Category Score:	1000	**6956**

Category: Management

	Work Package	Weight	Score
1	Project Management & Administration	300	2400
2	Systems Analysis	50	450
3	Systems Design	200	1852
4	Coding, Debug & Unit Testing	150	930
5	Interface Testing	50	322
6	Integration Testing	50	360
7	Data Conversion	0	0
8	Acceptance Testing	150	1110
9	Cutover & Parallel	50	355
10	Operations Support	0	0
	Vendor's Category Score:	1000	**7779**

Category: Cost

	Work Package	Weight	Score
1	Project Management & Administration	120	816
2	Systems Analysis	200	1620
3	Systems Design	250	1975
4	Coding, Debug & Unit Testing	230	1702
5	Interface Testing	50	345
6	Integration Testing	50	320
7	Data Conversion	0	0
8	Acceptance Testing	50	311
9	Cutover & Parallel	50	372
10	Operations Support	0	0
	Vendor's Category Score:	1000	**7461**

Vendor's Total Score: | N/A | **22196** |

EXHIBIT 10-18

TECHNICAL PROPOSAL VENDOR COMPARISON SUMMARY

Category: TECHNICAL

Vendor ID:

	Work Package	Weight	VA	VB	VC	VE	VF	VG	VH	Average
1	Project Management & Administration	50								
2	Systems Analysis	150								
3	Systems Design	400								
4	Coding, Debug & Unit Testing	150								
5	Interface Testing	50								
6	Integration Testing	50								
7	Data Conversion	20								
8	Acceptance Testing	80								
9	Cutover & Parallel	50								
10	Operations Support	0								

VENDOR'S TOTAL

EXHIBIT 10-19

TECHNICAL PROPOSAL VENDOR COMPARISON SUMMARY

Category: TECHNICAL

Vendor ID:

	Work Package	Weight	VA	VB	VC	VE	VF	VG	VH	Average
1	Project Management & Administration	50	375	255	200	255	225	340	260	273
2	Systems Analysis	150	1125	780	1170	735	465	1065	855	885
3	Systems Design	400	3040	1640	3120	2080	1200	2674	2280	2291
4	Coding, Debug & Unit Testing	150	1140	720	915	795	330	1110	720	819
5	Interface Testing	50	360	255	240	250	140	380	255	269
6	Integration Testing	50	355	245	230	225	100	340	300	256
7	Data Conversion	20	120	110	110	110	46	132	114	106
8	Acceptance Testing	80	616	352	520	384	128	640	464	443
9	Cutover & Parallel	50	370	200	250	260	115	275	305	254
10	Operations Support	0	0	0	0	0	0	0	0	0
	VENDOR'S TOTAL		7501	4557	6755	5094	2749	6956	5553	5595

Exhibit 10-20 contains a Technical Proposal Vendor Comparison Summary of the scores with the weights removed, thereby leaving the average gradation score for each work package.

Exhibit 10-21 compares every work package as a deviation from the mean for that work Package. Averages and deviations from the mean are useful ways of comparing vendor differences. It's often easier to see patterns in the information.

6. From Exhibit 10-20 we see that vendor VA had consistent average raw scores above 7, except data conversion. Perhaps he anticipated that the customer had to do this anyway, and down-played his contribution here. Vendor VB was also consistent, though with more modest average scores. Vendor VC had really good scores in the most important Work Packages 2-4, but was closer to just satisfactory in all the others. Vendor VG was less consistent than vendor VA, but remained in striking distance.

In the three most critical areas of Work Packages 2-4, three vendors: VA, VC and VG, had averages of 7.6, 7.3 and 7.1 respectively.

7. In Exhibit 10-21 the individual variances from the mean score for each work package highlight again that vendor VC was superior in really only three work packages, and just close to the mean in the others, while deficient in WP 1.0. Remember though that in this evaluation the mean is still above satisfactory. In other evaluations, the mean could be below satisfactory, meaning there were fewer superior proposals.

MANAGEMENT PROPOSAL VENDOR COMPARISON

The panel chairman enters the management scores onto the summary sheet.

Exhibit 10-22 contains a completed Management Proposal Vendor Comparison Summary.

Exhibit 10-23 contains a Management Proposal Vendor Comparison Summary of all the scores with the weights removed, thereby leaving the average gradation score for each work package.

Exhibit 10-24 compares every work package as a deviation from the mean for that work package.

The following discussion will examine the scores in Exhibits 10-22, 10-23 and 10-24. Since the BB&T evaluation team decided not to evaluate Work Packages 7 and 10 in any management proposal, the weights were originally distributed to only eight work packages.

Because percentage differences can vary considerably, depending upon what term is used in the denominator to measure the relationship, throughout this chapter we measure the percentage difference between two vendors' scores with the mean score as the denominator.

1. The average or mean score of all vendors is 5656, or over six hundred points over 5000 which would be a fully satisfactory response. This indicates a competitive situation. If you subtract the lowest score from the sum and then re-average those remaining, the mean score is 6016, a good score on the gradation scale.

EXHIBIT 10-20

TECHNICAL PROPOSAL VENDOR COMPARISON SUMMARY
COMPARISON OF AVERAGE SCORES

Category: TECHNICAL   **Vendor ID:**

	Work Package	Weight	VA	VB	VC	VE	VF	VG	VH	Average
1	Project Management & Administration	50	7.5	5.1	4.0	5.1	4.5	6.8	5.2	5.5
2	Systems Analysis	150	7.5	5.2	7.8	4.9	3.1	7.1	5.7	5.9
3	Systems Design	400	7.6	4.1	7.8	5.2	3.0	6.7	5.7	5.7
4	Coding, Debug & Unit Testing	150	7.6	4.8	6.1	5.3	2.2	7.4	4.8	5.5
5	Interface Testing	50	7.2	5.1	4.8	5.0	2.8	7.6	5.1	5.4
6	Integration Testing	50	7.1	4.9	4.6	4.5	2.0	6.8	6.0	5.1
7	Data Conversion	20	6.0	5.5	5.5	5.5	2.3	6.6	5.7	5.3
8	Acceptance Testing	80	7.7	4.4	6.5	4.8	1.6	8.0	5.8	5.5
9	Cutover & Parallel	50	7.4	4.0	5.0	5.2	2.3	5.5	6.1	5.1
10	Operations Support	0	0.0	0.0	0.0	0.0	0.0	0.0	0.0	0.0

| | **VENDOR'S AVERAGE** | | **7.3** | **4.8** | **5.8** | **5.1** | **2.6** | **6.9** | **5.6** | **5.4** |

EXHIBIT 10-21

TECHNICAL PROPOSAL VENDOR COMPARISON SUMMARY
COMPARISON OF DEVIATION ABOUT MEAN SCORE

Category: **TECHNICAL**

Vendor ID:

Work Package	Weight	VA	VB	VC	VE	VF	VG	VH
1 Project Management & Administration	50	1.4	0.9	0.7	0.9	0.8	1.2	1.0
2 Systems Analysis	150	1.3	0.9	1.3	0.8	0.5	1.2	1.0
3 Systems Design	400	1.3	0.7	1.4	0.9	0.5	1.2	1.0
4 Coding, Debug & Unit Testing	150	1.4	0.9	1.1	1.0	0.4	1.4	0.9
5 Interface Testing	50	1.3	0.9	0.9	0.9	0.5	1.4	1.2
6 Integration Testing	50	1.4	1.0	0.9	0.9	0.4	1.3	1.2
7 Data Conversion	20	1.1	1.0	1.0	1.0	0.4	1.2	1.1
8 Acceptance Testing	80	1.4	0.8	1.2	0.9	0.3	1.4	1.0
9 Cutover & Parallel	50	1.5	0.8	1.0	1.0	0.5	1.1	1.2
10 Operations Support	0							
VENDOR'S TOTAL		**1.3**	**0.9**	**1.1**	**0.9**	**0.5**	**1.3**	**1.0**

EXHIBIT 10-22

MANAGEMENT PROPOSAL VENDOR COMPARISON SUMMARY

Category: MANAGEMENT

Vendor ID:

	Work Package	Weight	VA	VB	VC	VE	VF	VG	VH	Average
1	Project Management & Administration	300	2280	1530	1200	2040	1590	2400	1530	1796
2	Systems Analysis	50	385	255	205	220	255	450	255	289
3	Systems Design	200	1560	1060	800	820	1000	1852	1020	1159
4	Coding, Debug & Unit Testing	150	1200	810	480	660	735	930	750	795
5	Interface Testing	50	330	240	110	260	275	322	250	255
6	Integration Testing	50	350	245	120	255	240	360	250	260
7	Data Conversion	0	0	0	0	0	0	0	0	0
8	Acceptance Testing	150	1125	780	390	840	750	1110	735	819
9	Cutover & Parallel	50	400	260	190	275	255	355	250	284
10	Operations Support	0	0	0	0	0	0	0	0	0
	VENDOR'S TOTAL		7630	5180	3495	5370	5100	7779	5040	5656

EXHIBIT 10-23

MANAGEMENT PROPOSAL VENDOR COMPARISON SUMMARY
COMPARISON OF AVERAGE SCORES

Category: MANAGEMENT

Vendor ID:

	Work Package	Weight	VA	VB	VC	VE	VF	VG	VH	Average
1	Project Management & Administration	300	7.6	5.1	4.0	6.8	5.3	8.0	5.1	6.0
2	Systems Analysis	50	7.7	5.1	4.1	4.4	5.1	9.0	5.1	5.8
3	Systems Design	200	7.8	5.3	4.0	4.1	5.0	9.3	5.1	5.8
4	Coding, Debug & Unit Testing	150	8.0	5.4	3.2	4.4	4.9	6.2	5.0	5.3
5	Interface Testing	50	6.6	4.8	2.2	5.2	5.5	6.4	5.0	5.1
6	Integration Testing	50	7.0	4.9	2.4	5.1	4.8	7.2	5.0	5.2
7	Data Conversion	0								
8	Acceptance Testing	150	7.5	5.2	2.6	5.6	5.0	7.4	4.9	5.5
9	Cutover & Parallel	50	8.0	5.2	3.8	5.5	5.1	7.1	5.0	5.7
10	Operations Support	0								

VENDOR'S TOTAL	VA	VB	VC	VE	VF	VG	VH	Average
	7.5	5.1	3.3	5.1	5.1	7.6	5.0	5.5

EXHIBIT 10-24

MANAGEMENT PROPOSAL VENDOR COMAPARISON SUMMARY
COMPARISON OF DEVIATION ABOUT MEAN SCORE

Category: MANAGEMENT

Vendor ID:

	Work Package	Weight	VA	VB	VC	VE	VF	VG	VH
1	Project Management & Administration	300	1.3	0.9	0.7	1.1	0.9	1.3	0.9
2	Systems Analysis	50	1.3	0.9	0.7	0.7	0.9	1.6	0.9
3	Systems Design	200	1.3	0.9	0.7	0.7	0.9	1.6	0.9
4	Coding, Debug & Unit Testing	150	1.5	1.0	0.6	0.8	0.9	1.2	0.9
5	Interface Testing	50	1.3	0.9	0.4	1.0	1.1	1.3	1.0
6	Integration Testing	50	1.3	0.9	0.5	1.0	0.9	1.4	1.0
7	Data Conversion	0							
8	Acceptance Testing	150	1.4	1.0	0.5	1.0	0.9	1.4	0.9
9	Cutover & Parallel	50	1.4	0.9	0.7	1.0	0.9	1.3	0.9
10	Operations Support	0							
	VENDOR'S TOTAL		**1.3**	**0.9**	**0.6**	**0.9**	**0.9**	**1.4**	**0.9**

2. Vendor VC had a score of 3495 which falls at the adequate to fair level and which would infer correction is required. The score is surprising, given that vendor VC had the third highest Technical score! You want to ask: What happened? From Exhibit 10-23 you can see that the vendor just blew it. We can guess that he put together a great technical proposal team to propose the design, but has shown no follow through in the quality of personnel assigned to complete the job, nor has he created believability in his management process to deliver the product. It is this kind of analysis which picks apart those vendors who are all promises and no delivery. On this basis, vendor VC would be rejected.

3. Four vendors had fully satisfactory scores, vendors VB, VE, VF and VH. We previously rejected vendor VF for an unacceptable technical score. These four vendors are also somewhat below the mean score for this category.

4. Vendors VA and VG were again good to superior with vendor VG having the slightly higher score this time. From Exhibits 10-23 and 10-24 vendor VG has shown even greater strength in the first three work packages, including overall management process and control.

At this point in most proposal evaluations, the panel discussions and analysis would concentrate primarily on vendors VA and VG, with all other vendors put on hold for later analysis if required.

COST PROPOSAL VENDOR COMPARISON

The panel chairman enters the cost scores onto the summary sheet.

Exhibit 10-25 contains a completed Cost Proposal Vendor Comparison Summary.

Exhibit 10-26 contains a Cost Proposal Vendor Comparison Summary of all the scores with the weights removed, thereby leaving the average gradation score for each work package.

Exhibit 10-27 compares every work package as a deviation from the mean for that work package.

The following discussion examines the scores in Exhibits 10-25, 10-26 and 10-27. Since the BB&T evaluation team decided not to evaluate Work Packages 7 and 10 in any cost proposal, the weights were distributed to only eight work packages. We measure the percentage difference between two vendors' scores with the mean score (all vendors) as the denominator.

1. The average or mean score of all vendors is 5823 or over eight hundred points over 5000 which would be a satisfactory response. This indicates very cost-effective proposals.

2. Vendor VE had a score of 4258 which falls at the adequate to fair level and which would infer correction is required to make the costs acceptable. We had previously rejected this vendor.

EXHIBIT 10-25

COST PROPOSAL VENDOR COMPARISON SUMMARY

Category: COST

Vendor ID:

	Work Package	Weight	VA	VB	VC	VE	VF	VG	VH	Average
1	Project Management & Administration	120	648	600	600	540	612	816	1032	693
2	Systems Analysis	200	1260	1020	1020	960	1000	1620	1340	1174
3	Systems Design	250	1875	1275	1250	1050	1250	1975	1600	1468
4	Coding, Debug & Unit Testing	230	1725	1150	1127	943	1173	1702	1886	1387
5	Interface Testing	50	310	265	265	210	250	345	375	289
6	Integration Testing	50	310	250	260	175	250	320	355	274
7	Data Conversion	0	0	0	0	0	0	0	0	0
8	Acceptance Testing	50	300	245	250	175	250	311	290	260
9	Cutover & Parallel	50	300	265	250	205	250	372	310	279
10	Operations Support	0	0	0	0	0	0	0	0	0
	VENDOR'S TOTAL		6728	5070	5022	4258	5035	7461	7188	5823

EXHIBIT 10-26

COST PROPOSAL VENDOR COMPARISON SUMMARY
COMPARISON OF AVERAGE SCORES

Category: COST

Vendor ID:

	Work Package	Weight	VA	VB	VC	VE	VF	VG	VH	Average
1	Project Management & Administration	120	5.4	5.0	5.0	4.5	5.1	6.8	8.6	5.8
2	Systems Analysis	200	6.3	5.1	5.1	4.8	5.0	8.1	6.7	5.9
3	Systems Design	250	7.5	5.1	5.0	4.2	5.0	7.9	6.4	5.9
4	Coding, Debug & Unit Testing	230	7.5	5.0	4.9	4.1	5.1	7.4	8.2	6.0
5	Interface Testing	50	6.2	5.3	5.3	4.2	5.0	6.9	7.5	5.8
6	Integration Testing	50	6.2	5.0	5.2	3.5	5.0	6.4	7.1	5.5
7	Data Conversion	0								
8	Acceptance Testing	50	6.0	4.9	5.0	3.5	5.0	6.2	5.8	5.2
9	Cutover & Parallel	50	6.0	5.3	5.0	4.1	5.0	7.4	6.2	5.6
10	Operations Support	0								

VENDOR'S AVERAGE	**6.4**	**5.1**	**5.1**	**4.1**	**5.0**	**7.1**	**7.1**	**5.7**

EXHIBIT 10-27

COST PROPOSAL VENFOR COMPARISON SUMMARY
COPARISON OF DEIALTION ABOUT MEAN SCORE

Category: COST

Vendor ID:

	Work Package	Weight	VA	VB	VC	VE	VF	VG	VH
1	Project Management & Administration	120	0.9	0.9	0.9	0.8	0.9	1.2	1.5
2	Systems Analysis	200	1.1	0.9	0.9	0.8	0.9	1.4	1.1
3	Systems Design	250	1.3	0.9	0.9	0.7	0.9	1.3	1.1
4	Coding, Debug & Unit Testing	230	1.2	0.8	0.8	0.7	0.8	1.2	1.4
5	Interface Testing	50	1.1	0.9	0.9	0.7	0.9	1.2	1.3
6	Integration Testing	50	1.1	0.9	0.9	0.6	0.9	1.2	1.3
7	Data Conversion	0							
8	Acceptance Testing	50	1.2	0.9	1.0	0.7	1.0	1.2	1.1
9	Cutover & Parallel	50	1.1	1.0	0.9	0.7	0.9	1.3	1.1
10	Operations Support	0							

VENDOR'S TOTAL	VA	VB	VC	VE	VF	VG	VH
	1.1	0.9	0.9	0.7	0.9	1.3	1.2

3. Our two prime competitors had scores above the good rating. Vendor VA with 6728 and VG with 7461. The spread between these vendors is 12.9% from the mean. The score for vendor VG reflects the evaluators' judgments that vendor VG is providing a lot of management and technical quality for whatever cost he has quoted. Vendor VA is perceived to either not have technical performance cost effectiveness, is more costly overall, or some other factor is present.

4. Surprise! Vendor VH, previously providing just above fully satisfactory technical and management proposals, has received a score of 7188. Presumably, the high score is related to the cost effectiveness of a minimal solution for the client. With such a strong showing from a vendor which has not been rejected, it might be necessary to include vendor VH in the final comparisons.

FINAL VENDOR COMPARISONS

The final set of meetings for the evaluation panel is where all of the vendors scores are summarized. At this point in the analysis it is useful to stand back from the numbers and summarize the status of the vendors in a table that descriptively reflects the results of the previous analysis.

Table 10-3 contains a descriptive, rather than arithmetic comparison of the results of the evaluation so far.

TABLE 10-3
DESCRIPTIVE COMPARISON OF EVALUATION RESULTS

VENDOR	TECHNICAL SCORE	MANAGEMENT SCORE	COST SCORE
VA	Hi	Hi	Hi
VB	Fair	Sat	Sat
VC	Good	Fair	Sat
VE	Sat	Sat	Fair
VF	Unsat	Sat	Sat
VG	Hi	Hi	Hi
VH	Sat	Sat	Hi

Because of the quality of the best proposals, we can eliminate all the fair and unsatisfactory proposals. This would reduce the above table to the following:

VENDOR	TECHNICAL SCORE	MANAGEMENT SCORE	COST SCORE
VA	Hi	Hi	Hi
VG	Hi	Hi	Hi
VH	Sat	Sat	Hi

For completeness we'll take the summary results from Exhibits 10-19, 10-22 and 10-25 and consolidate them.

Exhibit 10-28 contains the consolidation of all of the summary category scores of all the vendors. This corresponds to row 6 in Exhibit 10-1.

From Exhibit 10-28 we see that vendor VG has the highest Raw Score, 22196 versus the next closest score of 21859, a difference of 337 or 2.0% from the mean. Vendor VH with a score of 17781 is almost 26% lower than VG from the mean, a significant difference.

However, the original intention of attributing more importance to the technical category, as is natural for this kind of procurement, must now be considered. This is accomplished by multiplying the raw scores by the Category Percentile Contributions of 65%, 20% and 15% respectively for the technical, management and cost categories. The results are found in Exhibit 10-29.

Exhibit 10-29 contains the final numerical evaluation results after the application of the Category Percentile Contribution Percentages have been calculated.

Now the results are reversed. Vendor VA has a final score of 7411 and vendor VG a score of 7197. The difference is only 214 now in the favor of vendor VA. This is a 3.8% difference from the mean. Vendor VH, with a final score of 5696 is 30% behind vendor VA. Vendor VH stayed in the contest somewhat longer than four other vendors (due to a low cost proposal which we'll see later), but will come in a distant third.

The differences between vendors VA and VG are too small to choose vendor VA directly by a strictly numerical comparison. The commentary on the technical proposal would have to be compelling to award the contract at this point to VA. We need to look further.

SENSITIVITY ANALYSIS

When the standings are close, the National Football League uses tiebreaker rules to determine who gets into the playoffs. We need to do something similar. The real dollar difference between the vendors may be the first tiebreaker, but we'll save that analysis for last.

Sensitivity Analysis is the process of adjusting weights originally assigned during the category or weight assignment processes to determine if the decision would be changed by changing category percentages or weight assignments.

Category Percentile Contribution Sensitivity Analysis

At the macro level, the simplest sensitivity test is to determine how much the final total results change with a change in the Category Percentile Contribution. From now on we'll consider only vendors VA and VG in our discussion.

Exhibit 10-30 contains six examples of different Category Percentile Contribution percentages. The "difference" is always calculated as (VA-VG).

Example 2 in Exhibit 10-30 changes the distribution to reduce the technical percentage and increase the management percentage. This halves VA's lead. Example 3 gives equal weight to management and cost and halves VA's lead again. When all categories are equal, vendor VG has the advantage. This is equivalent to the raw final scores calculated in Exhibit 10-28.

EXHIBIT 10-28

**FINAL VENDOR COMPARISON SUMMARY
RAW SCORES**

CATEGORY	VA	VB	VC	VE	VF	VG	VH	Average
Technical Proposal Score	7501	4557	6755	5094	2749	6956	5553	5595
Management Proposal Score	7630	5180	3495	5370	5100	7779	5040	5656
Cost Proposal Score	6728	5070	5022	4258	5035	7461	7188	5823
Vendor's Total Raw Score	21859	14807	15272	14722	12884	22196	17781	17074

EXHIBIT 10-29

FINAL VENDOR COMPARISON SUMMARY
AFTER CATEGORY PERCENTILE CONTRIBUTION CALCULATION

CATEGORY	CPC %	VA	VB	VC	VE	VF	VG	VH	Average
Technical Category Final Score	65%	4876	2962	4391	3311	1787	4522	3609	3637
Management Category Final Score	20%	1526	1036	699	1074	1020	1556	1008	1131
Cost Category Final Score	15%	1009	761	753	639	755	1119	1078	873
Vendor's Final Total Score		7411	4759	5843	5024	3562	7197	5696	5642

If we ignore the cost category, the technical advantage of vendor VA increases (Example 5). Finally, when management is ignored, and the technical and cost categories are given equal weight in Example 6, the advantage reverts to vendor VG. But neither of these options are really rational.

We know that when technology is concerned, vendor VA seems to have the advantage. When the cost evaluation is concerned, vendor VG received outstanding marks. Are there nuances within individual work packages that we haven't noticed before that can help solve our dilemma in choosing the winning vendor?

It appears we'll have to go back and reexamine Exhibits 10-19, 10-22 and 10-25 to determine whether a big tiebreaker can be found.

Technical Proposal Sensitivity Analysis

Five recalculations of weight assignments in the technical category were performed. The results are shown in Exhibit 10-31 as Examples 2-6.

The differences between the two vendors for each example are graphed in Exhibit 10-32.

The examples spread the original distribution of weights either more evenly (Examples 2, 5), or strongly skew the weighting toward analysis and design (Examples 3, 4), or toward the production and test activities (Examples 5, 6). Vendor VA retains a strong lead over vendor VG when the early phases of the project are emphasized. The margin is reduced however, when more emphasis is given to the latter phases.

There is no information of a startling nature here, and no indication that the original weight assignments were poorly conceived. Therefore, the results in the technical category should stay the way they are, and vendor VA should be considered to have a small but real lead over vendor VG in technology.

Management Proposal Sensitivity Analysis

Five recalculations of weight assignments in the management category were performed. The results are shown in Exhibit 10-33 as Examples 2-6.

The differences between the vendors for each example are graphed in Exhibit 10-34.

Here we see an interesting contrast. Although vendor VA had superior technical scores in the early phases, the management proposal scores are reversed. Vendor VG has a superior management proposal, particularly in systems analysis and design.

Vendor VA reverses the score however when a premium is placed on the Coding and the Test Phases (Examples 5, 6). We could guess that vendor VA wrote a terrific technical proposal, but the execution of the technical work in the early phases, as reflected in the Management Work Packages, was not as credible as vendor VG. On the other hand, vendor VA certainly seemed to devote more and better management attention to the testing and acceptance work. This could be because VA did not expect much of a contribution in these phases from the customer. Vendor VG might have understated his role because he expected quite a bit of help from the client.

In any event, the resultant scores swing quite a bit. It would seem that the original

EXAMPLE 10-30

CATEGORY PERCENTILE CONTRIBUTION ANALYSIS

EXAMPLE 1: ORIGINAL

CATEGORY	CPC %	VA	VG	DIFFER-ENCE
Technical Category Final Score	65%	4876	4522	354
Management Category Final Score	20%	1526	1556	-30
Cost Category Final Score	15%	1009	1119	-110
Vendor's Final Total Score		**7411**	**7197**	214

EXAMPLE 2: MUCH HIGHER MANAGEMENT

CATEGORY	CPC %	VA	VG	DIFFER-ENCE
Technical Category Final Score	50%	3751	3478	272
Management Category Final Score	35%	2671	2723	-52
Cost Category Final Score	15%	1009	1119	-110
Vendor's Final Total Score		**7430**	**7320**	110

EXAMPLE 3: EQUAL MGMT & COST

CATEGORY	CPC %	VA	VG	DIFFER-ENCE
Technical Category Final Score	50%	3751	3478	272
Management Category Final Score	25%	1908	1945	-37
Cost Category Final Score	25%	1682	1865	-183
Vendor's Final Total Score		**7340**	**7288**	52

EXAMPLE 4: ALL CATEGORIES EQUAL

CATEGORY	CPC %	VA	VG	DIFFER-ENCE
Technical Category Final Score	33%	2498	2317	181
Management Category Final Score	33%	2541	2590	-50
Cost Category Final Score	33%	2240	2485	-244
Vendor's Final Total Score		**7279**	**7391**	-112

EXAMPLE 5: COST IS NO OBJECT

CATEGORY	CPC %	VA	VG	DIFFER-ENCE
Technical Category Final Score	80%	6001	5565	436
Management Category Final Score	20%	1526	1556	-30
Cost Category Final Score	0%	0	0	0
Vendor's Final Total Score		**7527**	**7121**	406

EXAMPLE 6: COST = TECHNICAL

CATEGORY	CPC %	VA	VG	DIFFER-ENCE
Technical Category Final Score	50%	3751	3478	272
Management Category Final Score	0%	0	0	0
Cost Category Final Score	50%	3364	3731	-367
Vendor's Final Total Score		**7115**	**7209**	-94

EXHIBIT 10-31

TECHNICAL PROPOSAL SENSITIVITY ANALYSIS

EXAMPLE 1: ORIGINAL

	Work Package	Wgt.	VA	VG	Difference
1	Project Mgmt & Admin	50	375	340	35.0
2	Systems Analysis	150	1125	1065	60.0
3	Systems Design	400	3040	2674	365.5
4	Coding, Debug &Test	150	1140	1110	30.0
5	Interface Testing	50	360	380	-20.0
6	Integration Testing	50	355	340	15.0
7	Data Conversion	20	120	132	-12.0
8	Acceptance Testing	80	616	640	-24.0
9	Cutover & Parallel	50	370	275	95.0
10	Operations Support	0	0	0	0.0

VENDOR'S TOTAL 7501 6956 545

EXAMPLE 4: CRITICAL DESIGN EMPHASIS

	Work Package	Wgt.	VA	VG	Difference
1	Project Mgmt & Admin	0	0	0	0.0
2	Systems Analysis	300	2250	2130	120.0
3	Systems Design	400	3040	2674	365.5
4	Coding, Debug &Test	300	2280	2220	60.0
5	Interface Testing	0	0	0	0.0
6	Integration Testing	0	0	0	0.0
7	Data Conversion	0	0	0	0.0
8	Acceptance Testing	0	0	0	0.0
9	Cutover & Parallel	0	0	0	0.0
10	Operations Support	0	0	0	0.0

VENDOR'S TOTAL 7570 7024 546

EXAMPLE 2: FLAT PROFILE

	Work Package	Wgt.	VA	VG	Difference
1	Project Mgmt & Admin	100	750	680	70.0
2	Systems Analysis	100	750	710	40.0
3	Systems Design	200	1520	1337	182.8
4	Coding, Debug &Test	100	760	740	20.0
5	Interface Testing	100	720	760	-40.0
6	Integration Testing	100	710	680	30.0
7	Data Conversion	100	600	660	-60.0
8	Acceptance Testing	100	770	800	-30.0
9	Cutover & Parallel	100	740	550	190.0
10	Operations Support	0	0	0	0.0

VENDOR'S TOTAL 7320 6917 403

EXAMPLE 5: ENHANCED TEST ENVIRONMENT

	Work Package	Wgt.	VA	VG	Difference
1	Project Mgmt & Admin	50	375	340	35.0
2	Systems Analysis	50	375	355	20.0
3	Systems Design	200	1520	1337	182.8
4	Coding, Debug &Test	100	760	740	20.0
5	Interface Testing	200	1440	1520	-80.0
6	Integration Testing	200	1420	1360	60.0
7	Data Conversion	0	0	0	0.0
8	Acceptance Testing	200	1540	1600	-60.0
9	Cutover & Parallel	0	0	0	0.0
10	Operations Support	0	0	0	0.0

VENDOR'S TOTAL 7430 7252 178

EXAMPLE 3: DELETE LAST FIVE

	Work Package	Wgt.	VA	VG	Difference
1	Project Mgmt & Admin	250	1875	1700	175.0
2	Systems Analysis	250	1875	1775	100.0
3	Systems Design	250	1900	1672	228.5
4	Coding, Debug &Test	250	1900	1850	50.0
5	Interface Testing	0	0	0	0.0
6	Integration Testing	0	0	0	0.0
7	Data Conversion	0	0	0	0.0
8	Acceptance Testing	0	0	0	0.0
9	Cutover & Parallel	0	0	0	0.0
10	Operations Support	0	0	0	0.0

VENDOR'S TOTAL 7550 6997 553

EXAMPLE 6: PRODUCTION EMPHASIS

	Work Package	Wgt.	VA	VG	Difference
1	Project Mgmt & Admin	0	0	0	0.0
2	Systems Analysis	0	0	0	0.0
3	Systems Design	200	1520	1337	182.8
4	Coding, Debug &Test	400	3040	2960	80.0
5	Interface Testing	200	1440	1520	-80.0
6	Integration Testing	200	1420	1360	60.0
7	Data Conversion	0	0	0	0.0
8	Acceptance Testing	0	0	0	0.0
9	Cutover & Parallel	0	0	0	0.0
10	Operations Support	0	0	0	0.0

VENDOR'S TOTAL 7420 7177 243

EXHIBIT 10-32

TECHNICAL PROPOSAL SENSITIVITY ANALYSIS

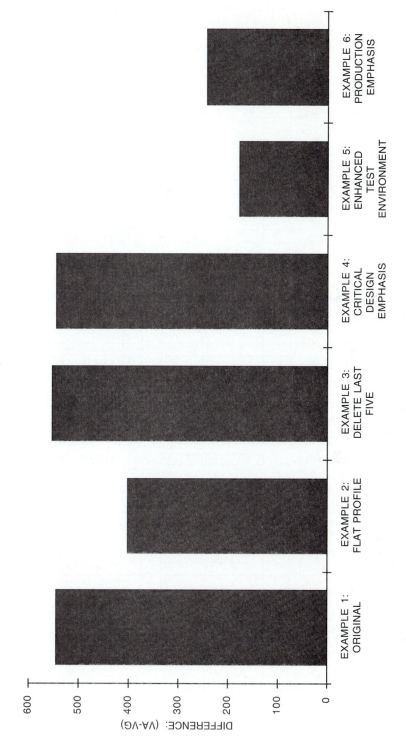

EXHIBIT 10-33

MANAGEMENT PROPOSAL SENSITIVITY ANALYSIS

EXAMPLE 1: ORIGINAL

	Work Package	Wgt.	VA	VG	Difference
1	Project Mgmt & Admin	300	2280	2400	-120.0
2	Systems Analysis	50	385	450	-65.0
3	Systems Design	200	1560	1852	-292.0
4	Coding, Debug &Test	150	1200	930	270.0
5	Interface Testing	50	330	322	8.0
6	Integration Testing	50	350	360	-10.0
7	Data Conversion	0	0	0	0.0
8	Acceptance Testing	150	1125	1110	15.0
9	Cutover & Parallel	50	400	355	45.0
10	Operations Support	0	0	0	0.0

VENDOR'S TOTAL | 7630 | 7779 | -149

EXAMPLE 4: CRITICAL DESIGN EMPHASIS

	Work Package	Wgt.	VA	VG	Difference
1	Project Mgmt & Admin	0	0	0	0.0
2	Systems Analysis	300	2310	2700	-390.0
3	Systems Design	400	3120	3704	-584.0
4	Coding, Debug &Test	300	2400	1860	540.0
5	Interface Testing	0	0	0	0.0
6	Integration Testing	0	0	0	0.0
7	Data Conversion	0	0	0	0.0
8	Acceptance Testing	0	0	0	0.0
9	Cutover & Parallel	0	0	0	0.0
10	Operations Support	0	0	0	0.0

VENDOR'S TOTAL | 7830 | 8264 | -434

EXAMPLE 2: FLAT PROFILE

	Work Package	Wgt.	VA	VG	Difference
1	Project Mgmt & Admin	200	1520	1600	-80.0
2	Systems Analysis	100	770	900	-130.0
3	Systems Design	100	780	926	-146.0
4	Coding, Debug &Test	100	800	620	180.0
5	Interface Testing	100	660	644	16.0
6	Integration Testing	100	700	720	-20.0
7	Data Conversion	100	0	0	0.0
8	Acceptance Testing	100	750	740	10.0
9	Cutover & Parallel	100	800	710	90.0
10	Operations Support	0	0	0	0.0

VENDOR'S TOTAL | 6780 | 6860 | -80

EXAMPLE 5: ENHANCED TEST ENVIRONMENT

	Work Package	Wgt.	VA	VG	Difference
1	Project Mgmt & Admin	50	380	400	-20.0
2	Systems Analysis	0	0	0	0.0
3	Systems Design	0	0	0	0.0
4	Coding, Debug &Test	100	800	620	180.0
5	Interface Testing	250	1650	1610	40.0
6	Integration Testing	250	1750	1800	-50.0
7	Data Conversion	0	0	0	0.0
8	Acceptance Testing	250	1875	1850	25.0
9	Cutover & Parallel	100	800	710	90.0
10	Operations Support	0	0	0	0.0

VENDOR'S TOTAL | 7255 | 6990 | 265

EXAMPLE 3: DELETE LAST FIVE

	Work Package	Wgt.	VA	VG	Difference
1	Project Mgmt & Admin	250	1900	2000	-100.0
2	Systems Analysis	250	1925	2250	-325.0
3	Systems Design	250	1950	2315	-365.0
4	Coding, Debug &Test	250	2000	1550	450.0
5	Interface Testing	0	0	0	0.0
6	Integration Testing	0	0	0	0.0
7	Data Conversion	0	0	0	0.0
8	Acceptance Testing	0	0	0	0.0
9	Cutover & Parallel	0	0	0	0.0
10	Operations Support	0	0	0	0.0

VENDOR'S TOTAL | 7775 | 8115 | -340

EXAMPLE 6: PRODUCTION EMPHASIS

	Work Package	Wgt.	VA	VG	Difference
1	Project Mgmt & Admin	0	0	0	0.0
2	Systems Analysis	0	0	0	0.0
3	Systems Design	200	1560	1852	-292.0
4	Coding, Debug &Test	400	3200	2480	720.0
5	Interface Testing	200	1320	1288	32.0
6	Integration Testing	200	1400	1440	-40.0
7	Data Conversion	0	0	0	0.0
8	Acceptance Testing	0	0	0	0.0
9	Cutover & Parallel	0	0	0	0.0
10	Operations Support	0	0	0	0.0

VENDOR'S TOTAL | 7480 | 7060 | 420

EXHIBIT 10-34

MANAGEMENT PROPOSAL SENSITIVITY ANALYSIS

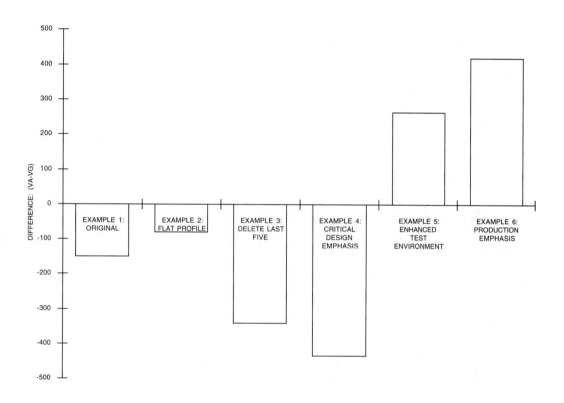

weighting may have unduly emphasized the General Management and the Design Work Packages. Example 2 may be more reflective of what the weighting should have been. However, even in this example, vendor VG is superior, though both vendors are much more than just satisfactory throughout.

It seems that a re-visit to the worksheets is required. Even that may not be sufficient. Fact-finding with each vendor may be the only way to really understand the differences in their management proposals.

Cost Proposal Sensitivity Analysis

Five recalculations of weight assignments in the cost category were performed. The results are shown in Exhibit 10-35 as Examples 2-6.

You can immediately see that there is no redistribution of weight assignments in the cost category that would have any influence on the superiority of vendor VG. So it seems that we are where we started. One vendor is superior in technical merit, while the other is superior in management and cost performance. Why is that so?

REAL COSTS ANALYSIS

Ultimately, a vendor decision distills down to the price in dollars you are willing to pay. Let's look at what the vendors originally proposed in their dollar pricing summaries.

Exhibit 10-36 lists the vendors' total proposed price to BB&T.

Exhibit 10-37 graphs the quoted prices for the work package portions of the proposals.

Exhibit 10-38 graphs the total prices quoted by the vendors.

We can make the following observations about the prices:

1. If we had not required that the labor effort for the work packages be separately itemized, we would have no basis for choosing a winning vendor except to choose vendor VH (Exhibit 10-38), based upon the vendor's total price. As we discussed under the cost proposal sensitivity analysis above, vendor VH received quite a good score for his cost proposal, and it is evident why. His proposal is more than $120 thousand lower than the next lowest. Considering technical merit, one can infer that vendor VH proposed minimal changes to his existing system. His cost category score and low price are indicative of a minimum effort project. Then when we examine vendor VG's work package prices (Exhibit 10-37), it's the lowest of all!

2. It appears that vendor VE's proposal might have been to mostly build a new system rather than doing material changes to an existing system. Even so, despite the high cost, he received adequate merit in all categories.

3. The remaining proposals are all bunched about the average, and the summary price leaves little to distinguish among them. We need to examine the cost detail to find clues to choosing the best vendor.

EXHIBIT 10-35

COST PROPOSAL SENSITIVITY ANALYSIS

EXAMPLE 1: ORIGINAL

	Work Package	Wgt.	VA	VG	Difference
1	Project Mgmt & Admin	120	648	816	-168.0
2	Systems Analysis	200	1260	1620	-360.0
3	Systems Design	250	1875	1975	-100.0
4	Coding, Debug &Test	230	1725	1702	23.0
5	Interface Testing	50	310	345	-35.0
6	Integration Testing	50	310	320	-10.0
7	Data Conversion	0	0	0	0.0
8	Acceptance Testing	50	300	311	-11.0
9	Cutover & Parallel	50	300	372	-72.0
10	Operations Support	0	0	0	0.0

VENDOR'S TOTAL | 6728 | 7461 | -733

EXAMPLE 4: CRITICAL DESIGN EMPHASIS

	Work Package	Wgt.	VA	VG	Difference
1	Project Mgmt & Admin	0	0	0	0.0
2	Systems Analysis	300	1890	2430	-540.0
3	Systems Design	400	3000	3160	-160.0
4	Coding, Debug &Test	300	2250	2220	30.0
5	Interface Testing	0	0	0	0.0
6	Integration Testing	0	0	0	0.0
7	Data Conversion	0	0	0	0.0
8	Acceptance Testing	0	0	0	0.0
9	Cutover & Parallel	0	0	0	0.0
10	Operations Support	0	0	0	0.0

VENDOR'S TOTAL | 7140 | 7810 | -670

EXAMPLE 2: FLAT PROFILE

	Work Package	Wgt.	VA	VG	Difference
1	Project Mgmt & Admin	125	675	850	-175.0
2	Systems Analysis	125	788	1013	-225.0
3	Systems Design	125	938	988	-50.0
4	Coding, Debug &Test	125	938	925	12.5
5	Interface Testing	125	775	863	-87.5
6	Integration Testing	125	775	800	-25.0
7	Data Conversion	0	0	0	0.0
8	Acceptance Testing	125	750	778	-27.5
9	Cutover & Parallel	125	750	930	-180.0
10	Operations Support	0	0	0	0.0

VENDOR'S TOTAL | 6388 | 7145 | -758

EXAMPLE 5: ENHANCED TEST ENVIRONMENT

	Work Package	Wgt.	VA	VG	Difference
1	Project Mgmt & Admin	50	270	340	-70.0
2	Systems Analysis	50	315	405	-90.0
3	Systems Design	100	750	790	-40.0
4	Coding, Debug &Test	100	750	740	10.0
5	Interface Testing	200	1240	1380	-140.0
6	Integration Testing	200	1240	1280	-40.0
7	Data Conversion	0	0	0	0.0
8	Acceptance Testing	200	1200	1244	-44.0
9	Cutover & Parallel	100	600	744	-144.0
10	Operations Support	0	0	0	0.0

VENDOR'S TOTAL | 6365 | 6923 | -558

EXAMPLE 3: DELETE LAST FIVE

	Work Package	Wgt.	VA	VG	Difference
1	Project Mgmt & Admin	250	1350	1700	-350.0
2	Systems Analysis	250	1575	2025	-450.0
3	Systems Design	250	1875	1975	-100.0
4	Coding, Debug &Test	250	1875	1850	25.0
5	Interface Testing	0	0	0	0.0
6	Integration Testing	0	0	0	0.0
7	Data Conversion	0	0	0	0.0
8	Acceptance Testing	0	0	0	0.0
9	Cutover & Parallel	0	0	0	0.0
10	Operations Support	0	0	0	0.0

VENDOR'S TOTAL | 6675 | 7550 | -875

EXAMPLE 6: PRODUCTION EMPHASIS

	Work Package	Wgt.	VA	VG	Difference
1	Project Mgmt & Admin	0	0	0	0.0
2	Systems Analysis	0	0	0	0.0
3	Systems Design	200	1500	1580	-80.0
4	Coding, Debug &Test	400	3000	2960	40.0
5	Interface Testing	200	1240	1380	-140.0
6	Integration Testing	200	1240	1280	-40.0
7	Data Conversion	0	0	0	0.0
8	Acceptance Testing	0	0	0	0.0
9	Cutover & Parallel	0	0	0	0.0
10	Operations Support	0	0	0	0.0

VENDOR'S TOTAL | 6980 | 7200 | -220

EXHIBIT 10-36

VENDOR PRICING COMPARISON SUMMARY

$=(000)   Vendor   ID:

COST COMPONENT	VA	VB	VC	VE	VF	VG	VH	Average
Work Package Proposal Costs	331.7	370.0	426.0	618.0	430.0	204.0	258.5	376.9
Software License Fees	160.0	100.0	75.0	35.0	125.0	320.0	95.0	130.0
Other Costs	0.0	35.0	60.0	0.0	15.0	36.0	17.0	23.3
Vendor's Total Price	491.7	505.0	561.0	653.0	570.0	560.0	370.5	530.2

EXHIBIT 10-37

VENDORS' WORK PACKAGE PRICES

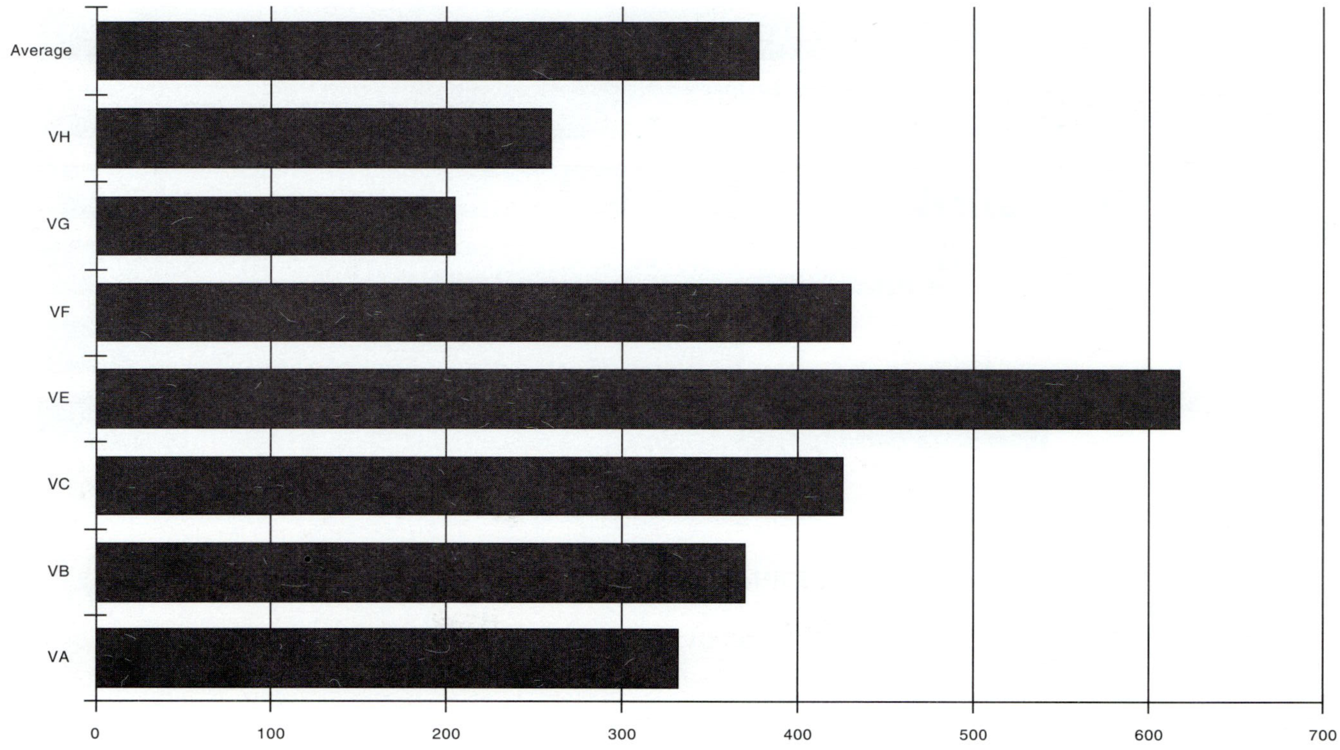

EXHIBIT 10-38

VENDORS' TOTAL PRICES

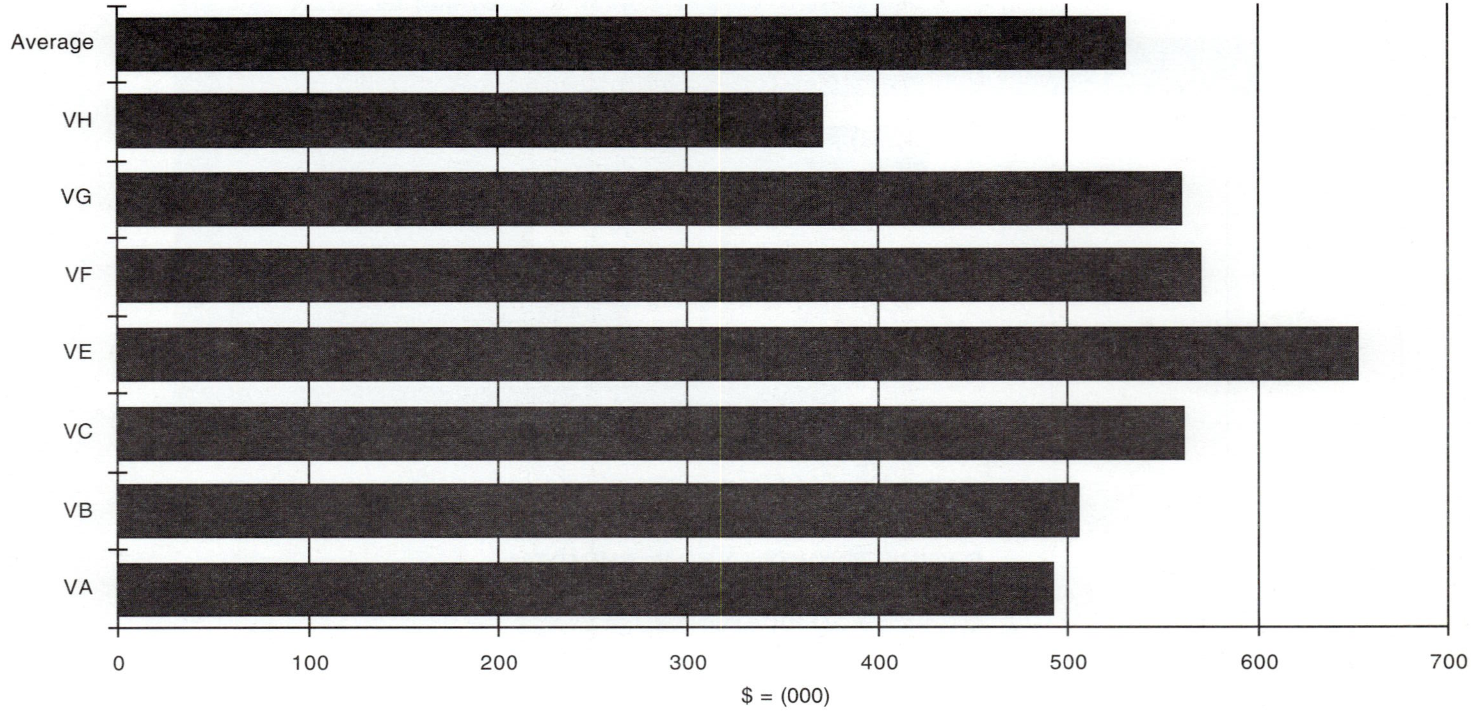

$ = (000)

At this point we'll just examine vendor VA and VG in more depth, assuming that an final average price (all vendors) of $530 thousand seems reasonable. However, the average price for the work packages of $377 thousand, and the software license fee average of $130 thousand needs to be examined.

Exhibit 10-39 contains a cost proposal comparison by work package line item prices for vendors VA and VG.

The grand total shows a difference of $68 thousand in favor of vendor VA. The Work Package costs favor vendor VG by almost $128 thousand. Examination of the other additional costs shows why the swing occurs. Vendor VG wants to charge BB&T a software license fee of $320 thousand! This exceeds vendor VA's quote of $160 thousand, and far exceeds the average of the seven vendors of $130 thousand. Wow!

Presumably, most of vendor VG's profit will be coming from the license fee. He is also charging for extra documentation and computer time, and must assume that BB&T won't provide sufficient computing resources. If vendor VG were selected, there is plenty of room for negotiation on the price components not included in the work packages. If vendor VG already has a set of clients who bought the software at the quoted license fee price, you won't have room for much price reduction. Vendor VG is either a bargain, or is too expensive, depending on the license.

In the actual work package customization work that must be done for BB&T, vendor VG proposes to charge much less than vendor VA. We need more information to determine if this pricing is appropriate.

Exhibit 10-40 contains the profile of resources for each work package that vendors VA and VG quoted to deliver the project.

In Exhibit 10-40 *Task Loading* refers to the number of persons who will simultaneously work on each work package. Vendor VA therefore will require the services of over 31 individuals, and vendor VG over 23. The same person could work simultaneously or serially on more than one work package. For simplicity we've assumed that different persons work in each work package. In nearly every work package, vendor VA requires more persons to do the work than vendor VG.

Task Duration reflects the scheduled elapsed time for each of the tasks. Since the schedule is defined by BB&T, both vendors have the same start and end dates. We will examine any differences in the schedules later.

The *Months Labor Effort* reflects the proposed work for each work package and is the product of the loading and the duration. Vendor VA has quoted 15 months more labor effort than vendor VG. Eleven of these are in overhead (project management and administration) and in system design.

How does 15 months more labor effort translate into $128 thousand in higher costs for vendor VA?

Exhibit 10-41 provides details on the salary and overhead rates quoted by each vendor. The column heading numbers refer to the Notes at the bottom of the Exhibit.

Annual Salary is the actual salary paid to each labor grade. For simplicity, we've assumed that every person in a labor grade is paid the same salary. The *Number of Persons* is the actual number of people who will work on the work packages. The *Annualized Salary*

EXHIBIT 10-39

COST PROPOSAL COMPARISON

($000)

#	Work Package	Vendor VA	Vendor VG	Differ-ence
1	Project Management & Admin.	84.4	62.2	22.2
2	Systems Analysis	30.9	13.2	17.7
3	Systems Design	68.8	18.0	50.8
4	Coding, Debug & Unit Testing	61.6	55.5	6.1
5	Interface Testing	28.1	15.0	13.1
6	Integration Testing	14.1	12.0	2.1
7	Data Conversion	3.8	1.0	2.7
8	Acceptance Testing	3.3	4.5	-1.2
9	Cutover & Parallel	13.1	9.0	4.1
10	Operations Support	23.8	13.6	10.2
	Total Work Package Costs	331.7	204.0	127.7
a	Software System License Fee	160.0	320.0	-160.0
b	Documentation Supplement		21.0	-21.0
c	Computer Time Usage		15.0	-15.0
	Total Additional Costs	160.0	356.0	-196.0
	Grand Total Cost Proposal	491.7	560.0	-68.3

Note: Rounding from original calculations accounts for addition anomalies.

EXHIBIT 10-40

PROJECT LOADING COMAPRISON

#	Work Package	Vendor VA			Vendor VG		
		Task Loading #Persons	Task Duration #Months	Months Labor Effort	Task Loading #Persons	Task Duration #Months	Months Labor Effort
1	Project Management & Admin.	2.25	5.0	11.25	1.5	5.0	7.5
2	Systems Analysis	3.0	1.5	4.5	2.0	1.0	2.0
3	Systems Design	4.0	2.5	10.0	2.0	1.5	3.0
4	Coding, Debug & Unit Testing	5.0	2.5	12.5	5.0	2.5	12.5
5	Interface Testing	5.0	1.0	5.0	4.0	1.0	4.0
6	Integration Testing	5.0	0.5	2.5	3.0	1.0	3.0
7	Data Conversion	1.0	1.0	1.0	1.0	1.0	1.0
8	Acceptance Testing	2.0	0.3	0.5	2.0	0.5	1.0
9	Cutover & Parallel	2.0	1.1	2.2	1.5	1.5	2.25
10	Operations Support	2.0	2.0	4.0	1.5	1.5	2.25
	Total Resources Required	31.25	17.4	53.45	23.5	16.5	38.50

EXHIBIT 10-41

LABOR RATE COMPARISON

($000)

	Vendor VA				Vendor VG			
Notes:	**1.**	**2.**	**3.**	**4.**	**1.**	**2.**	**3.**	**4.**
Labor Grade:	**Annual Salary**	**# Persons**	**Annual-ized Salary**	**Total Cost if Annual**	**Annual Salary**	**# Persons**	**Annual-ized Salary**	**Total Cost if Annual**
Senior Management	100.0	0.25	25.0	37.5	86.0	0.10	8.6	12.4
Project Mgr.	80.0	1.00	80.0	120.0	70.0	1.00	70.0	100.8
Administrator	30.0	1.00	30.0	45.0	25.0	1.00	25.0	36.0
Sr. Analyst	65.0	1.00	65.0	97.5	60.0	1.00	60.0	86.4
Analyst	50.0	2.00	100.0	150.0	50.0	1.00	50.0	72.0
Designers	60.0	2.00	120.0	180.0	50.0	1.00	50.0	72.0
Sr. Programmer	45.0	1.00	45.0	67.5	45.0	1.00	45.0	64.8
Programmer	38.0	4.00	152.0	228.0	35.0	4.00	140.0	201.6
Librarian	30.0	1.00	30.0	45.0	25.0	0.00	0.0	0.0
Test Mgr.	65.0	1.00	65.0	97.5	50.0	1.00	50.0	72.0
Test Support	40.0	4.00	160.0	240.0	25.0	3.00	75.0	108.0
Total Cost	**603.0**	**18.25**	**872.0**	**1308.0**	**521**	**14.10**	**573.6**	**826.0**

NOTES:
1. Base Annual Salary for this Labor Grade for this Vendor.
2. # of Persons who will be simultaneously required for any task.
3. The annual salary for these personnel.
4. The annualized salary times Benefits, Overhead and Profit Margin for these personnel on an annualized basis. Vendor VA has a mark-up factor of 1.50 times base salary, and Vendor VG has a mark-up factor of 1.44 times base salary.
5. The results in Exhibit 10-40 are based upon the mix of personnel required in each Work Package times the duration they work, times the Total Cost in this Exhibit divided by 12. For example, Work Package #1 for Vendor VA has a full time Project Manager (5 months), a full time Administrator, and a quarter time representation by Senior Management for a total of $84.4 thousand for Project Management and Administration.

converts the actual salary and the number of persons required to an annual cost for that labor grade for the project. The *Total Cost* reflects the addition of overhead, pension and other benefits, and the vendor's profit component for that labor grade.

It is essential that the RFP require project loading, labor grades and hourly (annual) rate information from the vendors. In the event that there are changes in scope later, or you wish to add support during operations, the quotations for the labor rates serve as a ceiling on what you will pay.

Reviewing the bottom line, we note that the *Annualized Total Costs* of vendor VA are $1.3 million (if every employee proposed worked all the time for the full year). Vendor VG's annualized costs are $826 thousand. At the macro level it is obvious that vendor VA pays his people much more, and has a higher mark-up (1.50 versus 1.44) than vendor VG.

Having the annualized costs for each labor grade is helpful in conducting what-if analysis on schedule delays. At any point in the schedule we can calculate the running rate cost increases for a slip in the schedule. No matter where a slip would occur in BB&T's schedule, it is reasonable to expect that vendor VA's costs will be 58% higher than vendor VG's costs.

Vendor VA has a member of senior management spending at least one week a month on the project, while vendor VG has senior management spending 2 days. Which is required? Since there is also a full time Project Manager, is such a role by senior management necessary for vendor VA? Shouldn't senior management's contribution be included in the overhead? Is the allocation of senior management time by vendor VA just another way of including profit? Is senior management representation by vendor VA worth an additional $25 thousand?

All this information explains why vendor VA's work package costs are higher than vendor VG. Higher wages, higher overhead margin and more persons assigned to the project account for the pricing difference.
All this information still does not help us choose which vendor to select.

Although if we were forced to choose at this point, with no other information to be made available, we would choose vendor VG, on the expectation that the software license fee could be dramatically reduced, and therefore vendor VG would have a substantial total price advantage over vendor VA. If all other things are equal, and a definitive case cannot be made for the technically superior proposal, we choose the lower cost vendor.

RISK ANALYSIS

But are all other things equal? Why does vendor VA require more personnel? Why does vendor VG want to charge so much more for the license? Is there a correlation between the license and the work package effort to be done?

Exhibit 10-42 contains a side-by-side Gantt Chart Schedule of the Work Package phasing of each vendor. Because each vendor proposed some start-up activities that varied, BB&T normalized each schedule to correspond to a start date of November 1.

EXHIBIT 10-42

COMPARISON OF PROPOSED SCHEDULES VENDORS VA AND VG

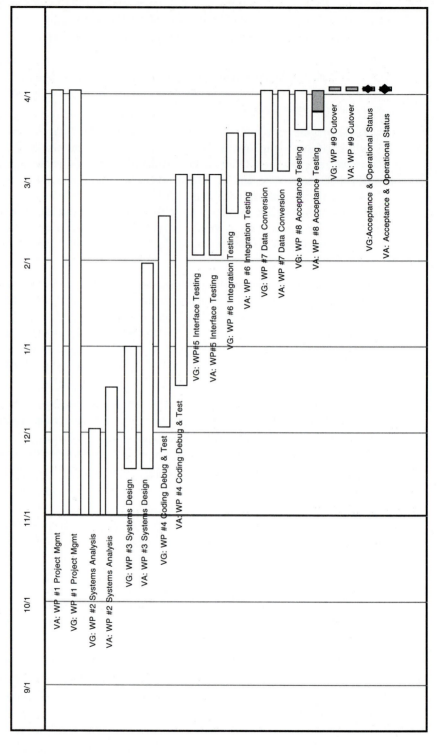

You can use Exhibit 10-42 or Task Duration (Exhibit 10-40) for the following discussion. Exhibit 10-42 has the advantage in showing the overlap in phases (work packages). Since BB&T is not buying operational support at this time, this work package has been left off of the schedule.

Note that vendor VA devotes one-half of a month more to Systems Analysis than vendor VG. Each vendor starts System Design at the same time, but vendor VG is finished a full month before vendor VA. Is there less to design? Vendor VA has a much longer duration for the Systems Analysis to be completed, inferring that the design could change as more analysis was completed?

Both vendors start Coding (Work Package 4) very early after the design has been started. VA has to wait until the analysis is finished, so this phase lags VG by half a month. In both cases, starting to code before design has started has high risk. Presumably this is necessary to meet the schedule dictated by BB&T.

Vendor VG has one month of overlap of Coding, Design and Test with Systems Design, and one and one-half months of effort following completion of design. Vendor VA has one and one-half months of overlap and only one month of clean coding after design is finished. If there are design problems, VA is more likely to have schedule delays due to the need to re-code software.

Vendor VG doesn't start Interface Testing until a month after Systems Design completion, allowing for coding to mature. VA starts Interface Testing the day after design is finished. There is significant compounding of risk in VA's approach.

Vendor VG devotes a full month to Integration testing, while vendor VA allocates just a couple of weeks. Vendor VG assumes Acceptance testing will take two full weeks while vendor VA is more optimistic, and the schedule reflects one week of slack time.

Which vendor has the greater risk in delivering the product? On the basis of all the above information, we think that vendor VA has much greater risk in delivering the project on time. Our reasons are:

1. Vendor VG is charging more for the software license because he has a much more robust existing software package. His technical proposal was ranked lower than vendor VA's because he did less design, not more. His approach was the more conservative, though less elegant.

2. Vendor VG needs to do less analysis and design because his existing software package presumably already fulfills many of the requirements desired by BB&T. It is firmer, requires fewer changes, and hence the schedule is less dependent upon additional design than vendor VA.

3. Vendor VG places stronger emphasis on Interface and Integration testing to ensure full compatibility with BB&T's existing wholesale banking software.

4. The overlap in dependencies upon prior phases of the project is less critical for vendor VG than for vendor VA.

One of the benefits that a comparison of proposed schedules provides is the understanding that each vendor must be consistent with itself throughout the proposal, otherwise inconsistencies would have been discovered in the evaluation process.

Because these vendors are consistent, you can rely on the information they have provided to truly reflect their expected execution of the project. Then you can make reasonable assumptions about the risks involved in selecting either vendor.

To calculate a final score, we might assign a completion Risk Coefficient to each vendor. We might assign vendor VG a probability of on-time successful completion of the project of 90%. We might assign vendor VA a probability of 75%. If we multiply these risk assessments times the Vendors Final Total Scores (Exhibit 10-29) we would have a final result (7411* 0.75) of 5528 for vendor VA, and a final result (7197 * 0.90) of 6477 for vendor VG. Vendor VG is now 16% better than VA, a noticeable difference.

Therefore we would select vendor VG as the successful vendor, and expect to negotiate the software license downward by about $150 thousand. Then, should the schedule happen to slip, the total costs would still be under what the costs would have been with vendor VA.

The evaluation panels argued far into the night about which vendor to select. It seemed that the partisans for vendors VA and VG were evenly split. The technical gurus, led by Peyton Somers, believed that VA's technical superiority was sufficient to choose it. Management advocates, led by Ulrich and Monk Eternic, felt that VG's overall proposal and lower risk made it the superior vendor.

Finally Fred Everet suggested that they reread the commentary side-by-side through the work packages to see if the verbal emphasis was sufficient to substantiate the numerical difference in the scores. They couldn't find adequate justification to unambiguously choose VA. Therefore, Fred suggested that given the substantial total dollar difference in the cost of the work packages, they should go with the lower cost VG on the assumption that the total price would be reduced. Everyone concurred. They sent the following recommendation forward for advisory committee and project review committee approval: Vendor VG is the recommended vendor, but only if the license fee can be reduced by $150,000. Otherwise negotiations with VG will be terminated, and VA will be the chosen vendor.

CONCLUSION

This chapter has covered an immense amount of material. The only way you will master it, is to use the methodology in your next technology procurement.

Table 10-4 summarizes the critical steps you must take to select the best vendor.

TABLE 10-4
VENDOR EVALUATION CHECKLIST

1. Choose Qualified Members of Evaluation Panels
2. Prepare Evaluation Questionnaires
3. Establish Fully Satisfactory Consensus
4. Create Schedule and Reading Sequences
5. Determine Category Percentile Contributions
6. Weight Work Packages and Sub-Work Packages
7. Choose Ternary or Gradation Scoring Range
8. Complete Evaluator's Worksheets
9. Evaluate Technical Proposals
10. Hold Technical Panel Review Session
11. Evaluate Management Proposals
12. Hold Management Panel Review Session
13. Evaluate Cost Proposals
14. Hold Cost Panel Review Session
15. Conduct Technical, Management and Cost Comparisons
16. Conduct Sensitivity Analyses
17. Determine Real Costs
18. Assess Risks
19. Select Vendor
20. Write Vendor Evaluation Report

## Chapter Eleven

NEGOTIATE THE BEST DEAL

You finally chose the vendor, wrote the Vendor Evaluation Report, and the advisory and the senior project review committees recommended approval. Management approved, subject to the negotiation conditions. Now, the accountable executive, project manager and the SCA have to prepare for contract negotiations.

Despite all the effort you've taken to limit uncertainties, there are a number of open items. The final technical design, vendor performance and exact schedule still have to be negotiated. These are important, but in the final analysis, negotiations are primarily concerned with money.

NEGOTIATING WITH MULTIPLE VENDORS

The example in the last chapter showed how two vendors were so close in capability that either one might be the best vendor. If you had the time, the best approach would be to carry the vendor selection forward. This would include fact-finding sessions to clarify any outstanding technical, management and cost issues revealed in the proposals, and other open items.

This is the best time to cover in depth the information in Chapters 3.0 through 9.0 (ref. Table 8-1) of the management proposal. Some of the topics, while not having any effect on the content of the technical proposal, could affect quality, schedule and total costs. After a few conversations, it is possible that one vendor will have a clear advantage or disadvantage because of some issue that was overlooked earlier.

A typical example would be where a vendor was negotiating with another client. If the vendor has limited personnel, it might be prudent not to award that vendor your contract because he might not have the resources you originally expected.

The situation changes also when the financial resources of a company have suddenly deteriorated, and the risk increases that the vendor will not be in business to complete your project.

Good financial things can also happen. If the vendor has a public offering of stock that improves financial stability, then that vendor might be preferred.

But what if you did all this fact-finding, and were still unable to choose the best vendor. The final option would be a pricing competition and contract award to the vendor with the lowest price.

Multiple vendor negotiations are common in government, where procurement statutes restrict awards and political interference is common. Negotiating a final contract for lowest price among the best qualified vendors is one more way to avoid political second guessing and political end-runs by the losing vendor. Because of political issues, a procurement process can take on a life of its own, as though the project had no real urgency or benefit to the taxpayer.

Multiple vendor negotiations will unquestionably get you the best price. But negotiations take time, effort, analysis and compromise. Since the relationship with each vendor is different, and your legal team may have its own agenda for each, a standardized approach to completing the negotiation can't be anticipated. Multiple vendor negotiations are almost never done commercially. You make your decision and accept the risk.

I recall one contract negotiation which was so lengthy that the project was completed before we were able to complete all the legal terms and conditions. The vendor was funded for each interim milestone using Letter Agreements. The final contract had no impact upon the original project. It served to govern maintenance and follow-on work. Yet, if both parties had not shown slow but continual progress toward reaching a satisfactory contract, our management would have held up the work. Letter agreements are discussed later in this chapter.

The time to negotiate a contract can't be predicted. If that is so, your recommendation to management must be based upon the assumption that the vendor provided his proposal in good faith. It is assumed there are no issues in the contract negotiations that will have a significant impact upon the schedule, performance or the maximum cost of the project.

This assumption is not always valid. There are many instances, particularly in the construction industry where "low-ball" bids are so prevalent, that any buyer who has a vendor start work before a completed contract is signed is foolish. In most systems procurements a good faith negotiation can be assumed.

If the vendor evaluation process indicates a clearly superior vendor, you would waste time and money by doing multiple negotiations. After all, the process you've followed virtually assures that you have found the best vendor, and contract negotiations should be a mere formality. Well, not quite.

PREPARING TO NEGOTIATE THE CONTRACT

The evaluation chairman again reviews the vendor's proposal, other documentation and the evaluation worksheets. The purpose is to find possible omissions in the proposal; identify erroneous assumptions, conclusions or mistakes; and isolate superfluous or constricting designs that will prohibit future improvements to the system.

This pre-negotiation review can enhance the final product and the probability of success. The project team has at its disposal the combined wisdom of all the vendors who submitted proposals. The information contained in the losing proposals can be selectively used to double-check the winning vendor's proposal against the best of all the other vendors' work packages. An "ideal" set of work components can be constructed from this information, and matched against the winning vendor. If the ideal system were too far from what the vendor proposed, no value would be served, because implementing the ideal system would be different in technology, management and cost from what was proposed (and won). The ideal component analogy is to surface items which, if implemented, might make useful enhancements (or reductions) to the already superior system at a cost effective price.

The use of a "common denominator" of ideas, techniques and tools culled from the distilled wisdom of other vendors makes a lot of sense. (That is also why work packages are important; it improves the ability for finding the ideal among many inputs.) Your intent is to reduce risk, increase performance if possible, and obtain the best possible result at the lowest reasonable cost. In no way should there be any intent to plagiarize other vendors' proprietary information. Extracting the essence of an issue and translating that essence into a perspective applicable to the vendor selected is a different matter.

An analogy might be the never-ending, fine-tuning in styling that automobile manufacturers seem to borrow from each other each year.

Thus from their own analysis and from the distillate of proposals reviewed, the negotiators will prepare a list of issues. They naturally fall into the technical, management and cost categories.

Exhibit 11-1 contains the list of negotiation issues that will be discussed in the following paragraphs.

TECHNICAL ISSUES

Conformance to Requirements

Sometimes the vendor apparently conforms to a requirement, when detailed analysis indicates that may not be the case. If the requirement must be met, you'll need to get a conforming design. Theoretically, the cost of the vendor's old proposal and the new conforming one should be indistinguishable. (At least that should be your negotiating position for the items that you find in error or omission in the vendor's proposal.)

You might find some requirements were ambiguous and need to be restated. The vendor will then re-submit his proposal on these points, presumably at a higher cost. The requirement can even disappear in the interval between the writing of the specifications and the evaluation. You can remove the requirement, and the costs associated with it.

When you verify that all requirements are satisfied, you can proceed to the next set of issues.

Performance Criteria

There may be differences between the performance the vendor proposes and your performance criteria. In that case, the vendor should be asked to validate the performance of his existing system as-is, using a suitable simulation or real workload in a customer's location.

EXHIBIT 11-1

TYPICAL NEGOTIATION ISSUES

TECHNICAL

- Conformance to Requirements
- Performance Criteria
- Testing
- Final Acceptance Criteria
- Delivery Conditions

MANAGEMENT

- Statement of Work
- Work Packages
- Schedule
- Reporting and Control
- Personnel
- Subcontractors
- Facilities

COST

- Change Control
- Contractual Terms and Conditions
- Termination
- Letter Agreements
- Master Agreements
- Final Price

The measurements should then serve as benchmarks for establishing testing criteria for the system.

After the benchmarks, you may find that achieving your performance goals may not be possible unless the proposed design is improved. The vendor will want to be reimbursed for that effort. Alternatively, you may accept some compromise to the original processing criteria to achieve a less complex, less risky solution. The ultimate measure of performance reasonableness will be an assessment of whether the system can process the workload within the time assigned for it.

The performance issue is less pressing today than it was a decade ago. Upgrading hardware today is often less expensive than forcing major performance optimization improvements onto software. Nevertheless, you must be certain that there is hardware available that will process the workload.

Testing

Testing is like planning. If you don't do it, you always suffer in the end. Negotiations must achieve a clear differentiation of overlapping accountabilities between the vendor and customer personnel. Secondarily, the process by which the testing will be conducted must be agreed upon from the very beginning, so fingerpointing can be avoided when test time approaches. The negotiating issue is to finalize which personnel will prepare what part of the test cases, test scripts and plans, and how regression testing will be conducted once errors are found and corrected.

> Perhaps there is no vendor alive who allocates sufficient time and resources to testing. Consider the endless progression of delays in IBM's release date of OS/2-V2, or Apple Computer's extended beta testing prior to its System 7.0 release. Other more current examples abound.

Final Acceptance Criteria

The requirements specifications usually have a pretty clear definition of what the acceptance criteria will be. Uncertainty arises about the rigor to which the criteria will be applied. This includes retesting of programs, the degree of interface testing following error corrections, and whether the customer will accept part of the system or reject it all, until all acceptance criteria are passed.

An impatient customer might say: "We'll go ahead with conversion and parallel while you, vendor, iron out the last glitches." There's a lot of risk to the customer here. The vendor may think he's now off the hook. But the risk may be lessened if the negotiations establish that the vendor won't get paid until all acceptance criteria have been met.

Delivery Conditions

The vendor could assume that acceptance testing will constitute delivery, and will be done on a stand-alone platform using converted, but not actual production data. The customer has to be clear about what constitutes final delivery of the product. This includes receipt of documentation, tapes or other media the deliverables shall take. The final contract must be explicit on this point.

Attention to detail of this nature will assure you that the vendor delivers everything he should, at the time and place he should. If you forget, you'll be paying for delivery of items you thought you had already bought, even after the project is formally complete.

MANAGEMENT ISSUES

Although the technical product is the most important deliverable in terms of results, negotiations on the management proposal are more important in assuring that the project is successfully delivered. Remember a fundamental axiom: If you can't manage and control a process, you have no chance to be technically successful. The most imaginative technological concept must fail if it can't be implemented.

> There are many examples of the consequences of managerial failure: the B-1B bomber; the Navy A-12; the Hubble Space Telescope; Drexel Burnham Lambert.

The project manager may be emphasizing the technological effort with his counterpart from the vendor. Assuring that the management proposal is explicitly included within the contract terms and conditions is the major responsibility of the accountable executive. As business representative of the customer, he or she must take direct responsibility to see that the vendor's management process can deliver the technology.

The issues that follow amplify upon the Management Proposal outline contents previously presented in Table 9-1.

Statement of Work

The RFP included your Statement of Work (SOW), or the vendor will have proposed his own version. In either case you will likely need to make some revisions to the SOW.

In high technology research and development (R&D) contracts, SOWs, which are restrictive on design, tend to be undesirable. R&D contracts almost require change as a part of the learning process, and an excessively restrictive SOW places an administrative burden on both vendor and customer. This happens as a direct result of having to have a contract change (SOW update) every time a technical change occurs.

Alternatively, high-cost overruns on many production contracts occur, because they are written when the system being procured should still be in a R&D phase.

Since our preference is to make the SOW subordinate to the detail in the work packages, the SOW should contain general umbrella provisions of work that incorporate all of the proposal. However, for those companies which want the SOW to be the controlling section in the contract, we'll develop the negotiation issues related to the SOW a bit more.

If the SOW does not say that the vendor will do something, then no matter what the design document states, the vendor is not required to implement it under the terms of the contract. Therefore, traceability of the SOW to the requirements specification is the only assurance you have that the requirement will be satisfied in the delivered product.

As negotiation proceeds, there will be hassles over the meanings of words and intended scope of effort. Both customer and vendor can benefit from spending the time to haggle over the intent and meaning of the SOW. Nuances of interpretation and gray areas of performance will be surfaced, and as a result, the parties will understand the degrees of freedom available to each. Even though it is not possible to include every activity within the SOW (or even within the work packages), the very process of negotiation will enable the vendor and the customer to understand each other. This level of understanding permits open communications during implementation.

The best SOWs are those in which customer and vendor walk away feeling that each of them has a certain degree of leeway to do their work. Each feels that the leeway is still somewhat undefined, but represents an acceptable level of give-and-take for the relationship.

A vendor might find that although he quoted a required level of support from the customer, he now needs additional services in computer time. Since this may be an additional burden upon the customer, he could require the vendor to adhere to his original quotation. (But that might not be in the best interests of project success.) With some adjustments by each, the customer will usually be able to accept the additional burden.

If the process has worked as it should, each organization will know just about where the line of final resistance is drawn, and each will be wary of pushing their desires beyond the compromise areas.

If an issue arises in which neither party can or will compromise further, then the proper time has come to exercise other avenues, such as contract change, descoping of the task, or management escalation. When the SOW has been well defined, including the compromise areas, the number of these latter instances will be minimal, and they will be settled in a thoroughly professional and friendly manner.

> ## If it's not included in the Statement of Work, it doesn't get implemented!

Work Packages

With the emphasis you've placed on work packages, the vendor should have no doubt about your commitment to them. Therefore, the only real negotiation issue is whether you want to include more sub-levels in the work packages for additional management controls, visibility or allocation of resources.

In Exhibit 9-1 we displayed work packages with two levels of task breakdown, with occasional third level detail. If each second or third level work package is backed-up by a list of tasks, a schedule and deliverables, then the essential requirements of work packages will be met for most medium sized projects.

Such a modest level of work package breakout will not be sufficient for major projects like building subway systems, spacecraft or major systems projects like the Federal Aviation Administrations's efforts to revitalize the Air Traffic Control System. These kinds of projects require five or six levels of breakout.

The key factor in determining the depth of the work packages is whether the content of each is understandable and executable by the person who has to do the work. If it isn't, then you should add levels until it is understandable. Discussion of the work packages provides input toward additional fine-tuning of the schedule.

Schedule

No vendor who wants to win is really likely to tell the customer that his projected schedule is impossible. Nevertheless, any vendor who signs a contract for what he considers to be an impossible schedule is stupid. He'll lose money, lose reputation and will certainly harm the client.

Negotiations are the time to really insist upon do-able, success oriented (although tight) schedules.

Baccarat Bank & Trust's schedule was considered to be unacceptable from the very beginning by Fred Everet. This is the time to enlist the vendor to provide the answer of whether the schedule can be met If it can't, then presumably the vendor has sufficient data within his work packages, pert charts and schedules to verify that the schedule can't be met. If the schedule can be met, but has a substantial probability of also not being met, then the entire bank has to create a contingency plan for that outcome.

By this methodology, bank management shouldn't shoot the messenger, since an outside source (the chosen vendor) has collaborated the risk in the schedule.

After extensive discussions, Orlando Gomez, President of Grand Systems Design, assures Fred that the April 1st cutover date is achievable. The negotiations proceed on that assumption.

Working to a schedule that reasonably qualified persons know is impossible, is demoralizing and demotivating to all who work on such a project. Not only does the project miss its impossible target schedule, but in all likelihood, it will miss a target date that would have been met if the schedule was reasonable from the beginning. There is a fine line between the enthusiasm of working toward difficult but achievable goals, versus the devastating effect of low productivity upon impossible goals. You and the vendor have to agree upon a do-able schedule, or it won't be met.

In this manual we used the same schedule to apply to all vendors. There are some occasions in which the customer will leave the schedule duration for the vendor to define. Whatever the schedules proposed, the schedule proposed by the vendors will be longer than the customer's expectation, and probably shorter than it will really take.

In a vendor evaluation having an open schedule, trying to determine a firm delivery date prior to completion of negotiations is futile. Therefore, the schedule as defined in the contract should count from the time the contract is signed, and only from that moment.

Sometimes the negotiated contract requires review and re-approval by management. The schedule should not start until management approval is obtained and the vendor is formally notified. If management delays for any considerable time, the vendor might insist (in order to manage resource scheduling) that he be given an additional 30 days preparation time at customer's expense, before beginning the work.

Reporting and Control

During negotiations you and the vendor should agree on reporting, and the degree of control of the vendor that you will have. Milestones and reviews must be confirmed. Customer and vendor must have a clear agreement about what constitutes customer technical supervision and management of the vendor.

Exhibit 11-2 provides a definition of what constitutes *Technical Supervision.* This definition is sometimes included in contract clauses. It establishes that the customer's project manager, working day-to-day with the vendor, is the source from which technical direction is given to the vendor. By the same token, no agreement between the project manager and the vendor can include any effort which is a change because these personnel are not authorized to enter into such agreements.

EXHIBIT 11-2

CONTRACT CLAUSE REGARDING TECHNICAL SUPERVISION

The parties agree that the maximum benefits obtainable from the work to be performed will be achieved only by the vendor having adequate flexibility to complete the work, while allowing for adequate customer supervision and advice.

The work to be conducted under this contract will be under the technical direction of the BB&T project manager whose duties and authority are defined in Exhibit 11-3. The vendor will permit the project manager and/or the SCA to review work in progress at any time during working hours. The vendor will communicate directly with the project manager on technical aspects of the work being performed. Analysis and project approach aspects within the scope of the contract will be authorized directly by the project manager to the vendor in accordance with Exhibit 11-3. The project manager's instructions may be either written or oral and then ratified by him or her in writing.

The project manager may not authorize project approaches that would require additional costs or any changes in the scope of work under this contract.

EXHIBIT 11-3

DUTIES AND AUTHORITY OF THE PROJECT MANAGER

1. The BB&T project manager may: issue directions to the vendor without the necessity of submitting these directions through the SCA if such directions are within the scope of work and within the costs for such effort provided for in the contract.

2. Assist the vendor in interpreting technical phases of contract drawings, specifications, or other customer furnished items.

3. Assist the vendor in obtaining such technical data or other information that may be needed by the vendor, and within the scope of customer furnished items.

4. Review the technical reports submitted by the vendor in accordance with contract terms and notify the SCA of acceptance or nonacceptance when approval is required.

5. Perform technical acceptance of all specifications and modifications to specifications, as prepared by the vendor in accordance with the contract deliverables.

6. Initiate requests for preliminary data necessary to keep BB&T management informed of the development status and problem areas prior to the issuance by the vendor of formal information.

The difference in role between the project manager and the systems contract administrator (SCA) should be clearly understood by the customer and vendor teams. A definition of these responsibilities and authorities should be a part of the contract.

Exhibit 11-3 contains the description of the duties and authority of the customer project manager as it applies to the contract.

The authority for executing contracts is the Contracting Officer or Contracting Authority. In this manual the SCA and the contracting officer are the same individual.

Exhibit 11-4 contains the duties and authority of the Systems Contract Administrator as it applies to the contract. See Chapter 3 for other SCA duties.

EXHIBIT 11-4

DUTIES AND AUTHORITY OF THE CONTRACTING OFFICER

1. The contracting officer or Systems Contract Administrator (SCA) is BB&T's official buyer of the services to be procured.

2. The contracting officer's signature is the only official signature obligating BB&T.

3. Bears legal responsibility for protecting the interests of BB&T.

4. Coordinates the efforts of the technical project manager, legal, auditing and management when necessary.

5. He or she is solely responsible for requesting systems or engineering change proposals from the vendor during the course of the contract.

6. Only the SCA can negotiate a proposal, accept a proposal, authorize a change in scope or award additional fees.

7. Monitors contracts for SOW, work package, milestone compliance, commitments and expenditures.

8. Authorizes payments to the vendor based on input from the technical project manager.

9. Initiates termination activity when necessary and negotiates such termination.

With these contract clauses included, vendor personnel will recognize legitimate requirements guidance from the project manager, and will know that contract amendments can only come from the SCA.

Personnel

The customer wants some control over the quality of vendor personnel assigned to the project. There will inevitably be some contention over the degree to which the vendor will permit this to occur. Certainly the vendor will be unwilling to relinquish his prerogative of management control over his own personnel.

When the vendor will work away from the customer, only those vendor personnel having management responsibilities will be offered for customer approval. When vendor personnel have extensive customer interaction, especially with business units or senior management, the customer will insist upon approving those vendor personnel by name. Usually this is to screen out vendor personnel who might cause cultural imbalance in the relationship.

Earrings on men just aren't acceptable in the hallways of certain companies.

The availability of customer personnel to assist the vendor in tasks requiring joint participation is a common issue. The project manager can mess up negotiations if he or she hasn't lined up support early enough. This usually happens when support is needed from organizations outside the project manager's direct control. When the vendor persists in having a contractual commitment for support, the project manager tries to evade the commitment, for he or she will now need to make some waves in the company. This doesn't happen if everyone has signed up for the project from the very beginning, and the concept of customer furnished services and support has been included in the RFP package.

Subcontractors

Our RFP did not allow provision for subcontractors. The contrary is more frequent, particularly in large and complex projects. The same rules and requirements that apply to a vendor's employees should apply to subcontractors.

The government can insist on these provisions, but such control is less likely in commercial projects. Nevertheless, you must be prudent in your review of the qualifications and experience of the subcontractors. You need to assess the additional risk you incur as a result of the vendor being dependent upon a critical subcontractor. If you determine you can handle the risk, then the issue disappears. If the risk is high, you must devote the time to negotiate sufficient control over the subcontractor to reduce the risk.

Facilities

Facilities fall into two categories. The first category relates to customer furnished items which are to be made available for the vendor team. This includes computer time, desk space, reproduction, telephones and other administrative support. This also includes provision for access control, security and off-hours working conditions. This category is only a matter of working out the details.

The second category applies to a situation in which hardware or facilities construction are themselves part of the procurement. There are interdependent roles associated with delivery, installation and initial operating states of computer or other hardware delivered for the project. If a computer room has to be designed, then issues related to fire detection and suppression, security access, raised floors, power, air conditioning, piped water and the responsibilities of many other vendors involved come to the fore. Responsibility for each must be established prior to contract signing. Alternatively, you might give the vendor a blanket variance from any delay caused by any of these facilities issues which impact performance or schedule.

Additional real and potential costs to the project are often identified when facilities issues are negotiated.

COST ISSUES

Cost or price is the ultimate measure of the value each party places upon their need or contribution. All contract negotiations include price maneuvering. If the above technical and management issues have been settled, the ultimate cost/price uncertainty will have been lessened. However, final price is not the only cost issue of importance.

Change Control

Very few contracts are completed without some changes. A prudent provision for a change process within the contract assures that work can continue in unaffected areas while change negotiations occur.

At some time during implementation the vendor is bound to say: "Hey, you want something new which I didn't propose, and that I'm not funded to do. If you want a change, I can give you a proposal which will define the additional deliverable and my price for it. Then we can process the change, get the contract amended, and then I'll do the work."

Sometimes you want to delete a requirement, or substitute one for another. The vendor's response will be: "The design on the old requirement is basically finished, so you don't get any money back. In fact, if you want to delete it, I'll have to go back and do some retrofit to restore the original condition. Then I'll do the new requirement or substitution. You'll have to pay me additional for all of that." Yes, you will end up paying for much of what the vendor claims.

If these situations are bound to occur, the contract must contain explicit rules governing the process of change identification, request for proposal, proposal and cost negotiation. The management of the change control process is solely under the authority of the SCA.

The larger and more complex the project, the more elaborate and deliberate and costly the change process alone will be, not to mention the actual cost of implementing the change. Each contractual change creates a ripple effect throughout the project which increases costs. Without a process to control change, chaos would result.

Project managers typically hate the change process. They perceive change control as impeding progress. They would rather try to work things out informally with the vendor. Wrong! It won't work, because the mechanism to assure it does work is missing. The proper approach is for the project manager (in response to a user, or a technical issue) to prepare a Change Request which is issued by the SCA to the vendor. The vendor prepares a Change Proposal. If the proposal is accepted, a price is negotiated, and the SCA issues an amendment to the contract incorporating the change. The SCA then issues a Change Order directing the vendor to implement the change. This process could be done overnight or it could take weeks. Even if the change process does slow down the project, it is far better to have the changes incorporated into a system that the user wants developed, than deliver a system which does not respond to requirements.

Manufacturing or architecture firms have extensive experience in tracking and charting changes through specifications, drawings and blueprints, and more recently through computer aided design (CAD) and electronic updates. By analogy, the systems change process should be conducted just as smoothly as executed by these professionals.

In any event, the vendor should have tunnel vision with respect to the changes. This means he should continue with the current design (excepting the items in question) as if the discussions on the changes were not occurring. Not all changes that are proposed get approved. Starting work ahead of approval might result in the vendor not being paid for that effort, and might impact the schedule as well.

Contractual Terms and Conditions

Although much of the contractual "boilerplate" is not a factor in the actual performance issues under the contract, several may have cost impacts. Control of proprietary information; confidentiality of trade secrets of each party; ownership of the original program and modifications thereto; cross-licensing of the resultant program; vendor advertising and use of client's name; all require negotiation with respect to each party's rights following project completion.

Most large firms will want to protect themselves from the failure of the vendor to perform the work, either because of forces beyond the vendor's control, or through errors, omissions, negligence, fraud or incompetence. Provisions for contingent liability, compensatory damages and performance bonds need to be negotiated.

The cost of the insurance to cover these requirements could be a substantial amount for a small vendor, and may even impair cash flow. Ultimately these costs are reflected back into the contract as an additional cost to the customer. The project manager and SCA have a responsibility to protect their company, but not to the extent that the protection is unrealistic considering the risk. Their assessment of vendor risk should ensure that a proper degree of insurance protection is afforded to their firm at a sensible cost.

BB&T's standard contract terms and conditions are included in Appendix A.

Termination

Everyone is success oriented, but disasters happen. The contract should require provisions for termination due to outside influences, acts of God, convenience of the customer, for cause, or for non-performance. In those cases where there is termination for other than non-performance, the contract will specify that the vendor will be paid for work conducted up to that date, irrespective of the deliverables provided.

Non-performance can only be determined by a review of work effort matched against the work packages, the statement of work, the schedule and the requirements specification. If the product has already been delivered, and the customer wants to withhold final payment for non-performance, he'll have to demonstrate through rigorous testing with previously agreed test cases that the system doesn't work in accordance with requirements and performance criteria. Unless rigorous acceptance testing is built into the contract, the customer has no option but to pay the vendor in full for the project. Traceability to the original requirements, and matching of the acceptance testing against the as-built design, is the only fail-safe way you have of demonstrating to a court that the vendor has not produced a system conforming to the requirements.

Some of the most bitter contract disputes in recent memory have been related to non-performance of delivered but not accepted systems. If it's possible that you won't accept the system (presumably because of the original intrinsic risk), then you should have a termination strategy satisfactory to both parties. From the vendor's viewpoint, it may be willing to give up some profit, but it would certainly expect all costs to be paid by the customer.

Note, that unless the SOW actually states that the vendor <u>will deliver a system that will perform all the requirements,</u> he can do the work, not meet the requirements, and still win the court case because you just hired him to do work, not deliver a working system. A responsible vendor should also insist that the customer have a solid testing program. He wants to have the pride of delivering a product that meets requirements, and wants to protect himself from irresponsible claims of non-performance. Above all, the vendor wants to get paid for his labors without a hassle.

The termination terms and conditions are every bit as important as any other negotiating issue, and once negotiated, hopefully never invoked.

Both vendor and customer desire to have a successful implementation. If unsuccessful, both lose. However, even if success is not achieved, there are differences in the way in which an unsuccessful project is terminated. The worst "solution" is through the courts. A termination in which the vendor is paid most but not all of the fees due him, and the customer keeps a not quite optimal system, will leave both parties unhappy and unsatisfied. At least neither will be permanently scarred.

Letter Agreements

In a contract negotiation, it is common practice for the SCA to issue a Letter Agreement to the vendor. A *Letter Agreement* is normally a one page, start-work order committing the customer to pay the vendor a very limited sum for a limited amount of work over a limited time, subject to goodwill completion of the contract negotiations, or pending customer management approval of the contract.

Letter agreements allow the project to get rolling while some of the final details are ironed out. They should not be issued if there is any doubt whatsoever that a satisfactory final contract cannot be negotiated.

Because letter agreements constitute a formal beginning date for the schedule, both parties should have been organized to proceed as though the full contract was executed. If either party is not ready, issuing a letter agreement is an invitation to schedule delay. Large projects in particular are vulnerable to a cascading series of schedule slips when letter agreements are used because neither party wants to commit all the resources they originally intended. Progress is made in bits and pieces, not according to the original schedule. In such an instance letter agreements are a lazy person's stratagem. They are not sufficiently protective of the customer or the vendor.

Letter agreements seem to work very well for consulting assignments that involve report deliverables rather than systems.

Master Agreements

Corporations with many procurements have contract clauses embedded into standard blanket terms and conditions that require mandatory compliance by the vendor. Many vendors also have their own terms and conditions in their own blanket contracts. Negotiating a compromise acceptable to the legal staffs in either organization can be a long and frustrating process.

The parties may try to negotiate a single comprehensive *Master Agreement* governing the non-technology issues when a continuing relationship beyond the initial project is anticipated. Such master agreements often have global applicability governing services and support from vendor offices in many countries. The master agreement is managed from the headquarters country of one or both of the parties. This avoids the need to negotiate a new contract in every single country in which the parties do business.

When a new task or project is to be negotiated, the master agreement governs the relationship, with the technical, management, cost and performance clauses appended as an annex or exhibit.

Final Price

The final price is after all the final price. Well intentioned, experienced people can disagree quite vehemently on the final price. Even after all other factors have been negotiated, differences between the vendor's price and what the customer wants to pay will still exist. Strategies for achieving final agreement on price are covered in the next sections.

On rare occasions the customer may feel that the vendor has understated his costs, and may ask the vendor to enhance that level of effort with increased costs. On other occasions the customer may feel that the vendor's price was a fair price for the product, and will pay it. But doing so would take all the fun, drama and excitement out of that final test of strength, the actual pricing negotiation.

THE DRAMA OF NEGOTIATIONS

There is nothing as stimulating, exciting and demanding as the confrontation between two well prepared businesses negotiating a multi-million dollar contract. The aura is akin to a prizefight. The adrenaline flows when you are negotiating on the ragged edge of your nerves for a system which you must have, and the vendor is playing pricing hardball.

> One could say the smoke filled room reeks of stale cigars, but no one smokes anymore, so that bit of drama is out. However, in years past, I recall one contracting officer who only smoked during negotiations to induce the vendor to concede early, so he could escape the smoke!

Even in friendly negotiations the atmosphere can get embroiled in acrimonious accusations, irony, and hyperbole, as well as periods of great humor. Keep in mind that negotiations, to paraphrase Shakespeare, are a "stage" and the participants "actors on it." The whole purpose of conducting this drama is to ensure that the cues are known, the script rehearsed, and the play goes to its conclusion leaving the audience (namely the buyer) happy. Therefore, regardless of what we present in the rest of this chapter, you should consider the tactics as merely ancillary to achieving your goal.

Above all, contract negotiations have to be conducted in a success oriented spirit. The ultimate price paid must not be so restrictive to the vendor's profit that he is unable to have flexibility in how issues are resolved during the implementation. Restated in another way, the "uncle" principle applies. Either side is responsive to the others needs until one party says "uncle!" At that time, change proposals and other mediation are required. A major part of the negotiation process is to determine and understand where the uncle level is for each party.

DETERMINING YOUR PRICE

Analysis of the Vendor's Proposal

The vendor's response to the RFP is not only structured by how you've forced him to conform to your formatting guidelines, but also by the standards and processes of his organization. The vendor is a captive of his own environment. That captivity will dictate the way he proposes cost packaging, labor effort, labor grades, overhead, administrative costs and profit. The final result comes from many hours of internal coordination.

The vendor proposal manager has to justify the proposed price to his or her own management. As a consequence, the vendor must have prepared enough backup documentation that the traceability, accuracy and legitimacy of the price quotations are beyond question. What is not beyond question, is whether that legitimacy and accuracy reflect the appropriate level of work to respond to the requirements.

The review of the proposal by your project team, matching requirements against design, management and costs, will reveal whether the vendor has embellished certain tasks with too much "effort" thereby increasing his revenue. Inconsistencies and excesses within the vendor's own presentation will be exposed. These will serve as the tools of the frontal attack on the vendor's pricing proposal to convince him to reduce his final price.

> There is no one more embarrassed than a vendor who cannot defend his inconsistent and technically indefensible presentation. There will be examples in every proposal, no matter how well the vendor scored in the evaluation. It is the task of the negotiating team to find these inconsistencies, areas of risk and excess resource allocations.

> I recall one negotiation where nine subsystem interface specifications were proposed by the vendor in one part of his proposal. However the design work packages contained only eight interfaces. Needless to say, adjustments were made

If you can find the fat, you force the vendor to take unproductive resources out of your project. Since profit is normally a percentage of revenue, his profit is also reduced, though his profit margin may remain the same. As a result the vendor will still make money, though not as much as he hoped when he loaded up on resources hoping you wouldn't find the excess.

Competitors' Pricing Analysis

Refer again to the presentation on Real Costs Analysis in Chapter 10, particularly Exhibits 10-36 through 10-41. From the review of vendor VG compared with vendor VA, a negotiating position that will seek to substantially reduce the license fee should take the highest priority.

The negotiating team would also review other vendors' costs at the work package level to try to find an optimum labor effort to complete each work package. This optimum labor effort (and cost) might then form an "ideal" baseline which would be your opening offer, or best possible contract for you. You are unlikely to achieve your opening offer because this vendor had a pretty good price anyway, but at least you know from your research what the theoretical minimum costs might be. If you want to be a value shopper, then you have to do price comparison shopping to find your best deal. The proposals you received are your pricing comparisons. Use them.

In the simple example we presented in Chapter 10 it is not immediately evident that there is much to gain by conducting such a detailed analysis of each vendor's pricing.

However, consider larger projects than those in Exhibit 10-36, where the pricing proposals are in the millions, not thousands, and you will see that a nickel and dime negotiating baseline based upon a theoretical lowest price per work package could have millions of dollars of savings potential.

> ## If you want to be a value shopper, then you have to do price comparison shopping to find your best deal.

Vendor's Negotiation History

If the vendor and your company have done business before, review the systems contract administrator's archives on the negotiation strategy and results of previous negotiations. You will want to have a statistical appreciation of the vendor's negotiating positions, willing and unwilling areas of compromise, and ultimate settlement position. You can't rely too much on the actual price since there are major differences in scope, schedule and nature of projects over time. Inflationary factors have to be considered as well. The review should at least allow an estimate as to whether the vendor has a history of overpricing, underpricing, or whether he comes in pretty close to the final contract price.

If the vendor has a history of low-balling his price, but then negotiating extremely aggressively on change orders, you will want to emphasize the complete integrity of your requirements in the negotiations in order to reduce the probability of change orders. On that basis you may even decide to be a bit more generous in negotiating the base contract price.

You should also note whether the vendor overran any previous contracts and why. Your counterparts may have negotiated too aggressively, causing the vendor to eliminate required skills or other resources, thereby leading to increased risk and longer schedules

You can even find cost saving opportunities at the work package level. Some vendors will hide substantial additional profit in categories like maintenance, spare parts and operations support. These are usually the least defined categories in the RFP, and the vendor can expect that by the time these phases arrive, he will have spent the money, and you will need change orders to continue his assistance. If you are aware of this strategy, you can remove these costs in the base contract, or defer them until you need them.

Sometimes a vendor proposes a cost component that you just can't accept. Yet the vendor, on the basis of his experience, also insists that it be retained. Strong minds and strong wills can quickly lead to impasse. Perhaps the best solution is to try the vendor's approach with one work package to see how it works. If it is found necessary, you increase the contract for all work packages accordingly. If the costs are found not to be necessary, then you've only spent a little, while maintaining harmony with the vendor.

In a prolonged negotiation on a major defense systems procurement, the vendor proposed that his software department would have a liaison person attached to each of 20 hardware subsystems. We eliminated the role.

After two years into the project, we found that the vendor was right. Identification of a specific point of contact within the software organization for the hardware interface would have facilitated communications within the vendor's organization. More importantly, hardware designs that could not be computer controlled could have been identified earlier, and some change orders for hardware redesign eliminated. The cost impacts were about equivalent to the money originally saved, but the schedule could have been improved by three months if we had used the liaison personnel. The adage is, the customer is not always right.

Negotiations involve people, and the vendor's current negotiation team may be different from the past. That shouldn't matter to you. You will be prepared for any type of negotiation, but if there is a fundamental characteristic to the vendor's cost packaging or negotiation strategy, you will be doubly prepared. Interestingly, the vendor may be totally unaware of his own pricing and negotiating tendencies.

Determination of Target Price

The *Target Price* is the price you expect to pay after all negotiations are completed.

You don't buy a refrigerator or car without having a price in mind. Sometimes you do better than your expected price, sometimes you do worse. Sometimes you even walk away from the deal. The same is true in negotiating technology contracts.

Since price is directly dependent upon how well the negotiations on technical and management issues proceeded, the vendor's price established in the original proposal may no longer be valid. Therefore, you will need to have received his updated price quotations for any changes you've agreed upon.

The strategy for negotiating the contract price is based upon a principal of fairness. You want a quality product and are willing to pay a reasonable and fair cost plus profit to the vendor to deliver the product. The issue to be negotiated is what constitutes fair cost and fair profit.

Using everything you know about industry norms for salaries, benefits, overhead and profit, you construct a model of what you think is the vendor's baseline position. The vendor's baseline position is the absolute minimum cost for the vendor to do the work described in the proposal. Constructing a baseline cost for each work package, you build up what effectively constitutes the vendor's "no-go" position. Trying to negotiate a contract price lower than the vendor's baseline will result in the vendor terminating the negotiation because he would lose money. This method provides one of the boundary conditions for the negotiation.

Note that your estimate of the vendor's baseline and his actual baseline may be quite different. Your objective in negotiations is to learn enough about the vendor's true baseline to be able to make increasingly accurate revisions to your estimate.

Secondly, using the information you've collected concerning the ideal or optimum solution, you derive a set of costs for each work package which would reflect that data. The resultant costs may be higher or lower than your baseline estimate. Because these costs are referenced from the competitors' best prices, these are known as your Reference Position.

The information from the original proposal, revised proposal, baselines, and reference position are compiled into a worksheet.

Exhibit 11-5 displays a *Contract Price Negotiation Worksheet*. It contains this information plus additional negotiating positions that are discussed in the following paragraphs. The information in Exhibit 11-5 uses the data for vendor VG originally presented in Exhibit 10-39.

If you have a fixed budget, then that budget becomes your "no-go" price. Alternately, if your choice of vendor is dependent upon a successful contract negotiation requiring you to obtain a specific reduced price, then your no-go position is that price. If you can't agree at the no-go price, then you would open negotiations with the vendor who came in second in the evaluation.

Establishing your no-go price creates the second boundary condition for the negotiation. Somewhere between the boundary conditions a contract price will be negotiated.

For example, we noted in Exhibit 10-39 that vendor VG had a license fee of $320 thousand. If your position was that you would never pay more than $220 thousand for the license, that would be your no-go position. This is reflected in column 11 in Exhibit 11-5.

Rather than terminating negotiations, it would be better to find an area of compromise on the license fee: perhaps paying a one-time price and an annual maintenance fee; negotiating away your rights to sharing in the resale of the improved software; or some other off-pricing method which essentially gives the vendor most of his income, but at a slower pace.

If your vendor is an approved government vendor with a price schedule in the General Services Administration Catalog, that schedule price is by law the lowest you would be able to negotiate.

Negotiation requires a counterproposal, and since the vendor has already made a proposal, the opening counteroffer must be made by you. Your opening position which includes markup and profit (Column 8 in Exhibit 11-5) will be close to your estimate of the vendor's baseline price (Column 5), at least for the work package items.

After the expected outrage from the vendor, you'll begin poking at the inconsistencies in the proposal, trying to get some pricing concessions in these areas. Your strategy should be to slowly back down in your demands (based on reasonable arguments or evidence from the vendor) to arrive at what we would call Fallback Position #1 (Column 9). If the negotiation is complex or for great sums, you may have several fallback positions. Each fallback position would constitute a concession on your part to the vendor, and presumably some concessions on the vendor's part.

EXHIBIT 11-5

CONTRACT PRICE NEGOTIATION WORKSHEET

($000)

#	Work Package	Original Proposal	Revised Proposal	Est. Vndr. Baseline	Revised Baseline	Reference Position	Opening Position	Fallback #1	Target Price	No-Go Price
1	Project Management & Admin	62.2	66.6	40.0		50.0	42.0	48.0	55.0	65.0
2	Systems Analysis	13.2	15.8	11.6		12.0	10.0	12.0	14.0	15.8
3	Systems Design	18.0	24.0	19.0		20.0	18.0	20.0	22.0	24.0
4	Coding, Debug & Unit Testing	55.5	60.0	40.4		45.5	40.0	50.0	60.0	60.0
5	Interface Testing	15.0	15.0	12.0		10.0	10.0	12.0	14.0	15.0
6	Integration Testing	12.0	18.0	10.0		12.0	10.0	11.7	15.0	18.0
7	Data Conversion	1.0	4.0	1.0		0.0	1.0	1.8	2.5	4.0
8	Acceptance Testing	4.5	7.0	3.0		2.5	4.0	5.0	5.5	7.0
9	Cutover & Parallel	9.0	9.0	5.0		1.5	5.0	5.4	6.3	7.5
10	Operations Support	13.6	13.6	5.0		0.0	3.0	5.0	8.0	8.0
	Total Work Package Costs	204.0	233.0	147.0		153.5	143.0	170.9	202.3	224.3
a	Software System License Fee	320.0	320.0	70.0		120.0	90.0	130.0	170.0	220.0
b	Documentation Supplement	21.0	27.0	10.0		10.0	0.0	12.0	15.0	15.0
c	Computer Time Usage	15.0	18.0	8.5		0.0	0.0	10.0	15.0	18.0
	Total Additional Costs	356.0	365.0	88.5		130.0	90.0	152.0	200.0	253.0
	Grand Total Cost Proposal	560.0	598.0	235.5		283.5	233.0	322.9	402.3	477.3

Fallback #1 (Column 9) with a work package price of $171 thousand is still $62 thousand away from the vendor's proposal price of $233 thousand. This is a discount of almost 27%. You would need very good evidence that the vendor padded his proposal to have any hope of getting the vendor to even discuss this offer. Even a target price for the work packages of $202 thousand (Column 10) is an unrealistic expectation of 13% reduction.

If the vendor is convincing enough, you'll ultimately fallback to your Target Price (Column 10), which is what you would have expected to pay.

Although market forces will ensure that a vendor will be forced to offer his product at a competitive price, that does not preclude the possibility that a vendor's product could be so good that he can charge a significant, if not predatory, premium for it. You may find that you have very little negotiating room.

It may be that the vendor is still unwilling to concede at your target price, but insists on his original proposal. If you don't have rational reasons to insist on your price, then you'll have to concede to the vendor's superior negotiating skill. There's nothing wrong with that. After all, he is your chosen best vendor. However, if you've decided on a no-go price that is below the proposal price and the vendor won't concede, then you'll have to negotiate with much stronger tactics (walk-outs, temporary cancellations for consultations, threats of termination) or actually terminate the negotiations entirely.

In this example, your no-go price is more likely to be the final price. The example serves to illustrate the point that the buyer has to be realistic in his expectation of what can be accomplished at the bargaining table.

Exhibit 11-5 contains a negotiation scenario of penurious negotiation tactics by the customer. It is so out of line with the quality of the proposal that the vendor might consider that you're negotiating in bad faith, and he may dig in his heels or walk out of the negotiations.

Because both parties earnestly want to do the project, negotiation termination is quite unlikely between commercial entities where the total dollar amount is under a million dollars.

However, there are many instances in public works projects where the vendors' prices are so far beyond the bureaucrats' expectations of cost, that negotiations are terminated. Invariably these problems are caused by inadequately defined requirements to establish a reasonable cost estimate for the total project from the very beginning. In anticipating a pork barrel project, a political figure announces what is a low-ball expectation of the cost to complete, then has to eat crow when the real costs are known. To save face, the process is started all over again.

Descoping of Work

If you really must reduce the final price you will pay for the product, the best alternative is to step through the proposal, item by item, and eliminate those items that are optional features or functions, and the cost associated with them. This is called descoping of the work.

In the work package example in Chapter 10, Work Package #10, operations support was not even evaluated. Presumably BB&T planned to descope this effort all the time, but wanted to know what the vendors' offerings were. Therefore, the requirements for a quotation were included in the RFP. From Exhibit 11-5 we see that the negotiators are willing to pay up to $8 thousand (Columns 10 and 11) for the support, but not beyond that price. Work Package 10 0, therefore, is a prime candidate for descoping of work.

The process of descoping would generally follow completion of the negotiations, so both parties know the final total price including all proposal items. The vendor knows the maximum revenue he will receive if all items are purchased. Then you might say: "We have a firm price for Work Packages, 7.0, 10.0, 3.1.2.2, 4.1.2.2 and 5.1.2.2. We think they are optional, and we want to remove them from the contract. Therefore, the price for the contract will be reduced by the amount we previously agreed to." Generally the vendor has no choice but to agree to the descoping.

However, in software modification contracts, the optional software may be actually fully or partially embedded in existing code. The contractor will balk at accepting the descoping, either because he incurs a cost to remove it, or you will be getting something you're not paying for. Since it is impossible to know everything about the package you're buying, it's quite likely that what is rationally descopable in logic, may not be practically descopable. The vendor will convince you to change your mind.

Furthermore, if you're too rigorous in descoping, the vendor may say: "You have descoped my proposal so much it no longer looks like my original proposal. The residual level of effort you have already negotiated me into leaves me no flexibility to guarantee that I can deliver the quality product I originally proposed. I require these tasks to spread my work flow and staffing profile for the whole project. You have given me additional management problems. I want more money in order to handle these problems, or I wish to withdraw from the negotiations. This is not what you asked for, and it is not what I proposed."

Massive descoping can also have a major financial impact upon a small business vendor that gave you its best proposal to win the competition. Now is not the time to cut indiscriminately. Descoping should be viewed as a surgical activity, not a bludgeon. You do not cut out huge portions of a proposal to achieve a target price. Too much work has gone into preparing a good RFP and getting good proposals to now play games with the entire package.

Most vendors will not object to descoping small portions of the contract. They'll anticipate increasing their revenue and profits later through the change order process. In addition, some descoped items can always be deferred beyond completion of predecessor milestones. Operations support is a good example. Support for data conversion (WP 7.0) is another candidate.

> Descoping has value and purpose; use it with discrimination and caution.

NEGOTIATION TACTICS

In the friendly, small city world of BB&T, hardball negotiations doesn't make a lot of sense. Two parties want the project to succeed. Since the RFP and evaluation process was so elaborate, there really is very little left to argue about. But, there are circumstances in negotiations where there are significant differences between the parties, the dollar amounts are massive, or the risks are high for all.

So we need to examine the Machiavellian world of negotiating one-upsmanship. This is grand theater played at a conference table. For practical and psychological reasons, the SCA always schedules the negotiations on the customer's premises. You want your experts quickly available, and you want your logistical support to provide you maximum comfort. The vendor will have to endure all the minor and major inconveniences of operating on the other guy's turf.

> The home field advantage is no joke in professional sports, particularly basketball, so the home field advantage operates in business as well. As the customer, you do have certain perks, use them.

Negotiating Schedule

A careful manipulation of the schedule can give you a negotiation edge. A "schedule" for the negotiations should be prepared by the contracting officer and delivered to the vendor in advance of the negotiations. The schedule will list the agenda of items to be negotiated, and their estimated times. The "schedule" will always be shorter than the contracting officer's expectations. In fact it may be considerably understated. The purpose is to place a sense of urgency upon the vendor to compromise because the schedule is "running late." In reality, there is no timetable for negotiations.

> Japanese negotiators have exploited the schedule driven urgency of Americans for decades. They provide every amenity for their guests, entertaining lavishly, thereby creating fatigue. They know when return tickets are booked and recognize that the American's own "timetable," implied by their return flights, creates a psychological urgency to complete the negotiations before it is "time" to depart. As the negotiations drag on, and the departure date draws near, the Americans' "face" requires results rather than achievements, so they capitulate on key items in the negotiations.

There is no timetable for negotiations.

The contracting officer will schedule the negotiations to begin at the most opportune time for his team. Two thoughts apply here. The first would be to tell the vendor to appear as early as possible on a Monday morning (7:00 a.m.) because "it will take a long time to finish." Alternately, you might ask the vendor to appear at midweek, again early in the morning under the assumption that the negotiations will "only take a day or two."

In the first case the vendor may be apprehensive that he has to devote a whole week for negotiations, when his previous understandings were that negotiations are a mere formality. If he's from out of town, he may have to find lodgings the night before, or wake up early to get to the meeting at the scheduled time. Furthermore, he and his negotiating team have probably spent a portion of the weekend preparing for the unknown.

In the second case, the vendor will arrive with confidence that negotiations will be completed rapidly, only to find himself working through the following weekend when they do not.

In order to maintain the sense of urgency, the negotiating schedule will permit no interruptions. This includes scheduled breaks, biological breaks, lunches, or other periods to "touch base with the office." If you are going to drive a hard bargain, you don't want to give the vendor the impression that you are wasting time with a casual schedule, or throwing money about by providing opulent meals or settings. If people need to attend to personal or business issues outside of the negotiations, then they excuse themselves for a period of time. Meanwhile, the negotiations continue in their absence. Thus, a negotiating team is required, not a negotiating individual!

The sessions will begin early and end late. Dinner hour will certainly be inconvenienced, with sessions ending typically after 8:00 p.m., even if that means a commuting problem. The objective is to cause your negotiating opponent to be willing to compromise in your favor, by creating a situation of maximum urgency and stress.

Physical Environment

Ambiance or the lack of it has a great deal to do with how we feel about our activities. When the environment is pleasant, cheerful and comfortable, we tend to be at ease with ourselves and those with whom we are dealing. In a negotiation requiring fine-tuning and minor pricing adjustments, a pleasant, comfortable ambiance is conducive to goodwill and prompt conclusion of the negotiations. Everything is focused positively.

On the other hand, in tense negotiations, such as labor union contracts, where the issues can become acrimonious, a physical layout which inflicts maximum stress can hasten the conclusion of negotiations, if less than amicably.

> One negotiation involving hundreds of millions of dollars between a contractor and the government was conducted in a 15' x 30' room, with limited air conditioning, no windows, government issue steel folding chairs, crammed with 40 people, and the only door to the room far on the customer's side, so the vendor personnel had to climb over lots of bodies to exit the room. And nearly everyone smoked in those days.

Such Spartan conditions are sometimes necessary to convince a testy vendor who thinks he has a lock on your pocketbook, that you are serious about obtaining substantial reductions in price. When parties have substantial differences, uncomfortable surroundings can act as a sufficient irritant and stimulus to generate pressure to reach an agreement. Whether the ambiance accentuates differences, which can be discussed and agreements made, or whether it drives the parties to get rid of the pain and thereby compromise, it works. And sometimes this doesn't work at all, and everyone just suffers and remains intransigent.

When agreement is reached, the customer should ensure that the parties retire to more pleasant surroundings. There the negotiations can be treated as a just completed contest between athletes who respect each other. Food should be served, drinks poured, and the parties begin the process of behaving as one team immediately.

Anything said in anger or frustration by either party must be left in the negotiation room, and never brought up again. It's forgotten. It's history. Above all, it is certainly not personal. It's just a game.

Scripting the Negotiations

Coaches have their game plans. Hollywood has scripts. Businesses have contingency plans. Negotiations require some behavioral planning as well. Although the timing of some tactical maneuvers will depend upon the negotiating circumstances, a number of options in moving the action along are available.

You know the "good cop, bad cop" routine. One member of the negotiating team acts as the irritant in negotiations, another becomes the conciliator. The bad cop hassles the heck out of the vendor. Then he conveniently needs a break and leaves. The conciliator steps in and offers an option less severe than the bad cop, and the vendor accepts hurriedly before the bad cop steps back in the room.

Sometimes when the action gets too tense, some of the negotiating team storm out of the room in anger. The vendor, in fear of losing the contract, reconsiders some of his pricing. Even when both parties understand that the "walk-out" is staged, it does serve notice that the discussions are not making progress, and that both parties need to renew their efforts.

There are times in which the vendor is presented with counterproposals that require detailed recalculations of costs and profit. When such a circumstance becomes obvious, the contracting officer should offer an adjournment for whatever time is required. This reduces the tension. It also allows the vendor, from the comfort of a new venue, to reflect on the stress and inconvenience he's just endured. He often returns with an acceptable response.

Aside from these obvious tactics, a script is more than the agenda published prior to the meeting. The script for negotiations might have three scenarios, each to be applied at the appropriate time.

One scenario would be to plod methodically through the work packages, negotiating each item as it appeared. This will ensure eventual completion, but not rapid progress. The script will include back-up plans for rerouting the discussions around obvious stumbling blocks.

A second scenario is to move through the proposal on a technical functionality basis. Assume agreement is made on the systems analysis effort for Work Package 2.3. There may be causality of the work done in 2.3 upon Work Packages 3.3, 4.3, 5.3, etc. You could immediately jump to these work packages to see if a similar agreement can be negotiated. You try to make as much progress as you can while you are both satisfied with the issue. A series of consecutive agreements predisposes people to make further agreements.

Finally, you could take a shotgun approach to the negotiations. This is to probe how well prepared the vendor is in several areas, then concentrate the negotiation where you perceive him to be weakest.

The script is like a flow chart. It should provide the outline by which you will achieve your pricing strategy. It can have branches, detours, and do-loops for recurring problems, but it should lead to successful agreement with the vendor.

Scripting could be as simple as first offering the vendor a price which is fair and close to your target price. If he accepts, the negotiations are over. If he rejects the offer, you retract it and then start negotiating in earnest. After a while, the vendor knows that the best he can do is the first offering price, so he may give in. Such a script can save you a lot of time and effort, but you will unlikely get the best price.

Spokespersons and Speakers

There is a cardinal rule of negotiations. There is one, and only one, official spokesperson for the negotiating team of the customer. The Contracting Officer (SCA) is that person.

> ### The Contracting Officer is the only official spokesperson for the customer.

The contracting officer has extensive experience in negotiations, and although he or she is not a disinterested party, he or she is never emotionally involved in negotiations. As a consequence when things get heated, the contracting officer and the counterpart (if any) on the vendor's side can reach unemotional agreements on noncritical points, and can manage the agenda for the negotiations. The spokesperson is the only person who can agree to any of the contract clauses or prices by saying "done." The contracting officer never becomes involved in any part of the emotion related to negotiations. He must be totally cool throughout. Refer again to his duties and authority specified in Exhibit 11-4. He is the authorized representative of the customer. His only objective is to protect the rights of his employer. He has no vested interest in the project or the price, except the final price.

The spokesperson is supported by a number of other speakers and experts. The accountable executive may actually lead the negotiations himself, assisted by the project manager. Alternatively, and more likely, the thrust of the technological negotiations and pricing of technology will be led by the project manager. The accountable executive may observe the proceedings, interjecting his input from time to time. He may even absent himself from the majority of sessions, appearing only when his advice to the project manager or contracting officer is required.

Experts are called in to question the vendor about technical items in the vendor's proposal that will give further insight into the pricing of those items. Others may be financial experts who might challenge labor rates, overhead or profit margins. Legal representatives may be asked to present their opinions about certain terms and conditions. To negotiate successfully, you need a good team. That team must practice beforehand, and know and respect each other's role.

> ### Negotiations are a team effort, not an individual role.

At the point in which the speakers have agreed upon the issue and the price, the contracting officer will intervene and restate the agreement and price in contractual terms. His counterpart will acknowledge the agreement, which will then be recorded.

When all the issues and prices have been agreed to, the customer and vendor spokespersons will tabulate all of the agreements one final time, and recapitulate the final price. They will shake hands over the agreement, subject to management's final approval if that has not been delegated.

CONCLUSION

The contract represents a formal partnership relationship between the vendor and the customer. That partnership involves the commitment of resources by both parties to a day-to-day working relationship. There are enough difficulties in the technical, managerial and control aspects of such a partnership that they should not be compounded by a lack of rigor in the contracting process.

Through the use of strict contractual controls, both parties can work confidently with a clear understanding of the constraints and flexibilities applicable to each. Ambiguities are minimized, and as a consequence, they can concentrate on the job to be done, and not on the leverage each can obtain from the other.

In the final analysis, the basis of a contract is fairness to both parties, control of the project, protection of proprietary information and delivery of a working system for a fair price. The spirit of the project must be success oriented, and the customer cannot squeeze the vendor so tightly on price that there is no room for flexibility in the relationship.

Orlando Gomez, President of Grand Systems Design (GSD), hosted a pre-negotiation cocktail hour for the BB&T team. He was particularly gracious to Fred Everet and Monk Eternic. All that changed the next morning when he was adamant about getting full price for the license fee for the system. Gomez pointed out his cost of having to capitalize the systems investment in the original package, and the need to pay off debt related to borrowings for that purpose. He also insisted that the perpetual license included five years of maintenance.

Monk pursued other lines of negotiation. The technical discussions revealed somewhat more powerful capability than the BB&T staff had understood. That was a point in favor of the vendor. Management discussions showed that GSD was highly cooperative about all issues that BB&T had identified during their review.

Monk showed that BB&T's system had enough capacity to support GSD's development efforts, and computer time was not required, and BB&T would not pay for it. Gomez pointed out that he needed some contingency plan dollars for this purpose. Monk capitulated at $5 thousand. When the BB&T and GSD system standards were reviewed side-by-side, Gomez agreed that he could not justify an additional documentation fee beyond $10 thousand.

While this was going on, Fred met with Lisa Moore, Higby Wallace, and Hampton Oldsin, CEO of BB&T, to explain that they were unlikely to achieve a target reduction of $150,000 off the license fee unless they yield on other issues. He *explained that the progress made in other areas was very good, and the system seemed even better than originally expected. On that basis he requested he be allowed to pursue a strategy of limited license commitment that would reduce the immediate BB&T expense, while assuring a financially viable vendor. They outlined a new strategy, in which they agreed to a new no-go price and target price. This is reflected in Column 5 in Exhibit 11-6.*

EXHIBIT 11-6

BITS FINAL CONTRACT PRICE

($000)

1	2	3	4	5	6
#	Work Package	GSD Revised Proposal	Final Agreement	BB&T Target Price	BB&T No-Go Price
1	Project Management & Admin.	66.6	65.0	65.0	65.0
2	Systems Analysis	15.8	15.0	14.0	15.8
3	Systems Design	24.0	24.0	22.0	24.0
4	Coding, Debug & Unit Testing	60.0	60.0	60.0	60.0
5	Interface Testing	15.0	15.0	14.0	15.0
6	Integration Testing	18.0	18.0	15.0	18.0
7	Data Conversion	4.0	4.0	2.5	4.0
8	Acceptance Testing	7.0	5.0	5.5	7.0
9	Cutover & Parallel	9.0	6.0	6.3	7.5
10	Operations Support	13.6	8.0	8.0	8.0
	Total Work Package Costs	233.0	220.0	212.3	224.3
a	Software System License Fee	320.0	170.0	170.0	220.0
b	Documentation Supplement	27.0	10.0	15.0	15.0
c	Computer Time Usage	18.0	5.0	15.0	18.0
	Total Additional Costs	365.0	185.0	200.0	253.0
	Grand Total Project Cost	598.0	405.0	412.3	477.3
d	Future Years Maintenance		60.0		
	Total Obligation		465.0		

On the fourth day, Fred and Monk outlined a proposal for annual maintenance fees, and a reduced initial license fee. By evening Gomez gave some ground, and Eternic was able to close out the work package pricing. BB&T agreed to pay GSD $220,000 for the work packages. Fred insisted that they pay GSD a perpetual license fee of $170,000. However, they would also agree to 4 years of maintenance payments of $15,000 per year, after the first year of full warrantee. The final price would be $405,000 upon successful completion of the project. The additional fee of $60,000 for maintenance would be paid in years 2-5. BB&T's total obligation through year 5 would be $465,000. Column 4 in Exhibit 11-6 shows the BITS Final Contract Price.

Gomez fought furiously to bring the license fee total up to at least $250,000. BB&T began to indicate they would have to go back to vendor VA, Advanced Systems International, a key GSD competitor. As a face saving gesture, Monk offered that BB&T would waive all rights to future sales of the system using the enhancements they were buying, and would give Gomez a perpetual free license for that code. Gomez reluctantly agreed. They also agreed upon a performance bond. The next afternoon they signed the agreements, and went out to dinner together.

Neither got everything they wanted. Both got a good deal. That's what negotiations are about.

## Chapter Twelve

MANAGE THE VENDOR AND COMPLETE THE PROJECT

After you sign the contract, the vendor is on his way. Your project manager now assumes the responsibility to see that the vendor performs. Exhibit 11-3 in Chapter 11 addressed the duties and responsibilities of the project manager. In this chapter we want to examine some practical aspects of dealing with the vendor. The treatment is not exhaustive since there are many books on project life cycle management that adequately cover project management as a generic topic.

PROJECT START-UP

Though the project manager and his vendor counterpart have spent lots of time together, they haven't really had an opportunity to work together as a team. That can't happen until the contract is signed.

You need to get project momentum going, since there is often a desire to catch your breath after all that has already happened. You can't afford it. You and the vendor have to develop immediate rapport. We'd call this the "getting to know you" period. It also needs to be as short as possible so the vendor can get on with his work. It needs to be short so the customer doesn't interfere in the vendor's area of responsibility. If the vendor is using your premises, there will be a couple of days devoted to logistics. You'll get to know each other in that period.

If the vendor isn't using your facilities, facile coordination is more difficult. The project managers can eliminate a communications barrier if they agree on how coordination will be done. The best way to do this is for them to have formal schedules for meetings, rigid agendas, and attendance restricted to only those who must participate.

Within your current organization, consider the inertia that geographic separation contributes to productivity. Groups within 100 feet of each other on the same floor tend to share and work together. Separate the groups by as little as one vertical floor, accessed by elevator, and the overhead against teamwork increases as though they were a quarter of a mile apart.

A separation of a couple miles effectively adds an hour to any coordination schedule requiring face-to-face discussions. A separation of a hundred miles requires a full day of time to overcome the logistic barrier. Geography adds overhead to a project and it can add unplanned time to the schedule if not anticipated.

STATUS REPORTING

Before product delivery, vendor status reports are the only control element available to the project manager. Status reporting has to be regular and frequent enough that milestones and deliverable progress can be tracked and measured. For a three year project, monthly reviews are probably sufficient. For a one year or shorter project, biweekly, if not weekly reviews should be scheduled. The status report should cover the following topics.

Progress Versus Schedule

A project control room is a good way to keep track of the schedule of the project. Large scale displays allow the reviewers a full picture of the total schedule. Each work package task is listed along the left Y-axis, and progress against time is tracked on the X-axis. A graphic presentation of this kind is effective in keeping attendees focused on milestones and results.

Computer generated project scheduling and tracking systems are also important, and can contain details not contained in the big picture view. Emphasizing the computer gener-ated Pert or Gantt schedule during the review session can lead to nit-picking on tasks that have marginal impact on the final system. You need to guard against such myopia. The computer tracking system can be reviewed off-line, to ensure that the tasks correspond to the progress claimed during the review meeting.

When the vendor makes his presentation, you should use the questions in Exhibit 12-1 to assure yourself that you are not being given a superficial or inaccurate report.

Action Items

In any review there are bound to be questions that can't be answered immediately. These could be technical, administrative, managerial, cost or schedule. Any unanswered question must be recorded as an Action Item. The action item includes a description of the issue, the person assigned to answer the issue, and the date at which the response will be delivered. Every open action item is reviewed at each status review session. Any action items assigned that day are reaffirmed at the conclusion of the status review.

Red Flag Events

A "red flag" event is the name given to a missed milestone or major event. If the event does not occur on schedule the project is in danger.

The red flag has its etymology (perhaps) from the red capes used by matadors in the bull arena. It attracts attention.

Besides the standard critical path milestones that are obvious triggers of danger, there are several other events that should cause alarm.

EXHIBIT 12-1

CHECKLIST FOR REVIEWING STATUS REPORTS

- Is the vendor in control of this work package?

- Is the accomplishment or progress reported credible?

- Do the accomplishments reconcile to the requirements and to the statement of work?

- Do the results reflect theoretical validity, adequate analysis, quality design or sound implementation depending on phase?

- Are the labor effort estimates for this task still appropriate?

- Is the work package schedule still credible in light of this report?

- Does the accomplishment reported integrate into or with the other technology tasks to which it is linked?

- Does the accomplishment reported integrate into or with the schedules of other tasks to which it is linked?

- Is the entire project schedule still credible in light of this report?

1. Vendor Staff Recruitment

If the vendor has planned to recruit a key resource to contribute to the project, and has not done the recruitment by the target date, schedule slippage is almost certain. You must escalate the issue to your management and to vendor management as well.

2. Interface Specifications

System interfaces impact old systems, operations and the new system. The interdependencies among these elements increases complexity and risk. Any failure to maintain progress in the completion of system interfaces must be considered serious. All affected parties need to be informed of a deficiency, and their contributions sought to resolve the problem.

3. Documentation

No matter how elegant the design or coding, if the vendor is not keeping progress with the documentation corresponding to where he says he is, he is behind schedule. Many people discount the value of documentation in systems projects. Such an opinion is not warranted by experience. Invariably, delays in the production of system documentation reflect problems in design, problems in total quality, and possible problems in competency of programmers.

Late delivery of system documentation affects the generation of test plans and procedures, preparation of operational procedures, preparation of databases and conversion materials. The schedule must be affected by late documentation. Even at the risk of crying "wolf" a red flag alarm must be generated when documentation is late.

EARLY DELIVERABLES

One of the better ways of improving chances for success in systems projects is to complete a full cycle of reviews, milestones and deliverables before the project reaches full momentum. If a module or mini-project can be targeted for early delivery, the vendor's processes and vendor-client coordination can be debugged to ensure they are working as they should be. The more practice you have, the more likely you will be successful.

CHANGE CONTROL PROCESS

The best way to have change control work effectively is to have no changes at all. Unfortunately, that isn't always possible. The need to change the system can occur because of regulatory changes, user requests, new requirements or vendor initiated suggestions for enhanced capability.

The usual method for beginning the change process is for the source or the project manager to document the need for change in a *Systems Change Request* (SCR).

A more commonly used term is *Engineering Change Request* (ECR), often used irrespective of whether the change is equipment, software or procedures. Exhibit 12-2 contains an example of a completed SCR.

The SCR is forwarded to the systems contract administrator (SCA) who discusses the issue with the parties involved to determine if the change really must be made. When this is confirmed, the SCA will issue a simple letter to the vendor formally requesting a proposal, including technical design, schedule and costs to implement the change. The vendor responds with a *Systems Change Proposal* (SCP). The proposal is reviewed for technical merit, costs are analyzed, and a final price and schedule are negotiated. The SCA then directs the vendor to implement the approved change by issuing a *Systems Change Order* (SCO). The SCO is the official document that amends the contract. It is included in the contract documentation.

Until the SCO is issued, the vendor must continue work on the project according to the original contract. He might defer some work related to the area of change, but he can't do that for long. Not every systems change proposal results in an SCO. When an SCO is issued, the new tasks are incorporated into the schedule and work is started on the changes.

The chief challenge during this process is keeping momentum on the mainstream of the project, expediting the customer's process in rapidly processing the SCRs, SCPs and SCOs, and keeping track of the changes to work packages as a result of the changes. If a project has many changes, the sheer administrative effort to keep pace with change evolution is significant.

EXHIBIT 12-2

EXAMPLE OF A SYSTEMS CHANGE REQUEST

Contract No: 193-06	Page 1 of 1
Systems Change Request	Our Ref: **SCR 2.3.01**

Baccarat Bank & Trust
1400 Gambler's Square
Middletown, NX 00417

Mr. Orlando Gomez, President
Grand Systems Design
14 Empire Street
New City, NL 00019

Dear Mr. Gomez:

Subject: SCR for Proposal on Specification Change

1. In accordance with section 14 paragraph 6 of subject contract, you are requested to submit a proposal within 7 days for implementation of the changes defined in paragraph (2) below. You will be reimbursed for proposal costs on a time and material basis up to a maximum of $800.00 in accordance with paragraph 11 of section 14. You may implement the proposal only subject to our approval, and negotiation on costs and their approval, in accordance with paragraph 12 of section 14.

2. Reference SRS section 2.3, page 2-05, dated October 11, lines 8-10 should be amended to read:
"The performance summary report shall be available on a VDU screen at the operations console within 30 minutes of initiation of end-of-day processing. The proposed format of the screen contents shall be presented and approved at the Design Review."

For Baccarat Bank and Trust:

Monk Eternic
Systems Contract Administrator

MANAGING CRITICAL MILESTONES

REQUIREMENTS REVIEW

One of the first milestones is the requirements review. Despite all the previous analysis, the vendor may still have some questions about some requirements. A one day requirements review allows all outstanding unresolved requirements questions to be settled.

The review might also include presentations by the customer operations team to illustrate current operational procedures that may need to be considered in the final operational system.

The requirements traceability matrix should be finalized. This matrix provides a convenient reference tool for designers, reviewers, test personnel and the user, to track progress during development, and serves as an indispensable aid to ensure configurational stability of the system. The vendor can proceed to develop the system, and the customer can plan for the testing program to verify the systems adherence to requirements.

DESIGN REVIEWS

Sometime after project start, the vendor completes the systems analysis, and incorporates the knowledge learned or derived into design specifications. Design activity continues until the vendor has the equivalent of a blueprint, which represents the "design-to" objective. Just as the customer must approve blueprints in a construction project, he must also approve the vendor's design specifications.

In systems development projects, this is normally done by holding a design review. A *Design Review* is a formal meeting conducted by the customer to evaluate whether the vendor's design specifications can be approved. When approved, the vendor can code the software. The design review is a critical milestone in the project because this is the last time the customer can exercise any technical judgment concerning the quality and accuracy of the vendor's work. After this milestone, it's all in the vendor's hands until acceptance testing.

In very large projects, with many modules or subsystems, multiple design review sessions are common. Sometimes two phases of design reviews might be held. A Preliminary Design Review, and a Critical Design Review are held in governmental projects. The difference is the degree of specificity in the design available at a given time. Exhibit 12-3 lists some objectives of a Design Review.

Design reviews have two elements. The customer has to review vendor documentation required for this milestone. The collected wisdom, questions and issues resulting from the review lead to the second element, the design review meeting. The design review meeting allows the vendor to elaborate on his design using presentation materials about the design specifications. He responds to the customer's issues, and takes action items for those that cannot be resolved immediately. Assuming satisfactory answers, the design is approved and coding of the system begins.

EXHIBIT 12-3

DESIGN REVIEW OBJECTIVES

- Verify that all requirements have been incorporated into the design.

- Analyze the vendor specifications for design flaws.

- Verify that interface design is directly corresponding to interface specifications.

- Measure the vendor's progress against schedule for this milestone.

- Validate that test planning is consistent with acceptance criteria.

- Validate the detailed flow charts and logical structures against the requirements specifications and interface specifications.

- Verify all data elements and database specifications.

- Validate hardware allocations and timing in conformance to the design and performance requirements.

- Validate the human interface interaction for users of the system.

- Compare the proposed test plan against the requirements specification.

CODING

Fifty percent completed code is zero code completed. Ninety percent completed code is zero percent completed. You must constantly guard against believing programmer claims for percentile completion. The only way to insure that code is complete is to have the coding work packages subdivided, so that finite units of completed and debugged code are delivered by each programmer every week. The software delivered should be to a configuration controlled repository in the quality assurance unit of the vendor's organization. Programmers can't fiddle with the code after they've delivered it, unless there are substantial reasons why the code should be updated. If the programs are solely left in the programmers hands they might optimize it forever, and fail to make progress on other units.

The aggregated, debugged and documented code in a controlled repository is the vendor's best measure of progress. All other measurements are subjective.

ACCEPTANCE TESTING

The vendor is ecstatic. His programmers have completed their jobs, his testing has verified that the system works, and he's ready to get paid. He is finished. All that remains between the last 25% of his fee is you and your acceptance tests.

All people make mistakes. Pressure, stress, haste and ignorance lead to inadvertent errors. Shortcuts, sloppiness or incompetence are short of malfeasance, but the result is the same. Errors will exist in delivered programs. It doesn't really matter how they got there. They have to be detected and corrected.

The only way to objectively find mistakes is to have a totally disinterested team conduct the acceptance testing of the system. This quality assurance test team does a complete audit of the technical performance of the system. The project manager is near his final milestone: user happiness. He can't afford to blow away his career by conducting mediocre acceptance testing.

The test team will need to decide if the errors they find are catastrophic or minor. The vendor will immediately fix catastrophic failures. Testing will halt on that processing thread until the bug is fixed. Then the complete test will be run again to find if the fix introduced other errors. In large systems the propagation of newly introduced errors can spread like a virus. Regression testing from the last unambiguously, error-free checkpoint must be done to avoid the propagation phenomena.

When errors are not catastrophic, the test team will need to decide whether to continue testing, or wait for the vendor to fix the bug. The vendor will likely want to fix it on the fly. The test team may want to review the completed documentation first before retesting. The problem with minor errors is that if there are many of them, the result can be the same as a catastrophic error. Too many corrections, affecting too much of the program, cannot be fixed on the fly. Deliberate fixes must be planned and scheduled so that each minor bug is tracked and tested. It's best to delay further testing until all the minor bugs have been corrected. The testing, if continued, will likely find even more errors. The test team can go do other things instead of waiting around for the vendor to fix his code.

> Numerous errors can cause the user to doubt the credibility of the system to perform to his requirements. In anticipation of some testing problems, the project manager should explain how the pursuit of zero defects in the system during testing will lead to greater reliability of the system, fewer maintenance fixes when operational, and greater satisfaction with the system by the user and operators. A problem issue can be turned to an advantage.

Finally the system meets all acceptance test requirements. Only one issue remains. In order for the vendor to get paid, he has to deliver all the deliverables remaining, including all code and documentation updates reflecting any fixes implemented during testing. There is ample statistical data that lifetime maintenance costs will far exceed the cost of the initial program development. If the software cannot be maintained, updated and enhanced because of poor documentation, it is useless.

The original cash flow analysis supporting the investment in the system is irrelevant if the system doesn't survive lifetime projections made for its usefulness. It is this maintenance factor that makes high quality systems documentation so important. The system cannot be accepted without the complete package of documentation.

CONVERSION AND PARALLEL

The last step before operations is converting current manual and automated records and data into the format for the new system. The conversion can take a few weeks or several months. The project team is never staffed to do this job, but it is usual practice to have the same personnel who operate the current systems do the data conversion tasks. This is often done through overtime and weekend work.

Once the data is converted, existing systems and the new system operate in parallel until there is complete assurance that the new system produces accurate results for all transactions and entered data. If the acceptance testing suggests a high quality product, the parallel period can be brief. However, it usually is long enough to include one full period of processing, including month-end accounting and MIS reports.

The parallel operation is stressful to the operations staff. They must continue to operate existing processes, while at the same time, learn how to operate the new system. They debug the operations manuals and other procedures. Minor bugs are fixed. Finally, after a two to four week long parallel, everything works as planned and the system is cutover to full operations.

However, if the system has a catastrophic failure or serious data integrity problems, the parallel period can extend for months. Alternatively, the parallel can be stopped, and the vendor directed to fix the system. Then the customer will need another complete acceptance test, and another period of parallel. These situations are disastrous. The costs are enormous. The schedule is delayed by months, since new data must be converted in the interim. It destroys the vendor's credibility, and humiliates the customer project manager. It makes everyone unhappy and doubtful of the quality of the system, even if the problem is corrected, and no further discrepancies occur. The ultimate guidance is never enter conversion and parallel if there is any doubt whatever of the system's complete satisfaction of acceptance testing.

> Enter Conversion and Parallel in haste,
> repent unemployed at leisure.

OPERATIONS & MAINTENANCE

Before you pay the vendor the final fee, you'll need to decide whether you want to revisit the operations support work package that you deferred. In some system development projects where the new systems operational procedures are complex, it may be prudent to retain a few on-site, vendor support personnel for a few months to ensure operations staff are totally comfortable with the system.

Shortly after operations become routine, operations staff will identify new requirements for the system. They will also find some areas where performance or processing could be improved. This is a natural evolution of the learning process and the elapsed time between the initial requirements collection and system delivery. You may want to retain the vendor to do these changes until your staff is fully knowledgeable of the code and documentation as delivered.

In either case, you have the advantage of knowing exactly what the situation is before you commit any further funds to the vendor.

CONCLUSION

You're exultant over the results. You managed the vendor, your staff, and the user's expectations to deliver a system that everyone is pleased with. Congratulations.

Now make it easier on the next manager who has to do the same. Collect a complete copy of every document, contract, status report and whatever else may be relevant, and deliver the materials to the SCA. Write a vendor performance report that summarizes all the positive and negative aspects of the vendor's technical, management and cost performance. Convene the project team, operations personnel, users and management to conduct a post-mortem on your entire process, and to decide what was superior about each process you used to manage the vendor. Establish what didn't work as well as you expected, and why.

Then, have a party with the vendor and all who participated. You deserve to celebrate.

CASE STUDY

BB&T's Board of Directors convened for their early December meeting. Lisa and Fred were invited to make a report on the progress of Grand Systems Design in developing the BITS system. Fred displayed a Project Schedule Chart that showed all but one module was on schedule, and corrective action was in place to fix that. He showed that all deliverables were on time, and the quality was outstanding. The project costs were also on target. Every indicator pointed to success.

Lisa discussed the efforts in absorbing the Mimosa Street Bank personnel, and the planning for data conversion and parallel. She was pleased with the harmony the personnel from the two banks had achieved in working toward their goal.

The Board indicated their satisfaction with the progress and expressed their appreciation for the update from Lisa and Fred.

Three weeks later, Orlando Gomez, the GSD project manager, and three key GSD project personnel were on their way for a brief holiday skiing trip. Their privately chartered plane went down in a snowstorm and all were lost. The heirs of the business were not involved in running Grand Systems Design and the creditors forced an immediate bankruptcy.

BB&T received nearly a million dollars from the performance/completion bond posted by GSD as a final contract negotiation item. It was small compensation for having to go to the alternate vendor, VA and start all over. BB&T and Mimosa Street Bank were forced to delay the effective date of the integrated operation for six months.

Sometimes even the best plans and efforts don't work out just the way you thought. But even catastrophe can be compensated for, if you've been as cautious as BB&T was in their management of the vendor procurement process.

BB&T CONTRACT TERMS AND CONDITIONS

If a contract is to be negotiated with you (the Vendor) the following are the required standard clauses in Baccarat Bank and Trust's (BB&T's) terms and conditions for contract:

1.   This agreement made as of [date] is between BB&T and [Vendor].

2.   Term of Contract
The term of the contract will extend from [date] to [date] during which the Vendor will conduct the work specified in the Statement of Work and Work Packages (incorporated herein by reference) and deliver the Contract Deliverables specified in the Vendor's proposals and incorporated herein by reference.

3.   Supremacy of this Contract
The provisions, terms and conditions of this Contract represent the entire Contract of the parties with regard to the subject matter of this Agreement and supersede any prior Agreement not incorporated herein. In the event that any inconsistencies exist between this Contract and any prior written agreements, the terms of this Contract shall prevail. This Contract includes all BB&T documents and specifications and Vendor proposals referenced herein, as though they were physically incorporated.

4.   Right of Assignment
BB&T may assign all or any part of its rights to any successor party without prior consent of the Vendor. The Vendor may not assign any of its rights or obligations without prior written consent of BB&T except as may be specifically identified by amendment hereto.

5.   Change of Scope
If, subsequent to the date of this Contract, BB&T requests any significant changes in the scope of this Project as described in the Statement of Work, BB&T agrees to negotiate revised payments to the Vendor for the additional (or lesser) costs based upon the standard rates in effect at that time for any additional (or lesser) work performed by the Vendor as

the result of such changes and further to extend (or shorten) the term of this contract as necessary as a result of any such changes. Verbal or written requests by BB&T which might be construed by the Vendor as changes in scope cannot by undertaken without written authorization from the Systems Contract Administrator of BB&T.

6. Warranty by Vendor

The System and Deliverables will conform to the Requirements Specifications and Interface Specifications appended hereto and incorporated herein, and to the Statement of Work and Work Packages referenced documentation and said system shall perform the functions required within the performance criteria specified. The Vendor will correct errors that are documented by BB&T and reported to the Vendor at no cost to BB&T for one year from acceptance of the system.

7. Termination by BB&T

BB&T shall have the right to terminate work under this Contract any time upon 30 days prior written notice to the Vendor. The last day of such 30 day period shall be the Effective Date of termination.

8. Default

If the Vendor shall breach any provision of this Contract and shall not cure same to the satisfaction of BB&T within 15 days after notice thereof in writing, BB&T, at its option, may terminate further work under this Contract without further notice. As stipulated damages for such breach, the Vendor agrees that BB&T shall be entitled to retain any sums due but not yet paid, and recover any premium or increased cost incurred by BB&T in order to develop the Deliverable(s) within the specified schedule up to the full dollar amount paid to the Vendor by BB&T under this Contract.

    Vendor shall secure insurance policies to the benefit of BB&T in the amount of two hundred percent of the negotiated contract total price, in the forms of General Liability, Automobile Liability and Worker's Compensation, and shall post Performance and Completion Bonds in like amount for the benefit of BB&T.

9. Surrender

In the event of either default or termination, the Vendor shall immediately upon the effective date thereof turn over to BB&T all of the material developed under this Contract including but not limited to: equipment, programs, flow charts, working papers, narrative descriptions, reports, data, materials, etc.

10. Forbearance

The failure of BB&T to insist upon the performance of any terms or conditions of this Contract, to exercise any right or privilege conferred in this Contract, or the waiver of enforcing penalties resulting from any breach of any of the terms or conditions of this contract, shall not be construed as waiving any such terms, conditions, rights, or privileges, but the same shall continue and remain in full force and effect as if no such forbearance or waiver had occurred.

11. Governing Law

This Contract shall be deemed to be entered into, and shall be construed in accordance with, the laws of the State of _____ .

12. Indemnity

The Vendor herewith indemnifies and agrees to hold harmless BB&T from any and every expense, claim, damage or loss arising out of any claim that the Deliverables developed by the Vendor pursuant to this Contract constitutes an infringement or other violation of any rights of any other party pursuant to copyright, patent, or trade secret rights. If, as a result of such claim, injunction is entered against BB&T precluding any further use of the Deliverable(s), the Vendor agrees to refund promptly all sums paid by BB&T pursuant to this Contract.

The preceding sentence shall not apply if, immediately upon any issuance of a preliminary injunction, the Vendor either (a) obtains for BB&T the right to continue to use such Deliverables at no further cost to BB&T or (b) provides at no further cost to BB&T an equally satisfactory Deliverable which in BB&T 's opinion achieves the same objectives as such Deliverable and is equally practicable, and which does not infringe any copyright, patent, or trade secret protection.

13. Limit on Vendor's Liability

The Vendor agrees that, notwithstanding the form in which any legal action may be brought by BB&T against the Vendor, the Vendor shall be liable for general and special damages.

14. Penalty for Lack of Performance

Penalty for partial lack of performance or delivery by the Vendor in accordance with the provisions and work plan of this Contract shall be withholding of sums not yet paid for work not yet incurred, plus withholding of 10% of fees until performance is corrected. Irrespective of the foregoing, should the Vendor be unable to complete the system within the schedule, or the performance of the system does not materially meet the performance requirements specified, BB&T after 30 days of notification to Vendor and courts of such failure to perform, shall, on its sole judgment, execute the steps necessary to receive the benefits of the Performance and Completion Bonds posted.

15. Vendor Personnel

All Vendor personnel assigned to this Project must conform to the level of technical expertise required by BB&T and must be approved in writing by BB&T prior to being assigned under the contract.

16. Replacement of Vendor Personnel

Once assigned, the Vendor will not change personnel without 10 days prior written notice to BB&T unless such change in personnel is required through circumstances beyond the Vendor's control. In either case, BB&T reserves the right of approval as stated in the following paragraph.

The Vendor will provide the name and a specific outline of the qualifications 5 days prior to the assignment of the proposed alternative personnel. BB&T reserves the right to interview the proposed alternate personnel during this time. BB&T shall advise the Vendor within 3 days after an interview thereof as to whether or not such person is acceptable. If not acceptable, the Vendor will submit similar data and additional personnel until a satisfactory replacement is made. If satisfactory replacement cannot be made within the time required for replacement, BB&T reserves the right to terminate or renegotiate the Contract, at its option.

17. Independent Contractor

The Vendor agrees that at all times it will be the employer of its personnel engaged in the performance of this Contract. The Vendor agrees to arrange directly with such employees for all salary and other payments, and Vendor shall provide liability insurance covering such employees for damages caused, or contributed to, by its employees, and provide all workman's compensation, medical coverage, and other similar items required by any law, regulation or employment agreement.

18. Employees of Contracting Parties

Vendor agrees not to seek to employ any employee of BB&T during the course of the performance of this Contract.

19. Subcontracting

The Vendor agrees that all work which is to be performed under this Contract shall be performed by employees of the Vendor and that it will not subcontract any part of the work without the prior written approval of BB&T.

20. Nonuse of BB&T Name

The Vendor agrees that it will not, in the course of performance of this Contract or thereafter, use BB&T's name in any way as a customer of the Vendor without the prior written consent of BB&T.

21. Security of BB&T Information

All data relating to BB&T's business and customers which is acquired by the Vendor as a result of performance under this Contract will be safeguarded to the same extent that the Vendor safeguards data relating to its own business or to the requirements of BB&T, as attached hereto.

If such data is publicly available, or rightly obtained from third parties, the Vendor shall bear no responsibility for the inadvertent disclosure thereof.

22. BB&T Security Regulations

Vendor personnel will comply with BB&T security regulations. Vendor personnel, when deemed appropriate by BB&T, will be issued BB&T visitor's identification cards. Such cards will be surrendered if demanded by BB&T or upon conclusion of the Contract (whichever occurs first).

23. Confidentiality

The Vendor will undertake all necessary steps to protect the security and confidentiality, or patent, copyright, or trade secret protection, of all data information programs, materials, systems, techniques, ideas, procedures, or other matter provided by, or which is the property of BB&T.

BB&T will use the same procedures to protect the Vendor's property as it uses to protect its own proprietary data.

24. Proprietary Rights

Vendor agrees that all materials, ideas, programs, systems, or other items developed, produced, created or improved by the Vendor, or its employees in the course of performance of this Contract shall be at all times the sole property of BB&T and will not be disclosed to any third party by the Vendor, or used in any way by the Vendor without the prior written consent of BB&T.

25. Description of Deliverables
The Deliverables will be provided by the Vendor in accordance with the Requirements Specifications, the RFP Guidance Document, the Vendor Proposal, and as amended by negotiations and as appended hereto and make a part hereof.

26. Cost Procedures
If time and materials effort is included as part of the contract, Vendor personnel shall complete and submit invoices for work performed monthly. Time Sheets for the review and written approval of BB&T Project Manager will be included. The Vendor shall retain a copy of all such approved time sheets, and photocopies of all documents evidencing any additional expenses incurred under this Contract. These records shall be made available to BB&T auditors upon request.

27. Contract Management
The Vendor appoints as its executive contact _____ who shall have full authority to deal with BB&T in any and every regard concerning this Contract. BB&T appoints as its executive contact Mr. Monk Eternic, who has full authority to deal with the Vendor in any regard concerning this Contract.

28. Clause Names
Scope and intent of the clauses within this Contract are defined by the descriptive content of the clauses and not merely the clause title.

29. Authorization of this Contract
Both parties warrant that the entering into and performance of this Contract have been duly authorized by all necessary corporate action and will not result in a breach of any provision of its charter, bylaws, or any other agreement to which either is a party.

30. Notices
Any communications between the parties should be made only by registered mail or by courier receipts. The minimum total transit time baseline is 3 business days. Notices shall be delivered to the main current business address of the parties.

31. Payments
BB&T will award payments to the Vendor upon the satisfactory completion of effort and deliverables specified in the Statement of Work, the Specifications, and the Work Packages.

32. Ownership
In consideration for the contract granted by BB&T, BB&T is entitled to the deliverables, and documentation, and the Vendor grants to BB&T perpetual license at no additional fee other than the payments under this contract.

WORK PACKAGE DEFINITIONS

These Work Packages are illustrative of how you can specify what each vendor's effort must be. You will change these to meet your objectives when your project is different. Similar Work Packages have been used for telecommunications network projects and the renovation and cabling of major facilities.

1.0 PROJECT MANAGEMENT & ADMINISTRATION

Project Management & Administration is that Work Package in direct project support of the client assignment, not contained under any other work package, which relate to the vendor's management of the project from a project management and senior level management basis.

Project Management & Administration does not include ordinary overhead of the vendor in the general management of its personnel or its functions. For example, all financially related matters associated with time accounting, billing for services, credit processing and the like are normal and ordinary vendor activities which are not included in Project Administration.

1.1 Organization, Personnel & Controls

This Work Package includes all vendor activity related to the administration of each aspect of the vendor's activities: technical, management and cost administration and his client relations. This also includes the general management tasks related to overall management of the vendor's resources, execution of quality assurance and audit functions, and the recruitment of resources if required.

1.2 Scheduling

This Work Package includes maintenance and update of the project schedule, and day to day tracking of all vendor internal tasks and deliverables.

1.3 Contracts Administration & Change Management

This Work Package includes all direct labor related to vendor's contract officer maintaining oversight of contract compliance, and all effort related to the preparation of Software Change Proposals, and the negotiation thereafter.

1.4 Client Reporting

This Work Package involves the vendor's attendance at client meetings, interfaces to various components of the nontechnical side of the client's organization, and the execution of action items stemming from such meetings. It includes management preparation of reports and reporting deliverables for routine status reports.

Included are the vendor's senior management directly involved in client reviews, reports and reporting, quality assurance and technical reviews of work accomplishments under all other tasks. All work under this Work Package is directly related to the Assignment.

Client liaison does not include relationship meetings between vendor senior management and client personnel, or standard marketing calls of any kind.

1.5 Deliverables Production

All the nontechnical production effort required to prepare all deliverables for the client is included in this work package. Preparation activity can include typing, reproduction, tape copies, blueprints, or any media pertinent to the deliverable.

This Work Package does not include the technical or managerial creative effort to create the content of the deliverable. That effort is in the pertinent work package for that deliverable.

2.0 SYSTEMS ANALYSIS

Systems Analysis consists of the effort to perform technical trade off analyses and calculations required to validate that the design will meet performance requirements. The vendor's analysis efforts can include extremely detailed technical research, data collection, vendor inquiries for additional technical information, simulations, modeling and other mathematical analysis to provide the client with recommendations. Test beds of actual equipment are included in this Work Package. All Vendor analysis is documented. This task includes the management effort to produce the analysis and to prepare the deliverables required.

2.1 Hardware Capacity Analysis

This Work Package includes all effort to study and analyze the system's impact on computer hardware and operating system software, and includes the costs of machine time to conduct the study.

2.2 Hardware Performance Analysis

This Work Package includes all effort to model, study and analyze the system's operation on the computing hardware from a processing timeline requirement, and features an independent study of the computing environment to determine if the equipment has adequate power to process the system's transactions.

2.3 System Module Performance Analysis

This major Work Package includes all sub-Work Packages which model and analyze each module of the system on an individual basis to verify that it will meet its operating performance requirements.

2.4 Interface Performance Analysis

This Work Package consists of all sub-Work Packages which model and analyze each module of the system and its interface with the other systems it will interact with on an individual basis, verifing that it will meet operating performance requirements. This task also includes the effort to model each interfaced system to determine if the additional transaction and processing load will meet existing or new performance requirements.

2.5 Total System Performance Analysis

This Work Package involves all effort to model and analyze the final completed operating system within the hardware environment established to verify that it will meet its performance requirements.

2.6 System Reliability Analysis

This Work Package includes all effort to determine whether the system will meet its requirements for up time, recovery from an abort, and any other production delay causing suspension of the system. It also includes analysis of coding and documentation processes to ensure bug-free code generation.

2.7 System Security and Audit Analysis

This Work Package includes all effort to verify that the system will meet the security and auditability requirements that have been established.

2.8 System Analysis Deliverables

All effort to create and prepare the deliverables required for this Work Package use the content of the studies and analysis of the above tasks.

3.0 SYSTEMS DESIGN

Systems Design is defined by all tasks and sub-tasks used to design the vendor's system so that it will meet the requirements established in the Systems Requirements Specification, the Interface Specifications and other standards and requirements.

3.1 System Module Design

This Work Package consists of the work required to design each module of the system to meet the requirements allocated to it, and includes the design of each program, sub-program or other processing unit required to be designed within its respective module. The effort related to design of the vendor's solution and the modifications to the existing systems can include formats, databases, programs or screens, hardcopy output or interfacing files to other modules, interfacing programs or systems.

3.2 System Design Documentation Deliverables

This Work Package includes all effort to create and prepare formal deliverables, for each of the modules designed above. This task includes the preparation of the System Design Specification, Design Review Documentation, the Design Review Presentation, and the update of any design or action item required from the Design Review.

4.0 CODING, DEBUG & UNIT TESTING

This Work Package includes all the effort required to reduce the vendor's design solution to computer instructions, and their testing as units of delivered code.

4.1 System Module Code, Debug & Unit Test

This Work Package and all sub-work packages and tasks includes all effort to code, debug, document and test each programmable executable unit of the system, and the programs constituting assemblies of programs to the level of the constituted module.

4.2 Code & Documentation Deliverables

This Work Package includes all effort to collect, review, verify and correct all code and documentation and all other media required to be delivered under this Work Package.

5.0 INTERFACE TESTING

Interface Testing involves all effort related to the vendor's testing of the modules and software built with models or real interfaces from the client's other interfacing software systems.

5.1 Module and Interface Testing

This Work Package and all sub-work packages and tasks includes all required efforts to link and interface as required, each individual module of the system with each other interfacing module.

Module and Interface Testing also includes all required efforts to link and interface as required, each individual module of the system with each other interfacing system as specified in the Interface Specifications and the Systems Design Specification.

5.2 Interface Testing Deliverables

This Work Package includes all effort to collect, assemble and prepare all deliverables required.

6.0 INTEGRATION TESTING

Integration Testing includes the effort to install the system at the client's site.

It consists of testing all functioning parts of the vendor's system and the interfaces with other systems to validate correct processing after system installation.

6.1 System Timeline Testing

This Work Package includes the effort to verify the results of the systems analysis that real or dummy transactions processed by the system will meet the System Timeline production requirements established.

6.2 Interface Integration Testing with Modules

All of the vendor's efforts to link and process all of the systems modules with the installed interfacing systems of the client are included in this Work Package.

6.4 Input-Output Controls Testing

This Work Package includes all of the vendor's efforts to control the options for the execution of various system input and output streams, and to trap the results as required when the I/O are transient interfacing or interchange files without hardcopy output.

6.5 Integration Testing Deliverable

This Work Package includes the creation or collection, assembly and preparation of all materials required to be included as an integration testing deliverable.

7.0 DATA CONVERSION

This Work Package includes all vendor effort required to support the conversion of information from the old system formats into the required new system formats.

7.1 Operations Process Data Conversion

This Work Package and all sub-Work Packages includes all effort to convert operational transactions, tickets, data entry or resident databases into the form and format required by the new system.

7.2 Data Conversion Verification

This Work Package ensures that converted data has been accurately transferred to the new format without error.

7.3 Data Conversion and Database Deliverables

This task includes all effort to prepare the deliverables required for this Work Package.

8.0 ACCEPTANCE TESTING

Acceptance Testing includes all vendor effort to support the client in the complete testing of the new system and in verifying that it performs correctly according to requirements, within performance specifications, and according to approved design.

8.1 Systems Test Plan

All vendor effort to support the client in preparation of the Systems Test Plan and the preparation of all Systems Test Planning documentation and deliverables is found in this Work Package.

8.2 Systems Test Procedures & Script

This Work Package includes all vendor effort to support the client in the preparation of the Systems Test Procedures and Scripts and the preparation of the associated deliverables.

8.3 Database Verification Testing

This Work Package includes all vendor effort to support the client in testing the system's databases so they conform to test requirements.

8.4 Acceptance Test Criteria & Data

This Work Package includes all vendor effort to support the client in preparation, review and analysis of all criteria to be evaluated during the Acceptance Testing.

8.5 Systems Acceptance Test, Results & Reports

This Work Package includes all vendor effort to support the client in running the Acceptance Testing. It includes all vendor effort to correct any mistakes, errors, bugs or performance out of specification. It includes preparation of all regression test packages as required by the failures above. This task includes vendor preparation of all deliverables required by this Work Package.

9.0 CUTOVER AND PARALLEL

Cutover and Parallel includes the effort related to customer support while the new system becomes operational, and the verification of the accuracy of its processing as compared with the old system.

10.0 OPERATIONS SUPPORT

Operations Support are those services performed by vendor following the cutover and correspond to any client requested services in the Operations Phase of the Project.

10.1 Software Maintenance Support

This Work Package includes vendor effort to maintain the delivered software for new changes and enhancements.

This does not include any vendor effort to correct errors discovered in the system during the warrantee period. Such effort is for the vendor's own account.

10.2 Database Support

This Work Package includes the vendor effort to maintain, upgrade or change databases required by the customer after cutover.

10.3 Operational Procedures Support

All vendor effort to support the client in redefining or changing operational procedures or documentation after the system has become operational is included in Operational Procedures Support.

INDEX

Visits, vendor customer installations, 83, 119, 165

Weight assignment, 189-194, 10-23, 10-24
    sum, 189, 191-193
    work package, 189, 191, 193
        assigned weight, 189-193
        equal weight, 189, 191
Who talks to the vendor, 46
Win-win, 106
Work, descoping in contract negotiations, 268
Work breakdown structure, 144 (*see* work package)
Work package(s), 143-149, 171, 176-247, 254, 265-268
    assigned weight, 189-193
    benefits, 145-146
    contract negotiation issue, 254

definitions, 146, Appendix B, 292-297
equal weight, 189, 191
examples, (*see* work package, terminology)
fully satisfactory response or solution, 61, 180, 194-196
large system, 148, 161, 171
score, 200
small system, 147
subdivisions, 147, 148, 171
terminology example, cost proposal, 157
    management proposal, 154
    systems analysis, 149
    technical proposal, 152
Worksheet, 182, 184, 198
    evaluator, blank, 184
    evaluator, completed, 198